a–z of groups and groupwork

Professional Keywords

Every field of practice has its own methods, terminology, conceptual debates and landmark publications. The *Professional Keywords* series expertly structures this material into easy-reference A to Z format. Focusing on the ideas and themes that shape the field, and informed by the latest research, these books are designed both to guide the student reader and to refresh practitioners' thinking and understanding.

Available now

Mark Doel and Timothy B. Kelly: *A–Z of Groups & Groupwork*
Jon Glasby and Helen Dickinson: *A–Z of Inter-agency Working*
Richard Hugman: *A–Z of Professional Ethics*
Glenn Laverack: *A–Z of Health Promotion*
Neil McKeganey: *A–Z of Addiction and Substance Misuse*
Steve Nolan and Margaret Holloway: *A–Z of Spirituality*
Marian Roberts: *A–Z of Mediation*

Available soon

Jane Dalrymple: *A–Z of Advocacy*
David Shemmings, Yvonne Shemmings and David Wilkins: *A–Z of Attachment Theory*
Jeffrey Longhofer: *A–Z of Psychodynamic Practice*
David Garnett: *A–Z of Housing*
Fiona Timmins: *A–Z of Reflective Practice*

a–z of

groups & groupwork

Mark Doel and Timothy B. Kelly

palgrave
macmillan

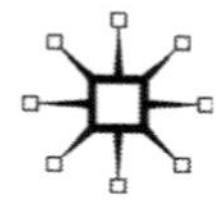

First published 2014 by
PALGRAVE MACMILLAN

Palgrave Macmillan in the UK is an imprint of Macmillan Publishers Limited, registered in England, company number 785998, of Houndmills, Basingstoke, Hampshire RG21 6XS.

Palgrave Macmillan in the US is a division of St Martin's Press LLC, 175 Fifth Avenue, New York, NY 10010.

Palgrave Macmillan is the global academic imprint of the above companies and has companies and representatives throughout the world.

Palgrave® and Macmillan® are registered trademarks in the United States, the United Kingdom, Europe and other countries

ISBN 978-0-230-30857-2 ISBN 978-1-137-31527-4 (eBook)

DOI 10.1007/978-1-137-31527-4

A catalogue record for this book is available from the British Library.

A catalog record for this book is available from the Library of Congress.

contents

acknowledgements

Groups are fundamental to being human. We grow up in groups, spend leisure and social time in groups and, by and large, work in groups. The influences on the experience and understanding of groups that we hope to share in this book are, therefore, enormous. We thankfully acknowledge all the family, friendship and professional groups to which we have belonged and continue to belong. In particular, we would like to acknowledge all those group members who, through our years of professional groupwork, have helped us to learn about the power and dynamism of groups, the joys and challenges of groupwork and the essential mystery of the chemistry of each and every group.

On a practical note, our sincere thanks to Catherine Gray, Vidhya Jayaprakash and the team at Palgrave for their help to bring this book and the A–Z series to fruition.

how to use this book

The book is written for anyone who wants to learn more about how to get the best from groups. It is natural to be curious about groups as they play such a central part in human life – family and friendship groups, social and leisure groups, team and work groups, community and neighbourhood groups and many others.

Most groups form naturally and the individuals in these groups do not consciously ponder what it is to be a group member. However, some groups are created specifically *as a group* for a very particular purpose. These groups make active and conscious use of the processes that occur naturally in all groups and they are often guided by a group leader who helps the group as a whole to realize its potential. This consciousness of group dynamics and group process is called *groupwork* – the understanding of what makes groups tick and the skills to make use of this understanding. When professionals in counselling, criminal justice, education, health, psychology, social work and other disciplines create groups and work with them, this is often referred to as *social groupwork*.

Whether you are leading a group or a member of one, a qualified professional or an untrained volunteer, we trust you can make good use of the book.

Using this book

The book uses an A–Z format for quick reference and ease, rather than organizing the content around clustered themes (such as Garvin et al., 2004; Gitterman and Salmon, 2009). There are 75 topics, each focusing on a discrete facet of groups and groupwork and nine of these entries give a more detailed treatment of their topic. Each entry stands on its own and contains cross-references to other related entries that are italicized in the text, as well as signposts to other related topics at the beginning of each entry. A comprehensive index enables the reader to search for themes across the book that might not be listed as a separate entry.

The A–Z format is designed so that the reader can dip in and out as needed, not as a sequential read from start to finish. We hope this means that a reader who, for instance, is considering the gender balance of a group can turn directly to that topic and follow up with the suggested reading. Of course, gender is related to other issues in groups, but the format of this book enables each reader to decide their own entry into it.

This A–Z emphasizes the essential elements that characterize groups and groupwork across the broad range of group practice. If you would like a brief introduction to the notion of when a group is a group and when it is not a group, turn to the *flash groups* entry first. Separate entries for groups with different populations (e.g. children's groups, women's groups, etc.) would have led to repetition, as group processes are similar across different groups; instead we have made sure that different kinds of group are used to illustrate the various topics. These issues are explored further in the **populations** entry.

Referencing and further reading

The book draws from a wide variety of groupwork traditions. We have produced a comprehensive, international bibliography that we hope will help readers to further their knowledge of groups and groupwork. In particular, the book benefits from the results of a complete literature review of journals such as *Groupwork: An Interdisciplinary Journal for Working with Groups* (published by Whiting and Birch); this international journal covers the whole span of groupwork across different professions, disciplines and continents.

Each entry aims to provide a succinct introduction to its topic. Guidance to further reading and any relevant website is given at the end of each entry as well as some citations within the text itself. All of these references are collected together in the full bibliography at the end of the book. In addition, there are extended bibliographies for four entries (*gender, methods and models, populations* and *settings*) in the appendix.

accountability

SEE ALSO **evaluation; groundrules; supervision**

Professions as a whole, and individual professionals specifically, are required to account for their actions much more publicly than they were once. On the positive side, this limits the opportunity for arbitrary, inappropriate treatment and oppressive behaviour by professionals; on the negative side, it has led to greater defensiveness and to risk-averse behaviour which does not always lead to the best outcomes.

The notion of accountability in groups needs to be understood in the broader social context. It is a concept with further complexity in the group context because of the variety of ways in which groups can be said to be accountable.

- First and foremost, group leaders are accountable to the group itself to ensure the physical and emotional safety of the group members. They are also accountable, in their role as leaders, for providing direction to the group (though the extent of this direction will vary from one kind of group to another) and for helping the group to achieve its purposes.
- Group leaders are accountable to the sponsors of the group. More often than not, these sponsors are the agencies that employ the group leaders. Group leaders must account for their time to ensure that is well spent. This means developing good systems of *evaluation* to ensure that accountability can be exercised and through *supervision* of their practice.
- Group leaders are accountable to their profession and to the broader groupwork community – to use the best practices available, guided by current research and to internationally recognized standards (AASWG, 2010).

- Group *members* are accountable – mainly to one another. Often, the group leaders will help members to develop *groundrules* that spell out the expectations that group members can reasonably expect of one another, which is another way of describing their mutual accountability and of exercising this accountability. Group members might also be accountable to people outside the group, such as family members, or other professionals, like health visitors or probation officers.

'Negative accountability' is important when things go wrong. This is not necessarily about allocating blame or 'covering your back', but it means that if, for instance, somebody in the group mentions an illegal action they have taken, they are aware beforehand that the group leader is accountable to the law and that such confessions would need to breach the group's usual expectation of confidentiality. It can, then, be important to discuss the notion of accountability with the group.

'Positive accountability' reminds groups of people and institutions outside the group who have a legitimate interest in the group. Group members can better understand the need to participate in evaluating the group if they know why this is important and for whom it is important – themselves and others.

Implications for practice

- Ensure group members have knowledge of what accountability means – perhaps by helping the group to develop groundrules which spell out what accountability means in practice;
- Develop a robust system of evaluation so that an accurate account of the group can be given to those who have not necessarily been a part of the group.

FURTHER READING

- AASWG (2010) *Standards for Social Work Practice with Groups*, 2nd edn (Alexandria, VA: AASWG) (available at www.aaswg.org)
- Bodinham, H. and Weinstein, J. (1991) 'Making Authority Accountable: The Experience of a Statutory Based Women's Group', *Groupwork*, 4 (1): pp. 22–30
- Manor, O. (1989) 'Organising Accountability for Social Groupwork: More Choices', *Groupwork*, 2 (2): pp. 108–122

activities

SEE ALSO **development; process; recreation groups; session**

The common understanding of the word activity implies some kind of *doing*. In groups, however, contemplation in *silence* can be described as 'an activity'. Some group sessions might consist solely of one activity, such as group discussion, but it is much more likely that any single group *session* will be made up of several different kinds of activity. Some groups, like arts and crafts groups, are 'Activity Groups' – their existence is focused around the activity itself (Finlay, 1999). However, in most cases, activities are used to help the group achieve a greater purpose.

Arts and crafts were typical of occupational therapy groups, with a focus on social and occupational interaction. Art therapy is a particular form of artwork that uses the arts to help people express emotions and to learn more about themselves and others (Maidment and Macfarlane, 2009; Otway, 1993; St Thomas and Johnson, 2002).

Discussion is probably the most common activity in a group. Even in a group that uses a wide variety of 'doing', it is usually important to carve enough time to reflect on the experience of the doing and to discuss its meaning beyond the activity itself.

Graphic activities help groups to balance the aural with the visual and flip charts can consolidate what is heard by making it seen. For instance, when people introduce themselves early in the group's life, the names can be written on flipchart paper, perhaps in a visual representation of how they are sitting in relation to one another; their reasons for coming to the group can be written in the 'group space' on the flipchart between their names. This helps to remind everybody of what has been said, especially for people who have hearing problems. Photographs with particular meaning to group members can prompt discussion (Craig, 2009). Taking a group photo at the end of each session and collecting them on a wall chart demonstrates the group's continuity and growth. Drawings and diagrams can help people to think about the closeness and distance of their relationships to family members and significant others; cartooning can be used to 'storyboard' a significant event, looking at what led to the event and what the consequences were.

Games and other forms of play are significant social behaviours that can be replicated in the group to help individual group members feel more like a group or team (Craig, 1988; Lee and Li, 2008). The balance between competition and collaboration prompts group members to think about these factors in their own lives outside the group and in the wider society. All groups need some *recreation* time.

The benefits of *physical activity* are well known generally. In a group, they can help to shake things up, literally, when a group feels stuck. Of course, the physical abilities of members of the group must be borne in mind. Relaxation exercises can help the group feel tranquil at the end of a session.

Although many activities will require planning and preparation such as the mask-making activities described by Lordan *et al.* (2009), some of the most effective activities are those that use *props* spontaneously. For example, a group with young offenders is re-enacting what happens when they get stopped for speeding and the chairs in the room are brought into play as a makeshift car. Anything that is used creatively to stand in for something else is a prop.

Simulation is the creation of a situation that resembles its real-life counterpart, such as flight simulators in airline pilot training. The group is an ideal theatre for group members to try different ways of responding to situations in their lives. Rehearsal, sometimes known as role play, can help people try different approaches in safety, knowing that they can stop the action at any point and that there are no consequences.

Guest speakers can be invited to address a group around a particular topic, such as sexual health, providing useful expertise. It is important that speakers are briefed so that they can tune to the group's needs and that there is time for the group to *reflect* on the input. Groups might want to make their own presentations and invite guests into the group to hear them. Depending on the focus of the group's presentation, this could be local politicians and senior managers, victims of crime or perhaps family members.

Computer-assisted games and programmes, pre-recorded video tapes and live recording all have their place in groupwork. Playing back a recording of the group rehearsing a difficulty, such as confronting a neighbour about noise, provides direct feedback that can have a big impact. *Virtual groups* use new technologies for their very existence, not just as a discrete activity within a group session.

The mix of activities, group shapes and the blend of spontaneous and planned activities all develop creativity in groups. Too many different activities and group members will be over-stimulated and find it difficult to make sense of how they all fit together; too few and the group is likely to become bored, listless and stuck. Too rigid a routine of pre-prepared activities and the group will feel mechanical and new opportunities arising from within the group will be missed; too unstructured and the group can easily drift and feel it is not being taken seriously by the group leaders. It is, then, this creative combination of activities that is so important to the group's success.

Why use activities in groups – and when not to use them?

When considering the use of an activity in a group it is always important to ask what its purposes are. To what extent does the activity serve its own purpose or some others? For instance, in a group that uses basket weaving activities, is the purpose largely to create baskets (for personal satisfaction or for sale to raise funds) or is it an activity designed to facilitate group *process* (a feeling of belonging, confronting taboo issues, rehearsing life changes, etc.). The two are not mutually exclusive and lie on a continuum. Groupworkers aim to harness group activities to group process, so that each set of activities in the group has a larger purpose, building the group *as a group*.

Activities should be planned according to the stage of *development* of each particular group – a process of *escalation*. Gentle naming games in the first session might build to a physical activity that involves some degree of touch when the group is sufficiently intimate for this; still later, group leaders might use photographs to confront group *taboos*, when the group is ready to discuss difficult matters openly.

So, there are some activities – such as those that require a degree of intimacy, disclosure or touch – that are likely to be less appropriate in the early stages of a group and, indeed, might be inappropriate at any stage with some groups. However, in many cases the same structure for an activity (such as the use of prepared photographs) can be used at different stages, though the content will vary according to the group's stage of development.

Implications for practice

- Create a balance between active doing and reflective discussion;
- Be clear about the purposes of an activity and whether it is congruent with the current development of the group.

FURTHER READING

- Bullock, A.and Bannigan, K. (2011) 'Effectiveness of Activity-Based Group Work in Community Health: A Systematic Review', *American Journal of Occupational Therapy,* 65 (3): pp. 257–266
- Doel, M. and Sawdon C. (1999) 'Action Techniques' in *The Essential Groupworker* (London: Jessica Kingsley), Chapter 7: pp. 130–159
- Hickson, A. (1995) *Creative Action Methods in Groupwork* (Oxon: Winslow Press)
- Norton, C.L. and Tucker, A.R. (2010) 'New Heights: Adventure-Based Groupwork in Social Work Education and Practice', *Groupwork,* 20 (2): pp. 24–44
- Streng, I. (2008) 'Using Therapeutic Board Games to Promote Child Mental Health', *Journal of Public Mental Health,* 7 (4): pp. 4–16

b

beginnings, middles and endings

SEE ALSO **activities; confidentiality; development; evaluation; groundrules; joining and leaving; outcomes; planning and preparation; purpose; sessions**

Although there have been many classifications of the phases of groupwork, the classic and simplest has been to characterize groups as having three major phases – a beginning, middle and ending.

When does a group begin?
It might seem obvious that a group begins at the start of its first *session*. However, all groups have important antecedents – processes and events that have led up to the first group session. The *planning and preparation* for the group might correctly be seen as part of the beginning, or engagement, phase (Manor, 2000). Where possible, group leaders should offer the group to potential members on an individual basis in advance of its beginning so that when the group gathers for its first session the members already know the group leaders. The initial contact with prospective members gives the group leaders a chance to test out their ideas for the group and to modify them in the light of the responses they get; it also means that group members already feel consulted and are perhaps beginning to feel some ownership of the group even before they arrive.

Before each session, and especially in advance of the first, group leaders should pause to consider how the group members are likely to be feeling – excited, nervous, hostile, expectant? This process is sometimes referred to as tuning in, when group leaders aim to understand the group from the members' point of view (of course, the group leaders might be sharing many of the same feelings, too). If group leaders can prepare in this way, they are more likely to understand what kinds of activity are likely to be most appropriate during the beginning phase of the group. It is important to remember that even towards the end of the group each individual session has its own beginning, so a similar tuning in helps in advance of all meetings of the group.

Typical group beginnings
The main purpose of the first session of a group is to provide opportunities to introduce the group members to one another and to the purposes of the group. In addition, the first session sets the tone for the group – the style of leadership and participation and a taste of the kind of group it is likely to be. Expectations of behaviour in the group might be discussed and agreed, especially. There should usually be discussion of *confidentiality*.

Instead of the classic round of individual participants introducing themselves, group leaders might decide to use some other *activities*. For example, 'introduce your neighbour', allows people to get to know the person next to them first, by pairs asking questions of one another and then introducing their pair to the rest of the group.

Usually the group leaders will make an opening statement of the group's purpose. This will already have been discussed with each individual member if the offer of groupwork was made in advance of the first session. It is important that group members are encouraged to discuss these preliminary purposes. Even if membership of the group is *involuntary* (e.g. by court order), participation and ownership need to be encouraged. Even with this mandated groups membership, there are some group *purposes* that can be negotiated. *Groundrules* for the group should be negotiated when group members are in a position to do this in a meaningful and participatory way.

Not all groups start from scratch. Ongoing groups have no formal beginning but it is important that these groups give themselves opportunities for a fresh start. If and when a new member joins this is a good time to review the group's groundrules (or establish them if none has been agreed) and to review its purposes. They may have changed since the group's life first began. Perhaps it is time to re-consider the name of the group – does it continue to reflect the group's purposes or is the group ready to be re-cast?

Middles
In the world of fiction, stories typically begin with an initial scene setting to introduce most of the central characters and plot lines.

Sometimes a story immediately grabs you and at other times the book seems slow to develop, but then something changes and you are immersed in the story, the plot thickens and all sorts of interesting things happen. At some point, a turning point or resolution is reached and the book ends. If it has been good, you feel sorry to put it down.

Groups are much the same. The scene setting (planning and preparation), is followed by a period where the central characters (membership) are introduced and the initial plot is established (beginnings). Then the story really gets going and the interesting things start to happen. In groupwork this is known as the middle phase. It is the period where group members work on the issues that brought them together and group purpose is realized. Difficulties may be faced and overcome as members work towards their shared goals. *Conflicts* (so central to a good story) may emerge and be resolved. Eventually, there is an ending when loose ends are tied up and the story is over – or perhaps there is room for a sequel.

There is another important element of this analogy. Though most stories follow this pattern, many great stories have different patterns. Some weave different elements together in an ebb and flow of plot, introducing new characters and different storylines. Groups, too, move back and forth without a clearly defined point at which the group moves from beginnings to middles or from middles to endings. Some groups are like soap operas – ongoing without a formal ending, though there are endings to plot lines and characters come and go.

The two most important decisions that group members must make are, first, whether or not to join and, second, whether or not to join *in*. Rather like a new year's resolution, it is easier to make the first commitment (to join) than to do work to do something about it (to join in).

Difficulties in groups can occur at any phase, but the struggle to make the commitment to join in means that obstacles are common in this middle phase. Some obstacles may arise from problematic communication patterns, *roles* or *structures*, often emanating from the group's beginnings and in need of review. Other blocks only begin to emerge in the middle phase because of difficulties being experienced in the group's work. For example, certain topics may become *taboo*, closing down and proving destructive to the group's dynamics. Differences of opinion may finally be aired, but result in conflict.

The central task of the worker during the middle phase is to help the group to identify these barriers, to name them for the group, and to work together to remove them so that the group can learn from them and move forward (Berman-Rossi, 1993; Heap, 1985). *Problem-solving* methods and other creative, nonlinear approaches are particularly useful in addressing group obstacles in the middle phase of groups.

The central *task* of group leaders in the middle phase is to help the group keep focused on its purpose, which usually means increasing the demands for work – on both individuals and the group as a whole. Resistance to this is not uncommon and the groupworker needs to consider whether this stems from group members' lack of *power* and control (so they do not feel they 'own' the group) or other causes. If the groupworkers are too focused on tasks and outcomes at the expense of feelings and process, the group can get stuck. Groupworkers need a skillful balance between supporting group processes and making demands for work towards group *outcomes*.

When do endings begin?

For groups that are time limited (that is, there is a specified number of sessions for the group), good endings begin at the beginning; the end of the group should be anticipated from the start. Keeping the end in sight helps focus the group and gives members a better idea of how near or far they are from achieving what they want.

'Open-ended' groups, as the name suggests, do not have an ending. It is usually difficult for professionals to give an open-ended commitment because of other demands on their time; after an agreed period to help the group to become self-sustaining, the leader might withdraw, available only if needed for some specific purpose. Open-ended groups need to beware of possible drift.

Sometimes there are endings for *individual* group members. For instance, a group for people with an addiction might have people *joining and leaving* at different times depending on their progress. In these instances it is important to mark the occasion of a person's last session; deciding how to celebrate is a good group exercise.

At other times a person's exit from the group is unplanned because their situation has changed without notice; it might even be a death. Whatever the circumstances of an unplanned and sudden ending for an individual group member, it is important that the *group as a whole* has the opportunity to discuss it. The situation faced by the person who has left might reflect the possible futures of many others in the group and they need the chance to air their feelings and to see how the group treats the memory of an ex-group member.

The nature of each ending is determined by the way in which the group has been experienced. If the group has not been given the opportunity to speak freely during its course, the final session might see a painful release of feelings; the more painful because it is the end and there is no opportunity to stand back and revisit at a later session. Productive endings, in which there is no unfinished business, rely on productive beginnings and middles. The temptation to leave discussion of any 'elephants in the room' until the last minute must be resisted. The group leader should explore their own feelings about the group's ending, too (Roman, 2006).

Getting the best from endings

First, we should note that endings can be difficult; this fact can take a group (and its leaders) by surprise when it has had a strong, positive, empowering experience. Think of a time you made a sudden and intense friendship, perhaps away on holiday. Most likely you swapped contact details and professed solemnly that you would keep in touch and meet up: the reality is probably that you both quietly let it go. The end of a group, especially one that has passed through strong emotions, ups and downs, is also a time when its members are likely to cling on to its memory, perhaps not wanting it to end. In general it is best not to extend a group beyond the agreed number of sessions – to make sure the group goes out at a highpoint. Of course, some long-term friendships do emerge from groups, but in most cases the ending where nobody wants it to end should be seen as a good indication of a success.

As noted earlier, it is important to anticipate the end of the group from the start, so that the ending process is as long as the group itself (a bit like life, really). If there is going to be a special session, a group outing for instance, ask the group to think about holding this as the penultimate session rather than the last. Generally it is nice for the last session to be the same pattern as the others, and any outing will no doubt generate lots of experiences that the group might like to debrief in the final session. Again, it is often better not to leave any group *evaluation* until the very last moment; if it is conducted in one of the later sessions, rather than the very last, it gives the group the chance to reflect on it and to add to it.

Endings are best seen as *transitions* and some group members might benefit from follow-up to help the transition (Benson, 2001; Shulman, 2009). Though some group members have achieved the necessary help and support in the planned number of sessions, others might still have some way to go. The decision about who can provide this support is something that needs to have been agreed in the planning and preparation for the group; another indication of how the best endings arise from thorough preparations.

Implications for practice

- Be aware of the three phases (beginnings, middles and endings) and their implications for activity in the group; but also be aware that there are not clearly marked boundaries between them and that each individual session of the group has a beginning, middle and end phase, too;
- Prepare for endings from the very beginning of the group; if the group is 'open-ended' build in new beginnings and staging posts that mimic endings.

FURTHER READING

- Berg, R.C., Landreth, G.L. and Fall, K.A. (2013) *Group Counseling: Concepts and Procedures.* 5th edn Kindle (New York: Routledge), Chapter 7 'Initiating a Counseling Group' and Chapter 8 'Maintaining a Group: Process and Development'
- Birnbaum, M.L. and Cicchetti, A. (2008) 'The Power of Purposeful Sessional Endings in Each Group Encounter', *Social Work with Groups,* 23 (3): pp. 37–52
- Cole, M.B. (2012) *Group Dynamics in Occupational Therapy: The Theoretical Basis and Practice Application of Group Intervention* (Thorofare, NJ: Slack Books)

- Gitterman, A.and Germain, C. (2008) *The Life Model of Social Work Practice: Advances in Theory and Practice*, 3rd edn (New York: Columbia University Press), Chapter 12 'Endings: Settings, Modalities, Methods, and Skills', pp. 414–446
- Shulman, L. (2009) *The Skills of Helping Individuals, Families, Groups, and Communities*, 6th edn (Belmont, CA: Brookes/Cole), Chapter 11 'The Beginning Phase in the Group'

C

cohesion

SEE ALSO **collective; dynamics; ending; group as a whole; group-think; process; purpose; taboos**

In a groupwork context, group cohesion is one of the elements of group *process* or group *dynamics*. It refers to the social and emotional connections or bonds among group members. It is a centripetal force that allows the group to focus on and work towards group tasks and goals (Crouch, Bloch and Wanlass, 1994). There is a reciprocal relationship between cohesion and task, as groups that work closely together tend to have increasing cohesion. Likewise, when groups successfully resolve a crisis or conflict, group cohesion tends to strengthen. In addition, cohesive groups are more productive (Beal *et al.*, 2003).

One of the central tasks of the groupworker is to foster the development of group cohesion (Berman-Rossi, 1993; Johnson and Johnson, 1994; Yalom and Leszcz, 2005). In the beginning of a group there is little cohesion (unless the group is already a naturally formed group such as in a school setting or residential facility). The groupworker must build connections and relationships between and among the group members. Having a clear group *purpose* that meets a shared need provides a fertile ground for the development of cohesion. In later phases, the worker's focus may change from making connections to helping the group remove the obstacles to the group's work and helping the members to make greater demands on each other. During the *ending* phase of work, the worker must help members disengage positively while maintaining a cohesive climate.

When a group has become cohesive it has become more than a sum of its parts. Members will be able to feel the 'groupness' of their *collective*. In cohesive groups, members will feel attracted or connected to the *group as a whole*, to the other members of the group and towards their shared tasks. In cohesive groups people will confront *taboo* subjects, share personal pain, be themselves, feel safe to challenge and be challenged. It will feel intimate and group members will experience a sense of belonging to the group. There can be a clear demarcation between those in the group and those outside the group.

Groups with high levels of group cohesion have been shown to have better outcomes. However, group cohesion can have a negative side as well. Strong cohesion can develop *group-think* (an uncritical acceptance of group norms) and if the group has negative aims or intentions such as gangs, cults, Nazi Youth Groups, the power of group cohesion can be channelled towards anti-social or extremely destructive ends.

Implications for practice

- Groupworkers can facilitate the building of cohesion by fostering connections among members;
- Helping the group focus on their common goals or tasks builds group cohesion.

FURTHER READING

- Beal, D.J., Cohen, R.R., Burke, M.J. and McLendon, C.L. (2003) 'Cohesion and Performance in Groups: A Meta-Analytic Clarification of Construct Relations', *Journal of Applied Psychology*, 88 (6): pp. 989–1004
- MacGowan, M.J. (2000) 'Evaluation of a Measure of Engagement for Group Work', *Research on Social Work Practice*, 10 (3): pp. 348–361
- Yalom, I.D. and Leszcz, M. (2005) *The Theory and Practice of Group Therapy*, 5th edn (New York: Basic Books), Chapter 3 'Group Cohesiveness', pp. 53–62

collective

SEE ALSO **democracy; group-think; power**

Humans are social beings. History has long been recorded as though it consists of a baton passed from one strong leader to the next, but this is a distortion: the truth is that human progress is much more dependent on our ability to engage with each other as social beings than on the behaviour of single men and women. It is reasonable to suggest that the civilizing of humanity and the development of *democracy* has come via its ability to harness the collaborative and collective instincts that are deeply ingrained.

Of course, group behaviour is not always benign; there is a negative facet of *group-think*. Mob behaviour alerts us to the potential danger of collective action.

Despite reservations about reactionary herd instincts, collective action has a long history of bringing oppressed peoples together to counter seemingly more powerful forces, sometimes with success and sometimes not – from the Peasants Revolt in fourteenth-century England to the collectivization of labour in the late nineteenth century and the collective civil disobedience that led to Indian independence in the mid-twentieth century.

Groups as collectives

Social groupwork relies on exactly the same kinds of human ability and instinct that we have been describing at the historical level. In its own modest way, small groupwork can enhance participatory democracy by enabling people to feel that their participation can make a difference and by gaining a greater understanding of other people's feelings and opinions. Group leaders model respect, tolerance and equality in the way they facilitate the group, and group members experience the power that can be generated through their collective activities. In some cases, this might result in collective action outside the group, for instance, in campaigning for better services for disabled people. In other cases the power might stay inside the group, with individuals feeling respect and being listened to in ways that are new to them.

Small groupwork is not generally an overly political activity, but the collective ideal that it embodies does implicitly challenge the acquisitive individualism and single-mindedness that is characteristic of developed capitalist societies. Perhaps there is an intuitive understanding of the vaguely subversive nature of social groupwork in the fact that it is rarely seen as 'the default' mode of professional delivery and that, frequently, a special case must be made by professionals to be allowed to create groups and conduct groupwork. The sense that there is strength in numbers can be unsettling, even challenging, both for individual practitioners and for the agencies that employ them.

Implications for practice

- Social groupwork has potential to be used at a social policy level as a tool to democratize civic society at a time when there is concern that active participation in democracy is diminishing;
- Group leaders should embrace the 'strength in numbers' aspect of groupwork and consider how groups can have an impact on their wider environment.

FURTHER READING

- Doel, M. and Sawdon, C. (1999) *The Essential Groupworker* (London/ Philadelphia: Jessica Kingsley), Chapter 1 'Why Groupwork?' pp. 11–32
- Kalcher, J. (2004) 'Social Group Work in Germany: An American Import and Its Historical Development' in C. Carson, A. Fritz, E. Lewis, J. Ramey and D. Sugiuchi (eds), *Growth and Development through Group Work* (New York: Haworth Press), pp. 51–72
- Williamson, T. (2008) 'Strengthening Group Decision-Making within Shared Governance: A Case Study', *Groupwork*, 18 (2): pp. 101–120

community groups

SEE ALSO **leadership; membership; process; purpose; residential groups; roles; sessions; social action; virtual groups**

The notion of community has been associated traditionally with a geographical area – local communities of people with a common interest in their neighbourhood. Changes, often seen as threats, to the neighbourhood can trigger individuals to come together; examples are concerns about road safety, proposals to bring outsiders into the area (such as establishing a hostel for homeless people), the building of a new supermarket. Some neighbourhoods are well organized, with a community group that is ongoing and proactive – perhaps organizing farmers' markets, bulb planting and with sub-committees to respond to specific issues as they arise. Tenants' groups are a localized form of community group, where the boundaries of the group are the local housing estate.

However, increases in individual mobility and new technologies make it easier for strangers to make contact with one another, and the idea of community has broadened beyond geography.

Communities of interest bring people from across the globe together around particular topics and concerns (Pollard, 2010) and, in professional life, communities of practice (Wenger, 1998) enable practitioners across continents and different professions to keep in regular touch as *virtual* communities drawn together by a common interest, perhaps in a specific method of practice such as groupwork.

Community development (known as community organizing in the US) has a long and illustrious history (President Obama was a community organizer). Groups of people in the community aim to achieve a place at the table *before* decisions are made rather than being the passive recipients of consultation exercises (Dyson and Harrison, 1996). Often a community group is formed around a single issue, but if it is to move from protest to power there is a need to develop a coalition of interests among people with shared values, perhaps nurturing allies among local political parties, too. If the issue attracts widespread support it transforms from a community group to a grass roots *movement*.

Community groups exhibit many of the features associated with social groupwork. There needs to be a *purpose* that will motivate members to take part (Muir, 2000); *leadership* is required and the relationship between the leadership and the *membership* needs to be negotiated and is likely to change during the life of the community group; the group dynamic and *process* will change as the community group matures; *roles* will be developed within the group, and often in community groups these will be formalized (chair, secretary, treasurer, membership secretary, etc.).

There are important differences between community groups and social groupwork, too. The boundaries of the former are more likely to be looser than those of the latter, so that membership fluctuates; community group meetings (as opposed to group *sessions*) will be larger, less intimate and those attending are likely to vary from one meeting to the next. As a meeting, rather than a session, the processes are likely to be more standardized, for example, following an agreed agenda and tabling motions and papers beforehand.

Community groups that attend to group process are likely to be able to work with *conflict*, change and *development* rather more successfully than those where the knowledge of groupwork is absent.

Therapeutic communities are established specifically to provide an oasis of safety in which the processes of group living are used for therapeutic ends.

Implications for practice

- Community groups are likely to have a wider but less stable membership than therapeutic groups;
- The outward-looking nature of most community groups (seeking change in their external environment) should not distract group leaders from the importance of group process within the community group.

FURTHER READING

- Drysdale, J. and Purcell, R. (1999) 'Breaking the Culture of Silence: Groupwork and Community Development', *Groupwork,* 11 (3): pp. 70–87
- Gitterman, A. and Salmon, R. (eds) (2009) *Encyclopaedia of Social Work with Groups* (New York: Routledge), 'Group Work and Community Context', pp. 267–280
- Tucker, S. (ed) (2000) *A Therapeutic Community Approach to Care in the Community* (London: Jessica Kingsley)

WEBSITE

- www.citizensuk.org and www.communitygroup.co.uk

confidentiality

SEE ALSO **groundrules; values**

Confidentiality is concerned with the limits placed around information and communication. Confidentiality is important because it encourages people to speak frankly. This openness is often the first step towards self-honesty, i.e. being able to confront your own demons and the reality of your situation. If you have trust in the person you are speaking to, and this trust includes a belief that they will respect your confidences by not telling others, you are more likely to speak freely. The importance of speaking openly is that it helps the speaker to develop beliefs and strategies that can ameliorate problems and heal traumas.

Confidentiality has limits. Social groupworkers do not have legal rights to privileged information, so if a crime is disclosed (whether in the group setting or one-to-one) there is a duty to report it. The reality of the group is that it is a semi-public gathering; the hope is that the group's boundaries will constitute the 'confidentiality bubble', but it is quite reasonable to expect that some of the group members will go home and talk about their experience of the group and that it will be difficult, therefore, to avoid revealing some of the details. Groups, then, are qualitatively different from personal encounters.

Raising the question of confidentiality with the group is an excellent way to open up the general issue of self-disclosure, personal and group boundaries and mutual expectations about how information will be handled by the group. Sometimes this might be formalized into *groundrules* for the group, though it is best to avoid a set of prescribed rules before the group has had a good opportunity to talk about these matters in depth and to get to grips with them.

Most people will nod their heads if asked whether they think matters discussed in the group should remain confidential. A better and more meaningful way to unpick what confidentiality might mean in practice, is to present the group with a number of brief scenarios that are realistic and could easily arise in the life of the group, and ask the group members to discuss what they think the issues are in each scenario and what they would do. This will help bring the abstract notion of confidentiality to life, reveal the group's *values* and expose interesting differences of opinion that will help the group to develop and individuals within the group to grow.

Implications for practice

- The idea of confidentiality should be introduced within the group early in its life – probably at some point during the first session of a new group;
- Scenarios that present dilemmas about the use of information are the best way to unpack what confidentiality means in practice to individual group members and to work towards a group consensus.

FURTHER READING

- Corey, G. (2011) *Theory and Practice of Group Counseling*, 8th edn (Belmont, CA: Brooks/Cole, Cengage Learning), Chapter 3 'Ethical and Professional Issues in Group Practice', pp. 71–94

- Doel, M. and Sawdon C. (1999) *The Essential Groupworker: Teaching and Learning Creative Groupwork* (London: Jessica Kingsley), Chapter 6 'The First Session and the Group Agreement', pp. 113–129
- Northen, H. (2004) 'Ethics and Values in Group Work' in C.D. Garvin, L.M. Gutiérez and M.J. Galinsky, *Handbook of Social Work with Groups* (New York: The Guilford Press), pp. 76–89

conflict

SEE ALSO **cohesion; development; methods; sub-groups**

Conflict is a group dynamic that occurs when there is a difference of opinion, or a disagreement regarding the work or functioning of the group. It may result in strife or friction between or among members of the group, or just raise the passions and energy level in the group. Conflict can emerge as a result of various factors: a power struggle; differing values, beliefs or norms; societal prejudices and differing individual differences (e.g. gender, race, ethnicity, sexuality, class) and/or differing ideas regarding the working of the group. The conflict can originate within the group or from outside (Benson, 1992).

Though conflict can be frightening for novice groupworkers, it should be seen as a natural and productive part of group life and group *development* (Canton, Mack and Smith, 1992). Conflict in groups can be a transformative element of the group experience and provide much of the energy in groupwork. In addition, intragroup conflict can actually increase group *cohesion*.

When conflict emerges, many members will suggest the democratic approach of voting. Here the majority wins at the expense of a minority, and this approach does not necessarily lead to the best outcome. Compromising is a second option. Here everybody gives up something, but again not always achieving the optimum result. A collaborative approach requires dialogue and careful listening skills (sometimes called a dialectical process, a concept that originates with Socrates and is further developed in Hegelian philosophy). Logical arguments begin with a thesis, followed by the opposing argument or antithesis. These are explored until a new perspective emerges. The new perspective is a *synthesis*. In groups, differences of opinion are to be expected, and can involve more than just two opposing points of view. It is through exploring those differences that members can begin to learn new ways of thinking and doing and tentatively reach a synthesis of their differences. Resolving conflict using a collaborative or dialectical process takes more time but can achieve a better outcome for the group and improved communication patterns.

Though conflict is a normal part of group development it can be destructive if it goes unrecognized or if it is not handled appropriately by the group and groupworker. The groupworker's role should be to help the group to bring conflict to the surface and to manage and use the conflict, rather than suppress or control it. This often means helping the members to understand that conflict is normal and will not normally destroy the group, especially if the group is well developed. The group should be helped to explore the differences and use the dialectical process. However, conflict can stir up powerful emotions in groupworkers, and these feelings and reactions may make it difficult for some workers to engage with group conflict. Yet by appropriately sharing their own reaction or feelings, groupworkers can help the group deal with conflict. The mediating function as described by Schwartz (1976) and Shulman (2009) provides some guidance: the worker's function is to help the primary messages of 'opposing sides' (whether individual group members or *sub-groups*) be communicated to and heard by the other sides so that communication, engagement and synthesis can occur.

The *problem-solving* approach offers useful steps to deal with conflict (Kurland and Salmon, 1998). Avoidance is a strategy that some groups and workers may try to use, but this strategy typically damages the work of the group in the longer run. As such, the worker must recognize the conflict and point it out to the group if it has not already acknowledged its existence. The conflict or problem inherent in the conflict must then be fully explored by the group and a mutually agreed definition of the problem should be reached. Next, the group must explore various ways to resolve the conflict before choosing their approach. Finally the chosen approach should be implemented and evaluated later to see if it worked. There are other *methods* of conflict resolution that are less linear and logical, such as 'sculpting' the conflict – giving it a visual and physical representation, often involving the group members' persons and positioning them to represent the conflict.

Implications for practice

- Conflict is normal in most groups and can be used to help the work of the group;
- Groupworkers help groups deal with conflict by recognizing it, helping the group explore the conflict, having faith in the group process and examining different solutions before implementing new plans or changes in the group's way of working.

FURTHER READING

- Northen, H. and Kurland, R. (2001) *Social Work with Groups*, 3rd edn (New York: Columbia University Press), Chapter 9 'Group Conflict', pp. 214–237
- Tindale, R.S., Dkyema-Engblade, A. and Wittkowski, E. (2005) 'Conflict within and between Groups' in S. Wheelan (ed), The *Handbook of Group Research and Practice* (London: Sage), pp. 313–328

contexts

SEE ALSO **community groups; individuals; power; role; setting; social action**

What goes on outside a group has an impact on what happens inside the group. The significance of these contexts for the group has sometimes been neglected, but it is gaining more recognition.

Individual group members spend a lot more time out of the group than in the group. Even if the group is in a residential or institutional *setting*, individual members are likely to spend much of their daily lives *not* in the group. This much is obvious but it can be neglected. Events outside the group affect what happens within the group. This is not just a question of somebody being in a bad mood when they come to the group because they have just had a family argument: one groupworker did not discover until four sessions into the group that two of the members were sisters-in-law, and this explained much behaviour that the groupworker had been at a loss to understand.

It is a two-way process – what occurs within the group should also have an impact outside it. A group member who is finding her self-confidence in the group and becoming more assertive will probably take this back into her relationships outside the group, where it may or may not be welcomed. If the group is likely to change the balance in its members' relationships outside the group, the group leaders need to consider how they might respond to this. Will significant others be invited to the group at any point? Will there be time within the group for members to consider how to prepare others outside the group for the likely changes?

Most groups that are led by professionals are sponsored by the agencies that employ them. It is important for the success of the group that the organization's support is sound. If further groups are planned, this support will need to be sustained. Developing a champion for groupwork within the senior management of the agency is helpful, though risky if that person moves on to another job. Embedding groupwork as part of the agency's continuing professional development programme makes it more secure and helps link groupworkers throughout one agency together in a network.

It is critical that groupwork is not perceived as a kind of hobby to be enjoyed just by favoured or canny workers. The exhilaration that groups can generate is also capable of alienating colleagues who are doing what might be seen as the humdrum day-to-day work and who feel they have been left out of the party. Finding ways to implicate colleagues and immediate managers, so that they can feel they share in any successes, is just as important a role for the groupworker as the skills they exercise within the group. If one single group is going to develop into a broader groupwork *service,* the goodwill and perhaps the direct involvement of others in the organization will be required.

The *power* dynamics, stereotyping and social roles that characterize the wider society are likely to be re-enacted within the group. In some respects, the group can be considered a microcosm of broader social forces. Oppressive social forces outside the group do not miraculously wipe their feet at the group's door. There may be no men present in a women's group, but this does not guarantee that the women have left internalized oppression outside the group. One of the purposes of the group, perhaps usually implicit, is to question the conventional social roles that its members experience outside the group and to learn how to challenge discrimination and oppression within the group, the better to counter it outside in the wider society.

Some groups have an outward-facing purpose; that is, they are formed in order to have a wide impact. *Community groups* and *social action* groups seek change in society rather than in themselves.

When they get very big, they are often called *movements* rather than groups, such as the disability rights movement and the movement for nuclear disarmament.

Implications for practice

- Group leaders should acquaint themselves as far as possible with group members' experience of the world outside the group;
- Group leaders should encourage champions for groupwork within the organizations that employ them, to help grow a strong and widely supported groupwork *service*.

FURTHER READING

- Doel, M. and Sawdon, C. (1999) 'No Group Is an Island: Groupwork in a Social Work Agency', *Groupwork*, 11 (3): pp. 50–56
- Liu, F.L.W.C. (2002) 'Closing a Cultural Divide: Enhancing Mutual Aid while Working with Groups in Hong Kong', *Groupwork*, 13 (2): pp. 72–92
- Yanca S.J. and Johnson, L.C. (2012) 'Generalist Social Work Practice with Groups' in A. Bergart, S. Simon and M. Doel (eds), *Group Work: Honoring Our Roots, Nurturing Our Growth* (London: Whiting and Birch), pp. 209–230

counselling groups

SEE ALSO **methods and models; therapy groups**

The Association for Specialists in Group Work (ASGW, 2000) describes four different types of group specialization, one of which is the counselling group. The others are task groups, psychoeducation groups and psychotherapy groups. The association acknowledges that there may not be a clear boundary between the four different types of groupwork specialization; however, they suggest that they do have characteristics that provide a professionally useful categorization. Groupworkers use similar skills, processes and techniques across all four specializations and similar theoretical approaches may be integrated into the different types of groupwork. Corey (2011) provides a differentiation between the four types, with a counselling group focusing on a specific problem or issue that members share. Though remedial action may be an aim, counselling groups are primarily concerned with growth and change, rather than intensive psychological overhaul. Group members may be facing problems in their general lives or having difficulties successfully navigating a life transition, but a counselling group does not focus on fixing problems or treating individual members. Rather, a counselling group has a here-and-now focus and the group provides a therapeutic milieu where members share and explore their current situations and develop the skills needed to overcome their difficulties – both current and future. The focus on the now and personal goals, the development of mutual aid and intrapersonal awareness and the translation of group experiences to actions outside the group are hallmarks of group counselling.

Group counsellors see the group as a microcosm of society, and as such, the group milieu recreates the members' external social world within the group. The struggles, issues, conflicts and problems that occur in the group mirror the experiences members have in the outside world; these experiences are recreated in the safe and supportive environment of the group where members can try new behaviours, gain insights into their behaviour and learn new skills to employ effectively outside the group (Gazda, Ginter and Horne, 2001).

Implications for practice

- The here-and-now focus in group counselling provides the opportunity for self-discovery as well as improving relationships with others;
- Counselling groups provide members with an opportunity to learn and test out new knowledge, skills and behaviours.

FURTHER READING

- Berg, R.C., Landreth, G.L. and Fall, K.A. (2013) *Group Counseling: Concepts and Procedures*, 5th edn (New York: Routledge)
- Corey, M., Corey, G. and Corey, C. (2010) *Groups: Process and Practice*, 8th edn (Belmont, CA: Brooks/Cole, Cengage Learning)
- Tudor, K. (1999) *Group Counselling: Professional Skills for Counsellors* (London: Sage)

co-working

SEE ALSO **differences and similarities; leadership; process; resources; values**

When the leadership of the group is shared among two or more people this is referred to as co-working or co-leadership (Hodge,

1985). There are many possible models: an exactly equal partnership between two groupworkers, each of whom takes the same *leadership* role in the group; a partnership in which different leaders take different roles; a collective of perhaps three or more groupworkers who might not all be present at every group session – and many other combinations (Doel and Sawdon, 1999, pp. 213–228).

The prevalence of co-working is difficult to know, but it is likely that it is more common in *community*-based groupwork than in clinical group practice. There are indications that co-working is the standard model in the UK, but not so in the US. A survey of a large English social work agency found that almost 90% of the groups were co-led (Doel, 2009a).

Co-workers can provide a good model of collaborative decision-making for group members. Invariably, group members are intrigued by the co-leaders' relationship and the way in which they work together. Group members can find it stimulating to have two sets of voices and two approaches, even benefiting from disagreements in the leadership, if these are resolved. Co-workers can share taking the lead for different parts of a group *session*, thereby playing to each other's strengths. They can share functions in the group; for example, whilst one worker is focusing on *task*, the other can attend to *process*.

Co-working enables a group session to take place rather than be cancelled if one of the leaders has to be absent. It is an arrangement that can provide the co-workers themselves with mutual support at all the stages of the work. Co-workers can present a more powerful front to the agency if this is needed – to make the case for more *resources* for the group, for instance, or to press to expand the groupwork service as a whole.

Groupwork is a semi-public forum and co-working is an opportunity for professionals to see one another in practice. Many community-based practitioners work in relative isolation and do not see one another at work: co-leading a group is an excellent opportunity to give and receive direct feedback and, as such, a good medium to promote continuing professional development. An experienced groupworker can mentor a novice by co-working in a group.

Diversity amongst co-workers is something to value, but if there are differences, say, in their *values* and beliefs and these are not understood or acknowledged, this can create turbulence in the group. Colleagues who get along fine in the context of the team might not be so compatible once they are co-leading a group. They can experience *differences* in how interventionist they are, or in how much they need to stick to an agreed structure. These differences could result in group members trying to split the leaders and to other fractures in the group. For success in the group, co-workers need to share a value system (for instance, that racism in the group should be tackled), even if they have differences about how this should be done.

Implications for practice

- The nature of the group leadership (sole or multiple) should be considered in terms of the best interest of the group;
- Co-leaders need to prepare themselves for co-working in a group, even if they know one another well.

FURTHER READING

- Brown, A. (1994) *Groupwork.* 3rd edn (Aldershot: Arena), Chapter 3: pp. 69–95
- Corey, G. (2011) 'The Challenges of Dealing with a System', *Theory and Practice of Group Counseling.* 8th edn (Belmont, CA: Brooks/Cole, Cengage Learning), pp. 46–47
- Doel, M. (2009b) 'Co-working' in A. Gitterman and R. Salmon (eds), *Encyclopaedia of Group Work.* Kindle edn (New York: Taylor and Francis)

d

democracy

SEE ALSO **community groups; leadership; power; social action**

The political dimension of groupwork is not particularly well developed or understood, yet there are at least two ways in which groupwork has strong associations with democracy. These are explored below.

Groups reflect the larger society in which they are situated: *power* relations in society resonate within the group, too. However, one of the purposes of groupwork is often to challenge what is considered normal and to create a different kind of society within the group.

People who experience oppression and relative powerlessness in their everyday lives find themselves with similar people – 'the same boat', it is often said. Group leaders nurture an environment inside the group where group members are listened to, treated with respect and participate in group decision-making. This might be quite different from the external world of the group members.

If the small group is developing well, it becomes more than a microcosm of the larger world; it starts to become something rather better than much of the larger world – participative, co-operative, inclusive, empowering and a model for active citizenship. In short, democratic.

Following the Second World War, small groupwork was used actively by the Allied occupying forces in Germany to aid the democratization of the fledgling German state (Kalcher, 2004). In addition to macro-economic policies such as the Marshall Plan, which sought to avoid the reparation mistakes of the First World War, there was great concern to build a sound, democratic civil society in the new Germany. There was recognition that this meant fostering a strong local democracy and that this, in turn, depended on the skills we see in successful small groupwork. Among the pioneers who put this policy into practice were German Jews, trained in social groupwork and returning to Germany from the US.

Whether the focus of the small group is *supportive* and *therapeutic* to cope with the common trauma of war, or functional and administrative to build inclusive experience of decision-making, small groupwork is a significant tool used to establish and support civic society.

In less dramatic times, models of groupwork such as *social action* and *community* development continue to nourish democratic societies by recognizing the links between the inclusive processes that characterize successful small groups and the levels of informed participation that are necessary to support political democracies.

The 2008 Obama campaign for the US presidency is an example of the way in which small group techniques such as the ability to help people to tell their stories, to reach out to one another and then to connect with a wider ideal produced a seemingly impossible result, the election of a black US president. 'For as long as I remember, the key to political power in Chicago has been keeping Whites, African Americans and Hispanics divided. Barack [Obama] learned that the key to opening the doors of power to others was to *connect* people. When we connect with one another at the level of our grief and hope, there is no power on earth that can keep us divided' (Kellman, 2012, p. 67).

In a much-used typography of *leadership styles*, the democratic style is noted as participative. *Leadership* is shared within the group and, though it is generally the preferred style, it does lengthen decision-making processes and does not neceassarily guarantee the best outcome. However, it is likely to deepen feelings of ownership of the group and broaden commitment to the decisions that are taken in a way that autocratic and laissez-faire styles do not.

Implications for practice

- Group leaders need to make explicit connections between processes inside the group and social processes outside the group;
- Policy makers should consider the relevance of groupwork to the development of a participative civic society.

FURTHER READING

- Fyfe, I. (2004) 'Social Action and Education for Citizenship in Scotland', *Groupwork*, 4 (2): pp. 42–63

- Glassman, U. (2010) 'Relevance of Group Work's Humanistic Values and Democratic Norms to Contemporary Global Crises' in D.M. Steinberg, *Orchestrating the Power of Groups: Beginnings, Middles and Endings (Overture, Movements and Finales)* (London: Whiting and Birch), pp. 136–147
- Kellman, G. (2012) 'The Power of Group Work and Community Organizing in the 2008 US Presidential Race' in A. Bergart, S. Simon and M. Doel (eds) *AASWG Symposium Proceedings, Chicago 2009* (London: Whiting and Birch), pp. 64–71

development

SEE ALSO **beginnings; cohesion; collective; conflict; endings; gender; ground rules; group as a whole; membership; models; planning and preparation; skills; structure; theories**

Group development refers to how the *group as a whole* changes and matures over time. There are many different explanations of how groups develop. Some are linear, staged approaches to development, others more cyclical. Linear approaches have been criticized for their rigidity and lack of fit with different types of groups.

In order to be most helpful, groups need to function well and members must remain reasonably focused on the purpose for which the group was formed. One of the central task or function of the groupworker is to help the group members work together as a *collective*. Understanding how groups change and develop over time can help the worker understand the dynamics that may be occurring in the group or getting in the way of the work at hand. In addition, different stages of group development require differential use of groupwork *skill* (Berman-Rossi, 1993).

Theories of group development

Many of the influential *theories* of group development were first published between 1955 and 1965 and these theories remain the dominant paradigm. In recent years, researchers have questioned the universality of these theories. Despite these criticisms, the models do provide a useful framework for understanding some group dynamics.

Bennis and Shepard (1956) developed a *model* of group development that was divided into two phases – both focusing on the resolution of anxieties for the group member. Each phase was divided into three sub-phases where members with different anxiety coping mechanisms took prominence. In Phase 1 the primary issues involve anxieties concerning *dependence and control*. Initially those members who Bennis and Shepard described as 'dependent' rely on the power and authority of the leader as a way to manage their anxieties. At some point other members who Bennis and Shepard describe as 'counter-dependent' revolt because they experience increasing anxiety with the authority and control being given to the leaders. A crisis ensues. Eventually, members who do not have anxieties around control and authority help the group to resolve the crises around authority and control. The group can then move to Phase 2 where issues of *intimacy* emerge as a preoccupation for group members. After surviving the crisis in Phase 1, some members feel overly close to the group and behave with increased emotional intimacy. Eventually those members that have anxiety around intimacy rebel and another crisis begins. A resolution-catharsis of the new crisis is brought about by those members who do not have intimacy issues. Once this resolution has occurred the group is then said to be a highly functioning group.

Later, Bion (1959) published his work on experiences in groups. Though Bion also identified intimacy and control as central to giving groups their energy, he did not see this development as linear; rather he recognized that these themes would occur in groups, and the group simply had to deal with them sufficiently to focus on the work of the group and they were never fully resolved.

In the 1960s the Boston Model (Garland, Jones and Kolodny, 1965) and Tuckman's (1965) model were published. Both of these models of group development focused on professional groupwork practice. Though they incorporated the power-and-control and intimacy themes, they added a professional helping component by linking the stages to tasks or activities that workers should do to help groups move forward.

The Boston Model has five stages:

Stage 1 – Pre-affiliation
Stage 2 – Power-and-control
Stage 3 – Intimacy

Stage 4 – Differentiation
Stage 5 – Termination

Stages 2 and 3 are similar to the Bennis and Shepard model of group development, though the Boston Model does not emphasize the internal psychological dynamics of individual group members. However, the Boston Model advanced understanding around the power-and-control and intimacy stages. The model recognized the uncertainty and ambivalence many people experience as they enter a new group, or any new social situation.

The pre-affiliation stage captures this initial anxiety and ambivalence; here new members struggle with making a decision to engage. Building on the concerns of earlier models with power-and-control and intimacy, the Boston Model proposed that the initial first blush of post-crisis intimacy was not true intimacy. This comes in Stage 4 when members develop a realistic appraisal of their fellow members, well-functioning roles are developed and the focus of the group is the work that brought them together. Finally, the Boston Model recognized the fact that many groups end and that a model of group development should include the notion of disengagement. In this final stage the group may regress to previous levels of functioning or deny that the ending will occur. The goal of the worker is to help the members adjust to the ending of the group.

Tuckman's model is also preoccupied with authority and intimacy. His model helpfully incorporates rhyming stage names: forming, storming, norming and performing and, added later, adjourning. Like the Boston Model, this model begins with an ambivalent or uncertain forming stage. Conflict is initially avoided and members search for common ground, build relationships and develop initial ways of working together. Eventually, conflict emerges due to dissatisfaction, sub-groups or differing ideas. This period of storming involves *conflict* and strife, and once again, it is expected that the group experiences conflict before a period of high functioning groupwork begins. As a result of the conflict, the group develops norms and productive ways of working, sometimes formalized as *groundrules*. Thus, the group becomes mature and reaches high levels of productivity. Finally, like the Boston Model the final stage involves explanations about group endings.

Critique of stages of group development theories

These models of group development have helped generations of groupworkers understand some of the dynamics that occur in groups. They highlight that the development of the group as a whole is dependent on resolving issues related to authority (usually between group members and the leadership) and relationships between group members. These models have also helped groupworkers to understand that conflict in groups is to be expected (Manor, 1996). However, the models have occasionally been unhelpfully interpreted as a blue print or road map for the development of all groups.

Not all groups develop as the models suggest and there are many factors that can influence this development (Caplan and Thomas, 1997). Group *structure* is one such influence. If a group has frequent and substantial turnover in *membership* it is unlikely to develop beyond the early stages of development, and yet, such groups can be beneficial for members if skilfully used (Galinsky and Schopler, 1985, 1989; Schopler and Galinsky, 1984). *Gender* is also likely to influence how groups develop. For example, some women's groups were found to develop a sense of safety and security before challenge and conflict could occur. Age, vulnerability and institutional context can make active conflict less likely to occur.

More recent research into group development suggests that, though authority and intimacy are important aspects of group life, the factors that influence how and if these themes emerge are numerous and more complex than previously understood. How these issues manifest (if they do) and how they are handled in the group will affect the levels of group *cohesion* and productivity and the overall development of the group. So, the order in which these themes arise (which concerned the early theorists) is not as important as how the groupworker and group members address them.

What is the difference between *stages of group development* and *phases of work*? The concept 'phases of work' refers to the time element and associated tasks required at each phase or work period. The phases of work are typically conceptualized as *planning and preparation, beginnings, middles* and *endings*, with their associated tasks and skills. Group development, though related to phases of work, concerns the underlying dynamics that unfold as the group grows and this can be quite separate from phases of work.

Implications for practice

- Groups mature and develop over time and require differential use of interventions at each stage of development;
- Conflict is a normative group process and, when successfully dealt with by the group, it can facilitate productive work;
- Each group develops differently and the groupworker's role is to help the group become mature and fully functioning.

FURTHER READING

- Kelly, T.B. and Berman-Rossi, T. (1999) 'Advancing Stages of Group Development Theory: The Case of Institutionalized Older Persons', *Social Work with Groups*, 2 (2/3): pp. 119–138
- McMorris, L.E., Gottlieb, N.H and Sneden, G.G. (2005) 'Developmental Stages in Public Health Partnerships: A Practical Perspective', *Health Promotion Practice*, (2): pp. 219–226
- Schiller, L.Y. (1997) 'Rethinking Stages of Group Development in Women's Groups: Implications for Practice', *Social Work with Groups*, 20 (3): pp. 3–19
- Tuckman, B.W. and Jensen, M.C. (1977) 'Stages of Small Group Development Revisited', *Group and Organizational Studies*, (2): pp. 419–427.
- Wheelan, S.A. (2005) 'The Developmental Perspective' in S.A. Wheelan (ed), *The Handbook of Group Research and Practice* (Thousand Oaks/ London: Sage), pp. 119–132

differences and similarities

SEE ALSO **cohesion; conflict; gender; race; values**

A group is an opportunity for people who are in similar circumstances to meet and to find out about others' experiences. To this extent groups are likely to be homogenous, i.e. focusing on similarities. The group's name might well reflect the circumstances that bring all the group members together: young offenders; women with mental health problems; support group for people caring for people with Alzheimer's. These similarities are strong factors in building intimacy and a sense of group *cohesion*.

Early in the group's life the leaders usually focus on helping members to explore similarities and what it is that brings them together. People are encouraged to tell their stories and relate them to the theme of the group, to find commonalities that strengthen the group's bonds and feelings of belonging.

Once the group has developed a sense of cohesiveness it is able to use this as a secure foundation to explore differences. Although all the group members might be young offenders, the nature and circumstances of their offences will vary and the group members may have different responses to their victims. A group for cancer survivors might include people who have experienced different kinds, some more recently than others. They will discover that they have varying degrees of support from family and friends and the meanings they attribute to their recovery from cancer will differ, if indeed they attribute any meaning at all. Some might see their religious faith as an important factor; others the support of their family; some the curative effects of their treatments; and others point to good fortune.

Heterogeneity (difference) in groups is important if there is going to be sufficient challenge. Members are likely to find the differences interesting and learn from them. Diversity can promote desirable and needed *conflict* in a group (Johnson and Johnson, 1994; Sullivan, 2004).

There are other ways in which the group can be described as homogenous or heterogeneous, such as the attributes of its members: *gender*, *race*, age, class, etc. The more similar these characteristics (such as a women's group), the more likely it is that the group will develop safety and intimacy. The more diverse the group (for instance, a group of people of different races) the more likely it is that there will be challenge and risk-taking. Safety and intimacy are beneficial as long as they do not settle into cosy and closed-minded; challenge and risk-taking are desirable if they do not escalate into aggression and hurt.

The balance, then, between sameness and difference in groups is important. Although we can be aware of the likely effects of sameness and difference, we cannot predict the chemistry of any specific group. It is usually wise to avoid a group that is very unbalanced (e.g., where there is only one man or where one person is much older than the rest of the group); even so, there are examples of such groups that are successful, too.

One study (Harmey and Price, 1992) discovered that, in groupwork with bereaved children, it was not necessary for children to share similar causes of sibling death in order to develop a shared understanding of each other's situations and feelings. However, it was necessary to avoid having a group in which there was only one child who is the sole surviving child in his or her family. No two people's needs are identical, but there should be sufficient common *purpose* that they can contribute to the proposed group and benefit from it.

Implications for practice

- Groupworkers should help groups to identify and work with sameness and difference;
- Even in groups whose biography is homogeneous, such as a group of white women, there will be differences – perhaps in their *values* and the beliefs that explain the circumstances that bring them to the group. Groups need to harness these differences in order to develop.

FURTHER READING

- Doel, M. and Sawdon C. (1999) *The Essential Groupworker* (London: Jessica Kingsley), Chapter 3 'Power and Oppression in Groupwork', pp. 50–67
- Rice, S. and Goodman, C. (1992) 'Support Groups for Older People: Is Homogeneity Or Heterogeneity the Answer?' *Groupwork*, 5 (2): pp. 65–77
- Smith, L.C. and Shin, R.Q. (2008) 'Social Privilege, Social Justice, and Group Counselling: An Inquiry', *Journal for Specialists in Groupwork*, 33 (4): pp. 351–366

difficulties in groups

SEE ALSO **conflict; context; development; individual; role**

One person's paralysing difficulty in a group is another person's interesting challenge. It is important, then, for groupworkers to recognize and acknowledge their own particular nightmare-in-the-group. Aside from the dread of violence and extreme aggression, which is commonly shared, what is it you most fear when anticipating joining or leading a new group: *silence, conflict, taboos,* scapegoating (Douglas, 1991).

Whatever the nature of the difficulty, it is important to try to understand it in *context*. Is it difficult behaviour that comes out of the blue or has it been building slowly? Is it behaviour that in a different context was helpful (e.g. a group member was highly participative at the start of the group and helped keep things going, but now dominates the group and prevents others from participating fully)? Do the difficulties that lie behind the behaviour come from outside the group or are they internal, part of the group's own dynamics?

Why is the behaviour difficult? Sometimes it is an *individual* in the group who is seen to be difficult and they can become labelled as the scapegoat, the deviant member, the gatekeeper, the clown, the monopolizer, etc. This tendency to describe people as though they were the *role* itself is not helpful. An understanding that these behaviours are much more fluid and volatile is a more accurate reflection of the reality in groups.

If groups are to develop they will need to confront taboos and this confrontation is likely to be uncomfortable and challenging. Some group members might want to rush into taboo areas whilst others are keen to keep the lid firmly closed; sometimes the whole group might defend against opening up these topics and it is the group leaders' behaviour that is 'difficult', as they lead the group towards difficult but crucial topics. 'Difficult' is, therefore, often a sign of the group's *development*, but the experience is uncomfortable and there is a strong impulse to avoid it.

What to do about difficulties in groups

The key to working with difficult behaviours in groups is to *understand* them and this, in turn, depends on the groupworker's ability to unlock the meaning of the behaviour, and to find a way to articulate this together with the group members. Of course, violent and aggressive behaviour needs to be stopped immediately, but if other behaviours that are experienced as difficult are suppressed this is usually a lost opportunity for the group to discover more about itself (Fatout, 1998; Kelly, 2004).

One of the most difficult challenges for the groupworker is to keep the focus on the group and not on the individual: it is important to remember to use groupwork, not casework (individual work) in a group.

It is important that groupworkers are honest with themselves about their responses to difficult behaviour and that they develop the confidence to work with these behaviours rather than trying to avoid them or bury them or see them as obstacles. It is likely that other group members are also experiencing these behaviours as difficult and they look to the group leaders to help the group as a whole make sense of them in a safe way.

Implications for practice

- Following an experience of difficult behaviour in a group, groupworkers should consider these six questions and discuss their responses with their supervisor or co-worker:
  1. What was the behaviour that you found difficult?
  2. What led up to the behaviour?
  3. How did it make you feel?
  4. What did you do?
  5. What would you have liked to do?
  6. How do you now explain the behaviour – what was it saying about the group and to the group?
- An understanding of the answers to these questions in one specific instance helps groupworkers to respond to future difficult behaviour in a group.

FURTHER READING

- Conyne, R.K. (1999) *Failures in Groupwork: How Can We Learn from Our Mistakes?* (Thousand Oaks, CA: Sage)
- Doel, M. (2004) 'Difficult Behaviour in Groups', *Groupwork,* 14 (1): pp. 80–100
- Lindsay, T. and Orton, S. (2008) *Groupwork Practice in Social Work* (Exeter: Learning Matters), Chapter 8 'Coping with Unexpected or Unhelpful Responses', pp. 109–119
- See *Groupwork* Journal (Whiting and Birch), 11 (1). This issue is devoted to difficulties in groups.

e

encounter groups

SEE ALSO **counselling groups; personal development groups; therapy groups**

The encounter group movement emerged in the 1960s and reached its crescendo in the early 1970s, when, as a movement it began to fade. However, encounter groups and offshoots continue to run in the present day. For instance, many religious denominations and personal development franchises have encounter-type groups. The terms encounter groups, T-groups, sensitivity training and other *personal development groups* are sometimes used interchangeably (see therapy groups and personal development groups); however, despite considerable overlap they are conceptually distinct. The encounter group movement developed after T-groups and Tavistock Training Groups and can be seen as an outgrowth of those types of groups.

Both the T-Group and Tavistock Training Group helped participants to learn about group dynamics, whereas encounter groups focused on helping participants encounter their true self. Unlike other personal development groups, the encounter movement did not distance itself from therapeutic models. Instead, it embraced some of the purposes and techniques of therapeutic models, but encounter groups used these techniques and purposes to help with 'normal' developmental issues in a humanistic manner, not focusing on 'treatment'.

Carl Rogers was the most significant influence on the encounter group movement. His approach to groupwork is a clear extension of his person-centred approach to working with individuals, which predates the encounter group movement. His humanistic approach to groups emphasized subjective personal experiences and members are able to speak about past or present experience, while the focus is on the here and now. There is not a clear distinction between therapy and personal growth. Members are encouraged to give honest feedback about how they experience other members (whether positive or negative) and group processes are used to facilitate the change process, rather than as a focus on analysis and learning, a difference from T-Group and Tavistock Training Groups.

Stoller (1972) and Bach (1967) added the element of time to the developing encounter movement. They called their groups *marathon group encounter* and facilitated intensive, time-limited but extended groups (e.g. over several days with few breaks). This created a sense of pressure, even fatigue, and was thought to help break through resistance and bring about change.

From these earlier roots, Schutz's (1986) *open encounter model* developed. Borrowing the marathon group encounter timeframe, Schutz developed an encounter method that recognized the importance of feeling states within the body and used physicality to work on dilemmas; issues and dilemmas would be represented in physical activities in the group. In addition, he used guided imagery and fantasy. An important task was to help remove the blocks that members had in their lives or their own personalities. These *activities* were used to help break through these blocks. Another concept in open encounter group model is the energy cycle. Here the leader is encouraged to go where the energy is in the group, rather than focus on an issue with no energy. Finally, fundamental interpersonal relations orientation (or FIRO) guides activities within the group. FIRO holds that there are three issues that have an impact on human relations: inclusion (do I belong or not); control (*power* and authority); and openness (intimacy). Activities are developed to examine and explore these three concepts as they manifest themselves within the encounter group.

Through these activities over an intense and extended, but limited period of time, group members are provided with an intense emotional experience. Members are given the space to work on any problems or concerns in their lives and they can use the group for their own purposes, whether for personal growth or psychotherapy.

The encounter group movement was not without its critics, with some evidence that encounter groups could cause psychological damage. Yalom and Lieberman (1971) identified that approximately 10% of encounter group members suffer damage, especially those with low self-esteem and overly high expectations of the experience. Encounter group leadership styles characterized by intrusiveness, charisma and a focus on the individual rather than group were more likely to cause damage.

Implications for practice

- The purposeful use of activities to help groups or individuals in groups can help remove blockages to individual or group growth;
- Focusing on individuals rather than paying attention to group process can be damaging to individuals.

FURTHER READING

- Peavy, R.V. (1971) 'Encounter Groups', *Conseiller Canadien*, 5 (4): pp. 245–299
- Rogers, C. (1970) *Carl Rogers on Encounter Groups* (New York: Harper and Row)
- Schutz, W.C. (1986) 'Encounter Groups' in I.L. Kutash and A. Wolf (eds), *Psychotherapist's Casebook* (San Francisco: Jossey-Bass)
- Weigel, R.G. (2002) 'The Marathon Encounter Group – Vision and Reality: Exhuming the Body for a Last Look', *Consulting Psychology Journal: Practice and Research*, 54 (3): pp. 186–198

evaluation

SEE ALSO **evidence base; manualized groups; outcomes; process; purpose**

Why evaluate?

Whatever the *purpose* of a group, whether it is softly vague or hard and explicit, it is important to know whether the group is achieving this purpose (reviews along the way) and has achieved it (an evaluation towards the end or afterwards). Primarily, it is important for the group members themselves, who might have a shared group purpose or specific individual ones that relate them to others through the group. In addition, groupworkers need to know how their *leadership* has helped or hindered the group's achievements and any sponsoring organization needs information about whether its *resources* (such as staff time) are being used effectively and how the evaluation of this group can aid the broader process of service review to improve the agency's services (Day, 2005).

There are wider constituencies, too. The local community and the families of group members might legitimately want to know how the group went. More formally, the stock of groupwork knowledge – the *evidence base* – is increased by groupworkers writing about groups and using the knowledge they gain from evaluations to develop scholarly groupwork (Gordon, 1992).

Who should be involved in evaluation?

As far as it is possible and appropriate, group members should be central in the design and execution of the evaluation (Preston-Shoot, 1988). Of course, groupworkers will use their experience and expertise, but should be open to the creative suggestions that the membership can make about the format of the evaluation. The group should discuss whether the evaluation is completed by the *group as a whole* or by individual members privately, or both.

Consideration should be given to the possibility of an independent evaluator, someone not connected to the group. This might seem unattractive at first – the feeling that the group is 'an object' of study – but, in fact, the involvement of someone who has not taken part in the group, but who knows about groups and group processes, can be quite a catalyst for the whole group to be reflective and see things anew.

When should evaluation take place?

Reviews of the group's progress, including the satisfaction or otherwise that group members are feeling, should be undertaken regularly. Indeed, a quick check-in and check-out at the start and finish of each *session* is often very helpful for the group. A more formal evaluation should take part later in the group, at a point when there is enough distance from the beginning to give meaningful judgement about the group's progress. However, this should not necessarily be the very last session – sometimes it is helpful for groups to have time to reflect on their evaluation. Follow-up evaluations, perhaps six months after the group has ended, are useful to see if the group has had lasting effects.

Manualized groups have a pre-determined programme and ready-made evaluation formats with prescribed points at which the evaluation should be executed. This aids standardization and validity, as the evaluation format has been tried and tested, but it can be at odds with the *values* of empowerment. What if the group does not want to use the prescribed format for evaluation?

How to evaluate?

There are two kinds of evaluation – finding out how the group has been experienced (*process*) and measuring how successful and productive it has been (*outcomes*). Both are of importance because they are linked. There are two ways of measuring: the one, *qualitative,* is associated with processes and the other, *quantitative,* with outcomes. Again, it is useful to use both methods.

An example of a qualitative measure would be a series of open-ended questions focused on the group's experience of itself as a group (sentence completion could be used, such as 'when I think of this group I think of... ').

Quantitative measures often try to measure changes, so members of the group might be given a questionnaire before the group starts or at the beginning, relating to their current feelings and behaviours, then asked to complete the same questionnaire at the end of the group, to see if there have been any changes. This is not proof that the group *caused* the changes, though it is important to find out whether members *think* the group is responsible for any changes.

A quantitative measure, such as a seven-point Likert scale, can be used to assess a qualitative item. For instance:

Tick the number that most represents your satisfaction with this group

1	2	3	4	5	6	7
highly dissatisfied	dissatisfied	fairly dissatisfied	OK	fairly satisfied	satisfied	highly satisfied

FIGURE 1 *Example of satisfaction rating using Likert scale*

Perhaps the simplest indicator of success in a group is, do the group members turn up?

Implications for practice

- Evaluation methods should take into consideration the ages and abilities of the group members;
- Methods should be congruent with each particular group and where possible not just consist of ticking boxes. Aim to be creative, such as asking group members to write a letter to themselves at the beginning of the group about how they hope to see themselves at the end of the group; at that point, group

members open their letters and write their response, perhaps sharing this with the group as a whole.

FURTHER READING

- Doel, M. (2006) *Using Groupwork* (London: Routledge/Community Care), Chapter 8 'Value', pp. 129–146 and Chapter 9 'Grow', pp. 147–170
- Gant, L.M. (2004) 'Evaluation of Group Work' in C.D. Garvin, L.M. Gutiérrez and M.J. Galinsky (eds) *Handbook of Social Work with Groups* (New York/London: Guilford Press), pp. 461–476
- Peake, A. and Otway, O. (1990), 'Evaluating Success in Groupwork: Why Not Measure the Obvious?', *Groupwork*, 3 (2): pp. 118–133

evidence base

SEE ALSO **evaluation; researching groups; scholarly groupwork; supervision; theories**

What counts as evidence?

Groupwork does not have a robust enough or sufficiently developed evidence base to support practice that is always – in the strictest sense of the word – 100% evidence-based. By this, we mean the type of evidence derived from randomized controlled trials and systematic reviews of the literature (Housen, 2009) – sometimes referred to as the 'gold standard' of evidence. The value placed on this 'gold standard' research is much contested within groupwork – and beyond. Many argue that this definition of evidence is too narrow. If we broaden the definition of what counts as evidence, groupwork has a rich body of knowledge available to inform practice with groups. This broader definition includes knowledge gained from quantitative studies other than only randomized control trials, qualitative studies, expert opinion, single group descriptions, theoretical and conceptual reviews in the literature, information in books on groupwork, evaluations by groupworkers of their own practice and the opinion of group members. Much of this is often described as 'practice wisdom'.

What is evidence-based groupwork?

Evidence-based groupwork is not a new model or *theory* of groupwork practice; rather, it is an approach to practice that attempts to apply the best available knowledge or evidence to your own practice and to evaluate the results systematically. The best evidence may include an understanding of the particular service user group, knowledge of the particular members in the group and awareness of the local context, as well as a more formal review of the relevant groupwork literature. As such, evidence-based groupwork is a mindset whereby empirical, theoretical and practice knowledge is applied to particular groupwork practice situations and then evaluated.

Several steps have been identified in the evidence-based groupwork approach. These include identifying a practice-based question (e.g., what is the best way to help this service user group?), then seeking the evidence to answer the question. Once evidence is found, it must be critically appraised and translated and applied to the practitioner's own practice context. This final step can often be difficult and can be helped by good *supervision*.

Where do you find evidence for groupwork practice?

The ability to source evidence has become much easier in the past 20 years. Many workers now have access to online resources such as Social Work Abstracts, Psychinfo, the Cumulative Index to Nursing and Allied Health Literature (CINAHL), ERIC, SCIE online and other electronic abstracting services. These databases are a good place to start when searching for groupwork evidence. They are becoming more widely available to practitioners through their employers and professional bodies, or through subscription services. Google Scholar and other similar internet search engines are also useful sources of *research* information. However, it is necessary to use critical skills to evaluate the merit of the evidence retrieved, especially from internet searches.

Practice guidelines and systematic reviews are increasingly available and can provide a good source of evidence. Websites such as the Cochrane Review and Campbell Collaboration and Joanna Briggs Institute offer searchable databases for qualitative or quantitative systematic reviews. Professional organizations and regulatory bodies often practice guidance.

Online communities of practice are becoming important sources of evidence. Such online communities often develop their own list of resources and sources of evidence. In addition, they can be of assistance in applying evidence to particular situations.

How can practitioners add to the evidence base?

As indicated earlier, the groupwork evidence base needs further development. Researchers and scholars are working to develop this evidence base and practitioners, too, have an important role to play. If groupwork is making a difference at a local level, then we need to have this documented in a systematized way (Doel, 2006). Small-scale *evaluations* and systematic demonstrations of change over time can be used to justify group services at a local level, and they can also be used cumulatively to add to the stock of knowledge about groupwork practice. Individual practitioners often find it difficult to add publication to their busy work lives; however, there are potential academic partners to help develop *scholarly groupwork* – to help turn evaluations of groupwork into publishable articles.

Implications for practice

- Evidence-based groupwork practice requires formulating a question about your own practice and then searching for and appraising relevant research and groupwork literature;
- Translating research findings to your own practice may require creatively adapting research to the local environment;
- Supervision and communities of practice are good places to find support for implementing research into practice.

FURTHER READING

- Barlow, S.H. (2010) 'Evidence Bases for Group Practice' in R.K. Conyne (ed), *The Oxford Handbook of Group Counseling* (New York: Oxford University Press), pp. 207–230
- Leszcz, M. and Kobos, J.C. (2008) 'Evidence-Based Group Psychotherapy: Using AGPA's Practice Guidelines to Enhance Clinical Effectiveness', *Journal of Clinical Psychology*, 64 (11): pp. 1238–1260
- MacGowan, M.J. (2008) *A Guide to Evidence Based Group Work* (New York: Oxford University Press)
- http://www.evidencebasedgroupwork.com/

f

flash groups

SEE ALSO **leadership; planning and preparation; problem-solving; process; resources; roles**

Some groups are carefully planned, consisting of members who are recruited or sent, and they are led by trained groupworkers. This is the template for classic social and therapeutic groupwork. However, there are other kinds of group, such as naturally occurring groups and those that form spontaneously, usually in response to a crisis. These exhibit many of the elements of a classic group, even though they are not planned, they are not led by groupworkers and they have no formal membership or recruitment. The term 'flash group' has been coined to denote these spontaneous groups (Doel, 2007; Manor, 2007).

Let us take an example of a flash group. A train is making its way from one city to another, passing through remote countryside. The 40 or so passengers are sitting in silence, reading books, newspapers and iPads, listening to music through earphones, sleeping or gazing out of the windows into the night. It is a dark, very wet and windy evening. The driver announces that there are floods ahead and the train will terminate at the next stop, a village, and a coach will come to take the passengers the rest of their journey. The passengers disembark into horizontal weather and wander out of the tiny station into a gale and torrential rain to await the coach. Time passes and the passengers begin to talk with one another, sharing their doubts that any coach is coming. In small groups they discuss their options – find taxis, seek shelter in the village or possibly try to find a B&B; then the small groups consult with one another. Some use their mobile phones to see what information is available. Nearby, shelter is found for the older and more vulnerable people among them.

Quite quickly, a collection of 40 individuals has become a group, with people using their *resources* and pooling them, taking different *roles* – some taking the lead, others going to reconnoitre and return with the intelligence they have gathered. The individuals have rapidly become a *collective*, sharing concerns, discussing options, some showing *leadership*, all *problem-solving*. Though there is no named groupworker among them and no one has been elected to be a 'member' and it is likely to be temporary, it is nevertheless a group. Out of a flash flood has been born a flash group.

No doubt you can think of similar circumstances, not necessarily ones in adversity, where this kind of spontaneous group has quickly formed and been effective, despite the lack of *planning* and formal organization (Wilson, 2009).

The concept of flash groups has broader significance because it challenges the more precious notion of groupwork as a process that can only occur in very particular circumstances and only when facilitated by highly skilled practitioners – groupwork as an exclusive activity, one that is occasionally brought down from a high shelf and dusted off for special occasions. This is not to diminish the expertise of trained groupworkers who know how to use these *skills* to an advanced level, but it does serve to connect many more people to the notion and experience of groupwork. Group *process* is part of everyday living and human beings readily and naturally form groups, and are skilled at doing so.

Implications for practice

- The idea of flash groups normalizes groupwork and broadens the number of people who see themselves as engaged in groupwork;
- It is important to name 'acts of groupwork' so that more people identify themselves as groupworking.

FURTHER READING

- Doel, M. (2012) 'When Is a Group Not a Group?' in G.J. Tulley, K. Sweeney and S. Palombo (eds), *Groups: Gateways to Growth* (London: Whiting and Birch), pp. 129–138
- Jagendorf, J. and Malekoff, A. (2005) 'Groups-on-the-Go: Spontaneously Formed Mutual Aid Groups for Adolescents in Distress' in A. Malekoff and R. Kurland (eds), *A Quarter Century*

of Classics (1978–2004): Capturing the Theory, Practice and Spirit of Social Work with Groups (Binghamton: The Haworth Press), pp. 229–246

- Johnson, P. (2008) 'Debate: Flash Groups', *Groupwork*, 18 (1): pp. 10–13

g

gender

SEE ALSO **co-working; development; group as a whole; individuals; membership; planning and preparation; roles; sub-grouping**

Gender has been an important pre-occupation in groupwork literature for several decades and the number of publications on the topic is huge (see the appendices). Gender is often discussed as an issue in the *planning and preparation* phase of work when the composition of group *membership* is being considered, as it can have a profound impact on a group. Group members will bring with them the gender roles and stereotypes learned in the societies and cultures outside the group. As such, the gender balance of a group can influence the behaviour of *individuals* and the *group as a whole*.

On the other hand, there are times when gender *roles* are not present in the life of a group, so there are no clear rules about the best gender composition for groupwork practice. Instead, the gender considerations should be guided by the purpose of the group.

How might gender influence group planning and preparation? Consider two possible groups: one to help parents estranged from their children due to divorce to find ways to be better parents and another to help parents without custody of their children to find better ways to parent. How might the decision about the gender composition of each group be made? Often, it is on pragmatic grounds, after considering the pool of potential members – is there a preponderance of fathers, in which case it would perhaps be an all-male group, or is there more of a balance, in which case it would be a mixed gender group? Whatever decision is taken, the gender composition will have an impact on how members feel about each other and, in a mixed gender group, the potential for *sub-grouping* along gender lines.

There is evidence to suggest that in some mixed groups the needs of women become secondary due to gender role socialization

(Pendergrast *et al.*, 2011). There is also evidence to suggest that some men may do better in mixed gender groups. Such differences raise the possibility of recreating societal oppressive processes and structures within groupwork practice.

Feminist influence

Gender within groupwork has been explored beyond its role in group composition. Feminist groupwork, for example, has a long tradition, and early feminist groupworkers pioneered the use of groups to challenge patriarchy and empower women. However, women are not a homogenous group, nor are men, and the voices of many women were not necessarily heard. Black and minority ethnic women often have their own struggles and racism may be more prominent in their lives than sexism.

Gender can influence the stages of group *development*. The Relational Model of Group Development is based on a feminist theoretical framework, and it suggests that women's groups develop differently from men's groups or mixed-gender groups, requiring the development of a relational base before conflict and change occur (Schiller, 1997).

Gender remains a salient issue for consideration in groupwork, irrespective of the composition of the group membership, gender differences between workers and members, the gender balance of *co-working* or the oppressive gender-based social systems that have a broader impact on group members' lives. Understanding the role of gender in individual and group behaviour is essential knowledge for sound groupwork practice.

Implications for practice

- The gender composition of a group has an influence on individual behaviour;
- Groupworkers must help the group confront oppressive gender-based actions such as stereotypical role assignment, and consider the potential impact of gender-based sub-groups.

FURTHER READING

- Butler, S. and Wintram, C. (1991) *Feminist Groupwork* (London: Sage)
- Cohen, M.B. and Mullender, A. (eds) (2003) *Gender and Groupwork* (London/New York: Routledge)

- Garvin, C. and Reed, B.G. (1983) 'Gender Issues in Social Group Work: An Overview', *Social Work with Groups*, 6 (3–4): pp. 5–18

groundrules

SEE ALSO **activities; leadership; process; sessions; skills**

Groups develop norms of behaviour, i.e. what is considered to be acceptable in that particular group. Norms are important for group members to develop a sense of belonging and togetherness. However, a group's norms are not necessarily empowering or productive: it can develop norms of behaviour that are oppressive, coercive and not functional. For these reasons, group leaders often help the group early on to consider how it is going to behave and perform; rather than use the term 'norms' which is not generally known and which refers more usually to implicit expectations of behaviour, group leaders often introduce the notion of groundrules, which are explicit guides for behaviour.

Once group members understand what the purpose of groundrules are (perhaps by discussion led by the group leaders), different *activities* can be used to create them: one of the most common is to use flipchart paper and pen to collect suggestions about what group members think should be included in a list of groundrules. The first stage might just include collecting suggestions on the flip paper before going on to discuss them. This method, sometimes called brainstorming or quick thinking, enables the subsequent discussion to take in the whole set of suggestions. This can assist the quality of the discussion and help pace the timing, because everybody knows the range of suggestions.

The group leaders might suggest the group prioritizes six groundrules. Prioritizing starts the group members thinking about what is most important to them and it exposes any differences in thinking. This can be helpful for the group (and its leaders) to know from the start. Also, the process of prioritizing requires negotiation, making your case and listening to others, compromise, assertion, all the qualities and *skills* that will be needed in the group. It is a good rehearsal, and the discussion is more likely to mean that group members will remember the groundrules, because they will feel ownership of them.

Usually, the final version of the groundrules is written up clearly on flip chart and stuck to the wall so that they can be referred to in subsequent *sessions*. They provide an objective check, which makes any challenges to a group member's behaviour seem fair and legitimate.

What are the common mistakes with groundrules? First, introducing them too soon in the group's life. The group needs to be able to discuss the groundrules meaningfully and the beginning of the first session is usually premature, because the members are still finding their place in the group. Group leaders often want to establish groundrules as soon as possible, in the hope of pre-empting difficult behaviours from the start; however, if the group feels it has been coerced into a set of rules before it is ready, it is likely to reject them. If the group leaders anticipate that control is going to be problematic in the group (e.g. a group for young people with behavioural problems), it might be reasonable to introduce straightforward *rules* towards the very beginning of the group, whilst promising to re-visit these and refine when the group knows itself better.

Implications for practice

- Groundrules should not be prepared beforehand and presented to the group as a *fait accompli*. That is the difference between rules and groundrules. Rules are given to the members as a condition of membership ('no hitting'; 'no taking of drugs or alcohol'); groundrules are the norms of behaviour that the group members develop among themselves;
- The process of creating groundrules *as a group* can provide an excellent rehearsal for the participative methods that will be experienced throughout the group. This reflects the mix of rights and responsibilities that constitute life in the group – and outside it.

FURTHER READING

- Doel, M. and Sawdon C. (1999) *The Essential Groupworker: Teaching and Learning Creative Groupwork* (London: Jessica Kingsley), Chapter 6 'The First Session and the Group Agreement', pp. 113–129
- Lindsay, T. and Orton, S. (2008) *Groupwork Practice in Social Work* (Exeter: Learning Matters), Chapter 4 'Setting Up the Group', pp. 59–67
- Preston-Shoot, M. (2007) *Effective Groupwork*, 2nd edn (Houndmills: Palgrave Macmillan), Chapter 7 'Working with Groups', pp. 125–150

group as a whole

SEE ALSO **cohesion; individuals; methods; power; roles**

Groups are more than a collection of the *individual* members and, indeed, more than the sum of their parts. This can be understood if one compares a group to an orchestra (Whitaker, 1985). An orchestra is made up of many individual musicians, each playing their own instrument. Though each musician is expert with their instrument, when *they* begin to play together the result is more than the sound of many different instruments; rather *it* becomes an orchestra and the noise is heard as a symphony.

The orchestra is, therefore, the *group as a whole,* something quite different from its individual members. *They* are the group members and *it* is the group. To carry the analogy further, a conductor brings the best out of each individual musician *and* the entire orchestra, understanding how to create a symphony from the many while bringing forth the skills and talents of the individuals. The groupworker, too, must be concerned with not only the individual members of the group, but also the group as a whole. This has been referred to as 'the two clients' (Schwartz, 1976).

This ability of groups to become more than a collection of individuals gives groups much of their *power* and groupworkers must learn to recognize, encourage and work with this *group-ness.* Helping the group as a whole to develop and mature is one of the central tasks of the groupworker, perhaps *the* key role, and it often marks out the novice from the experienced groupworker. This includes working with members to develop a sense of *cohesion,* a group culture, *roles* and identity in the group. In short, a feeling of belonging to a group and belonging *in* the group. The ability to analyse the group as a whole behaviour is an important groupwork skill and is especially important when group problems emerge.

The 'whole group' is used as a method by some group analysts and 'whole community' *methods* are employed in some psychodynamic groupwork traditions (Harris, 2007; Ringer, 2002).

The group as a whole can be a powerful entity – one that can be either benign or malign. There are numerous examples across history, literature and professional discourse of the power of groups to influence people for better and worse.

Implications for practice

- Helping the group move from a collection of individuals to a sense of itself as a whole is a central role of a groupworker;
- The groupworker needs to consider how best to help members work as a group.

FURTHER READING

- Douglas, T. (1991) *A Handbook of Common Groupwork Problems* (London: Routledge)
- Kurland, R. and Salmon, R. (2005) 'Group Work vs Casework in a Group: Principles and Implications for Teaching and Practice' in A. Malekoff and R. Kurland (eds) *A Quarter Century of Classics (1978–2004): Capturing the Theory, Practice and Spirit of Social Work with Groups* (Binghamton: The Haworth Press), pp. 121–132
- Stacey, R. (2005) 'Social Selves and the Notion of the *Group-as-a-Whole*', *Group*, 29 (1): pp 187–209

group dynamics

SEE ALSO **development; group as a whole; process**

Dynamics is a word borrowed from the physical sciences and it refers to the study of the motion of physical objects or the changes in movement. It also refers to the study of how physical systems change and develop over time. In the 1940s, Kurt Lewin applied this concept from physics to the study of social groups and coined the term group dynamics. As in physics, dynamics in groups refers to the forces that move, change or influence individual behaviour in the group, the behaviour of the group as a whole, or have an impact on the development of the group. These group forces emerge as the component parts (the members) that interact with one another and form a social system. They result from the interactions that occur within the group, but are also influenced by the histories that group members bring with them into the group.

Toseland, Jones and Gellis (2006) helpfully conceptualize group dynamics as consisting of five social–psychological domains: communication processes and interaction patterns; attraction and *cohesion*; social integration and influence; *power* and control; and culture. We discuss these below.

1. Communication processes and interaction patterns are the bread and butter of groupwork. Understanding and influencing the verbal, non-verbal or virtual communication processes and the group's patterns of interaction are essential *skills* for groupwork practice, not just what is being said, but also the meanings behind the words and what might not be said. This understanding also entails recognizing who is communicating with whom, and responding to these observations. For example, is one *sub-group* communicating only with itself? If so, what does this exclusiveness mean? Are there certain topics that members seem to resist and, if so, what supports this resistance?
2. Interpersonal attraction and cohesion are important elements of group dynamics. Interpersonal attraction refers to the positive attitudes that attract group members to one another, influenced by proximity, propinquity, similarity and complementarity. Cohesion refers to the collection of bonds or centripetal forces that hold a group together – this includes interpersonal attraction and, additionally, commitment to the shared purpose and working together on tasks.
3. Social integration and influence refer to how accepted members are within a group and the ways in which members are able to affect the actions or behaviours of other group members. Group *roles*, norms and status fit within this domain.
4. From early days *power* and control have been well documented in the groupwork literature as significant elements in group dynamics (e.g. Bennis and Shepard, 1956; Bion, 1959).
5. Group culture refers to the beliefs, language, traditions, ways of working and values that group members come to share. A strong group culture can be palpable when *joining* an existing group.

Group dynamics is sometimes explained in psychoanalytical terms, rather than the social psychological approach above. For example, Foulkes, an early group psychoanalyst, outlined the group specific dynamics in group psychoanalytic therapy (Pines, 2000). Here the dynamics of individual psychoanalysis such as resistance and transference operate within a group matrix. Working through the meanings of such dynamics becomes part and parcel of the group. Group-specific dynamics include socialization, whereby a member is brought out of isolation through group sharing; this is *the mirror phenomenon,* seeing aspects of oneself reflected in the behaviours or problems of other members. Through this projection and identification, members are able to confront their own issues. The collective nature of the group matrix unleashes a powerful dynamic, *the condenser effect,* whereby deep, unconscious material becomes manifest more readily than in individual work. *Exchange* is another important group-specific dynamic; the members share information and understanding and this can lead to group resonance and the *chain phenomenon.* In this interpretation of group dynamics, whatever the topic or experience in the group, each member will resonate with it at their own developmental or fixation level (Pines, 2000).

Implications for practice

- Attending to group dynamics requires groupworkers to respond to the meanings behind the words, and to what is not being said, too;
- Influencing the verbal, non-verbal or virtual communication processes and ways or patterns of interaction are essential skills for groupwork practice.

FURTHER READING

- Forsyth, D. (1999) *Group Dynamics,* 3rd edn (Belmont, CA: Brooks/ Cole-Wadsworth)
- Hare, P., Borgatta, E.F. and Bales, R.F. (eds) (1955) *Small Groups: Studies in Social Interaction* (New York: Alfred Knopf)
- Toseland, R.W., Jones, L.V. and Gellis, Z.D. (2006) 'Group Dynamics' in C.D. Garvin, L.M. Gutiérrez and M.J. Galinsky (eds), *Handbook of Social Work with Groups* (New York: Guilford Press), pp. 13–31

group supervision

SEE ALSO **activities; group dynamics; process; supervision of groupwork**

All professionals' work is supervised, ideally in a regular reflective session. Supervision helps professionals to develop and it is meant to act as a safeguard for the quality of service. Individual supervision is the norm in most cases, but there are good reasons to consider group supervision (Ashmore *et al.*, 2012). These reasons are similar to those for groupwork in general.

Supervising staff or students in groups can provide a supportive environment for people in similar situations to share their concerns and their learning. The supervisees can learn much from one another: the supervisor may have the weight of experience, but the supervisees carry credibility with each other because they are all in the same boat. A group context provides more ideas and responses as well as an opportunity to rehearse situations and use group *activities*. There are often economic reasons for group supervision – that it is cheaper to supervise a number of people together rather than separately. However, this should not be the main driver, as the importance of developing the skills to supervise in groups might be neglected, with poor results.

However, *group dynamics* can inhibit learning as well as promote it. The group facilitator needs knowledge and skill to work with the group *process* as well as the subject matter of the group. Another potential disadvantage is the fact that each individual has less time in group supervision and it might not be possible for all members to feel they have been able to address their own particular concerns.

Peer supervision is an alternative to the line management and consultation models of supervision (Tribe, 1997). In this model, two or more practitioners meet together to reflect on their mutual practice and to learn from one another. It is a model that is especially congruent with the *supervision of groupwork* as it uses the group as a context. Decisions need to be taken about whether the peer supervision group will have any formal *leadership* (usually not if it is a meeting of peers) and agreement about *confidentiality*, so that members know what will stay within the supervision group and what might not.

Although there are similarities with the debriefing between *co-workers* after a group *session*, peer supervision is different in that it usually brings workers together who have not been working together, either with individuals or groups, and it has a more formal basis. The debriefing between co-workers consists largely of immediate matters arising from the recent *session*, whereas the peer group might schedule particular topics over a period of meetings, perhaps reserving some of the group's time for current matters.

Implications for practice

- Group supervision should be considered in tandem with individual supervision – the two are complementary, not mutually exclusive;
- Group supervision needs to be conducted by someone who has groupwork skills – a person who is trained in individual supervision is not necessarily skilled in group supervision.

FURTHER READING

- Atherton, S. (2006) *Putting Group Learning into Practice* (Birmingham: West Midlands Learning Resource Network/Skills for Care)
- Berteau, G. and Villeneuve, L. (2006) 'Integration of the Learning Process and the Group Development Process in Group Supervision', *Groupwork*, 16 (2): pp. 43–60
- Hawkins, P. and Shohet, R. (2000) *Supervision in the Helping Professions* (Buckingham: Open University Press)

groupthink

SEE ALSO **cohesion; development; differences; group as a whole; leadership; membership**

Groupthink refers to a psychological phenomenon that is said to be a potentially negative process in group decision-making, problem-solving or behaviour (Janis, 1972; Turner and Pratkanis, 1998). In groupthink members of groups too quickly or uncritically reach a consensus about a decision or course of action. It may also refer to the influence the *group as a whole* exerts on members to behave in certain ways.

There are many explanations for the occurrence of groupthink, but the principal one is group *cohesion*. Though typically viewed as a positive dynamic in groups, the pressures of group cohesion may prevent group members from expressing dissent or differences of opinion. Conversely, some group *development* theories suggest that fully mature and functioning groups can develop high levels of cohesion that allow and support differences.

Perhaps it is not that groups experiencing groupthink are too cohesive; rather they are insufficiently developed to embrace difference. For example, many theories of stages of group development include a period of pseudo-intimacy where *differences* are suppressed rather than openly embraced. Later stages of development would expect differences of opinion to be freely expressed without posing a threat to group coherence.

Some theories of groupthink suggest that it is more likely to occur with a certain type of group leader – for example, a charismatic leader who does not tolerate difference of opinion – or that it is the chemistry between certain types of *leadership* and the group *membership*.

How to get the best from groupthink? Though the empirical evidence for the concept of groupthink is contradictory and not well developed, it is a notion that is widely employed and appears to be useful. It is worth considering how to mitigate the worst excesses of groupthink – poor decision-making processes, suppressed dissent, etc. – in order to promote good groupwork practice. Possible strategies include:

- Inviting critical dissent – even assigning the role of devil's advocate to a group member. Six Hat Thinking is a good example (de Bono, 2000);
- Following a sound problem-solving process (e.g. Northen and Kurland, 2001, Chapter 8), which might include brainstorming and reviewing all options;
- A restrained leadership, so groupworkers refrain from prematurely voicing their opinions, being aware of their status and the power they hold in the group.

Implications for practice

- Encouraging and supporting differences of opinion can mitigate against damaging elements of groupthink;
- Engaging in in-depth exploration of problems and solutions can prevent groupthink.

FURTHER READING

- de Bono, E. (2000) *Six Thinking Hats* (London: Penguin Books)
- Janis, I. (1972) *Victims of Groupthink* (Boston: Houghton Mifflin)
- Turner, M. and Pratkanis, A. (1998) 'Twenty Five Years of Groupthink Research', *Organizational Behavior and Human Decision Processes*, 73 (2): pp. 105–115

h

health groups

SEE ALSO **counselling groups; self-help groups; therapy groups; virtual groups**

Groups are used broadly in healthcare, from group *therapy* for childhood psychosis to pain management *self-help groups*, from *counselling groups* in GP practices to yoga classes in neighbourhood centres. The value of a group milieu has long been familiar to Occupational Therapists. In mental health work, groupwork has for some time been recognized as a chance to alter the attitudes of individuals and with more persistent effects, primarily because the socialization that can occur in groups improves a person's social behaviour outside the group (Jones *et al.*, 1971; Lewin 1947b).

The medical model widely used in healthcare focuses on individual pathology – a diagnosis of an individual's illness, a prognosis of its likely course and a treatment plan to cure, alleviate or manage the illness. The challenge for groupworkers in health settings is, then, to incorporate the social model that is implicit in groupwork practice; i.e. the social construction of health and illness and its significance for the group and its *individual* members. Let us take the example of a group for cancer patients. The groupworker needs to consider how different kinds of cancer, different lengths of time since diagnosis, different prognoses and different lifestyles might impact on the group and what differences and similarities to plan for. The group is not just a convenient place to see people with cancers, but to provide a stage for them to explore their feelings with others. This requires knowledge of *group dynamics* and an ability to use them.

Self-help groups, and in particular *virtual* ones, are especially common in health. From the neighbourhood Alcoholics Anonymous meetings, many health groups have developed into online groupings of people who can be in touch with others anywhere in the world. With syndromes that are very rare and dispersed, the internet allows sufficient numbers to group together in ways that have never before been possible.

All groups should make provision for the possibility of disabled members (wheelchair access to the group meeting room, etc.) and health groups specifically for disabled people will need to ensure that there is sufficient support to meet the members' physical needs. Group settings have been a tradition for blind people and deaf people, though these groups have more often than not been a case of working with individuals in a group rather than actively using group *process*. Crafts, arts and socializing are important *activities* but groupworkers need to be active in helping individual members to *become a group*.

Implications for practice

- Groups need to incorporate social models, even when the individualized medical model is dominant;
- Virtual groups have much to offer patients with rare disorders who are dispersed far and wide, and those with limited mobility.

FURTHER READING

- Drum, D., Swanbrow-Becker, M. and Hess, E. (2011) 'Expanding the Application of Group Interventions: Emergence of Groups in Health Care Settings', *Journal for Specialist in Group Work*, 36 (4): pp. 247–263
- McCarthy, C.Y. and Hart, S. (2011) 'Designing Groups to Meet Evolving Challenges in Health Care Settings', *Journal for Specialist in Group Work*, 36 (4): pp. 352–367
- Radcliffe, J., Hajek, K., Carson, J. and Manor, O. (eds) (2010) *Psychological Groupwork with Acute Psychiatric Patients* (London: Whiting and Birch)
- *www.patient.co.uk/selfhelp.asp*. This website has details of 1832 UK healthcare support groups. Social care groups tend to be organized in localities.

history of groupwork

SEE ALSO **activities; democracy; educational groups; methods and models; recreation groups; social action; theories; values; virtual groups**

Groups are a universal human experience, so it is no surprise that groupwork is a worldwide phenomenon. However, there are indications that the social significance of groupwork differs between cultures and it would be a mistake to believe that one could transpose the structure of, say, a *health group* for cancer patients in the UK to a group for people with HIV-AIDS in Sub-Saharan Africa. We need more *evidence*, but there are indications that groups in societies that are highly collectivist, such as India and Africa, are seen as a forum where the individual voice can be given expression, and that groups in more atomized western societies are seen as places where people can join together to find their *collective* voice (Cohen *et al.*, 2012). This is not a rule – as can be seen from some western therapy groups where individuals 'find themselves' through the group.

In Europe and North America, modern groupwork has its roots in the nineteenth century, where early forms of social education, welfare and healthcare were more likely to take place in group settings, through the charity organization societies, settlement houses and ragged school movements. The early leaders of the settlement house movement were an eclectic mix of social reformers, socialists and philanthropists, mostly women, concerned with chaos in the social order. Unlike many reformers at the time, they attributed deprivation not to the moral failing of individuals, but to the wider social system. From the settlement movement, groupwork embraced the *values* of social causes: *democratic* ideals, working *with* people, women as leaders and mutual aid. Groupwork soon became associated with *community* movements, especially recreation and youth camps and from these organizations and experiences groupwork embraced fun and participative ideals; and *activities* became to be seen as a social process, an important means through which other objectives could be achieved, such as character building.

In the shadow of Second World War, some future influential groupworkers, largely Jewish, escaped from Nazi Europe and arrived in North America, where their ideas profoundly influenced groupwork practice. After the war many of these groupworkers spent time back in Germany using their groupwork *skills* to rebuild democracy (Kalcher, 2004). Continental European groupwork has also been heavily influenced by social pedagogy – activity led and highly creative.

Groups facilitated by professionalized groupworkers emerged from the 1940s onwards, often through adult education, group psychotherapy, child guidance clinics and residential therapeutic environments. The 1950s and 1960s saw the development of specific groupwork *methods and models*, in particular ideas of mutual aid and British groupwork burgeoned in the newly formed Social Services Departments in the 1970s, especially in 'intermediate treatment' programmes with young offenders and in the probation service. Family services agencies and other voluntary organizations incorporated groupwork practice in their service delivery. Even so, the prevalence of groupwork in the large, public agencies was mixed and groupwork has generally been seen as marginal, with individual casework as the default.

Although there is some evidence that 'professionalised' groupwork is in decline (Ward, 2004), *self-help groups*, especially in the fields of health and personal development, seem to be on the increase. New forms of groupwork not involving people being in the same room at the same time, but communicating virtually, are stretching traditional ideas of what a group is. It remains to be seen whether these communities of interest continue to satisfy the same need as groupwork has historically satisfied.

Implications for practice

- A knowledge of groupwork's roots can help us to understand current developments;
- Whilst embracing new possibilities for groupwork (especially virtual groups), we should not lose sight of the benefits of more traditional group forms.

FURTHER READING

- Brown, A. and Caddick, B. (1986) 'Models of Social Groupwork in Britain: A Further Note', *British Journal of Social Work*, 16: pp. 99–103
- Gitterman, A. and Salmon, R. (eds) (2009) *Encyclopaedia of Social Work with Groups* (New York: Routledge)
- Toseland, R.W. and Rivas, R.F. (2001) *An Introduction to Group Work Practice*, 4th edn (Boston: Allyn and Bacon), Chapter 2 'Historical Developments'
- *IASWG (International Association for Social Work with Groups): www.aaswg.org*

human development and groups

SEE ALSO **collective; gender; purpose; self-help groups; support groups; teamwork; work groups**

We are by our nature social beings. This hard-wired drive to be part of a *collective* is in part responsible for our evolutionary development as a species. Groups made it possible for humans to survive and this dependency on group life continues today, albeit in greatly different forms. Over the life course naturally occurring and formed groups play an important role in human development.

Infants are born into family groups and are dependent on these groups for basic biological survival needs (Germain and Bloom, 1999). The extended family group and parents' friendship groups provide emotional and physical support to new parents and social structures exist in most cultures to support new families. Beyond basic human needs, the kinship group begins the socialization process from the beginning of life. From an early age infants prefer to look at human faces as opposed to inanimate objects and, further, prefer familiar faces.

As toddlers and into early childhood, play groups become an important socialization experience for children – either in local neighbourhood groups or in nursery schools. At this stage of development, parallel play (rather than interactive play) is frequently observed, yet the dynamics of mutual aid have been seen in groups of 2–3 year olds (Berman-Rossi, 1995). In addition, even in parallel play children notice what other children are doing and modify their behaviour in line with the play of others. Even toddlers appear to be influenced by group culture and norms.

In adolescence the peer group takes on increasing significance for the development of the young person (Longres, 2000). Though the influence of parents and close family remain important, adolescence represents a time when the socializing importance of friendship groups can take precedence. The peer group provides a place where young people practise taking on adult roles, learn how to function in collectives, explore culturally approved *gender* roles, and learn about the culture in which they live.

In adulthood groups remain an important part of life. The world of work almost inevitably involves groups whether in task groups, *teamwork* or *work groups*. The socialization to the workplace continues through these groups. Group culture and dynamics are significant in places of employment and friendship groups remain an important influence throughout adulthood. Though many friendship groups derive from the world of work, others centre around shared interests, children and naturally occurring social groupings, such as neighbourhood groupings.

Groups remain important as people age. For the healthy older person, friendship groups may shift with the transition from work to retirement. Social *support* received from these groups is a significant component of well-being in ageing. If health declines, the opportunity to engage in collective activities may decrease at a time when the need increases.

Groups play an important part in human development across the life course, but this is rarely a smooth journey, with stressful transitions and traumatic circumstances. Naturally occurring groups can mitigate some of the negative effects, but there are times when this support is not sufficient to support people and they need the support of formed groups, i.e. groups that are created for a specific *purpose* (Gitterman, 2005a). These groups help their members to live with, or overcome, difficulties and problems in living. They may be led by professionals who are trained in the dynamics of mutual aid or they can be *self-help* groups.

It may or may not be part of the 'worried well' movement, but there is also a tradition of self-exploration in groups for people who may or may not have experienced life traumas, but who seek personal growth through the medium of group exploration, sometimes called encounter groups or T-groups (Rogers, 1970).

Implications for practice

- Naturally occurring groups occur across the life course and support transitions through developmental stages;
- When naturally occurring groups are unable to provide needed support, formal groups can be used by helping professionals to support successful negotiation of stressful life transitions.

FURTHER READING

- Germain, C.B. and Bloom, M. (1999) *Human Behavior in the Social Environment*. 2nd edn (New York: Columbia University Press)
- Gitterman, A. (2005) 'The Life Model, Oppression, Vulnerability and Resiliency, Mutual Aid, and the Mediating Function' in A. Gitterman

and L. Shulman (eds), *Mutual Aid Groups, Vulnerable and Resilient Populations, and the Life Cycle*. 3rd edn (New York: Columbia University Press), pp. 3–37

- Rowan, J. (1999) 'Crossing the Great Gap: Groupwork for Personal Growth', *Groupwork*, 11 (3): pp. 6–18

i

individuals

SEE ALSO **collective; group as a whole; groupthink; problem-solving; process; roles**

There is a philosophical contention that it is not really possible to know what another person thinks or feels and that, like it or not, we are confined to our own bodies and experiences, merely inferring that others feel similar feelings and think similar thoughts. However, advances in our knowledge, especially through social psychology, suggest that Descartes' famous dictum *I think, therefore I am,* would better be expressed as *We think, therefore we are.* Several influential social psychological experiments have pointed to the extraordinary *power* of groups to influence the way individuals see themselves and the world, for better and worse. *Groupthink* can often override individuals' beliefs and mass movements attest to this phenomenon at an even broader level than small groupwork.

Even so, people *join* a group as individuals and they leave as individuals. In western societies, at least, individualism is dominant. Whereas a group experience is highly communal, collectivized societies might be an opportunity for the individual to find his or her singular voice; in more atomized societies groups are likely to be valued for the chance to feel at one with others and for the many 'I's to become a 'we' (Cohen *et al.*, 2012]. Indeed, one of the 'soft' indicators of a group's success is when its members start to use the plural 'we' more than the singular 'I'.

Work with individuals in the group

There are groupwork scholars who bemoan the increasing tendency for groups to be a mere collection of individuals. They do not consider these to be 'real' groups, rather a convenient opportunity for the leader to work with a lot of individuals at the same time, rather than deploying group *process*.

Indeed there is a difference between 'individual work in groups' and 'groupwork'. Individual *problem-solving* in a mutual aid context can be very useful to all group members when connected to the *group as a whole* (Northen and Kurland, 2001; Steinberg, 2004). Some groups offer limited opportunities for 'full-on' groupwork; for example, a group of people who suffer from Alzheimer's might find it hard to make connections between one another and from one *session* to another, so it is more like working with a collection of individuals in the same room than a group. However, the mental capacity and fluency of the individual members will vary within one session and from session to session and there will be flashes of connection that experienced groupworkers can build on and even help to ignite. Many groups, whatever their *membership*, go through times of fragmentation when they do not work well together; and other times when they experience a strong, *collective* We.

Individuals frequently find themselves playing different parts in the group and they sometimes settle into recognizable patterns, such as 'silent member', 'dominant member' and the like. These are explored in more detail in the *roles* entry.

Implications for practice

- Groups have a different significance depending on the broader cultural context: an opportunity to explore one's own individuality or to forge a collectivity;
- Group leaders need to remember that the group members enter and exit the group as individuals.

FURTHER READING

- Cohen, C., *et al.* (2012) 'Global Group Work: Honouring Processes and Outcomes' in A.M. Bergart, S.R. Simon and M. Doel (eds), *Group Work: Honoring Our Roots, Nurturing Our Growth* (London: Whiting and Birch), pp. 107–127
- Doel, M. and Sawdon C. (1999) *The Essential Groupworker: Teaching and Learning Creative Groupwork* (London: Jessica Kingsley), Chapter 10 'The Individual and the Group', pp. 194–212
- Kurland, R. and Salmon, R. (2005) 'Group Work vs Casework in a Group: Principles and Implications for Teaching and Practice' in A. Malekoff and R. Kurland (eds), *A Quarter Century of Classics*

(1978–2004): Capturing the Theory, Practice and Spirit of Social Work with Groups (Binghamton: The Haworth Press), pp. 121–132

involuntary groups

SEE ALSO **beginnings; joining and leaving; purpose; skills**

Group members come to groups for a variety of reasons. It is probably safe to say that few people wake up one morning and say, 'This is a great day to join a group. I'll see if I can find one today.' Rather there are pushes and pulls that will lead people to join groups. For some they will recognize they have a problem, an unmet need, or some concern and search for a way to do something about it. They may come across a group as a possible solution and the promise of the group acts as a pull – *joining* a group as an active choice. These group members are said to have joined voluntarily.

Others come to groups because a professional recognizes that they have an unmet need or decides they have a problem and discusses the group as a possible way forward; this can be described as a *proffered service.* Yet others come to a group because they are required to by some authority; for example, a condition imposed by the courts, probation or parole. These group members are referred to as involuntary group members and groups developed for members required to attend are called *involuntary groups.*

There are different levels of voluntary and involuntary participation. The three categories – voluntary, proffered and involuntary – are not discrete and, in reality, members rarely fit neatly into one particular group. Most people will experience some ambivalence about coming to a group and, rather than three categories, it is better to consider a continuum. For example, members who come to a group voluntarily may be attending because someone close to them has given an ultimatum – 'either you do something about this or we are finished.' All actions are constrained in some respects.

Even when there is no compulsion to attend, group members may resent having to come and be unconvinced that there is really any problem. Likewise, some people may be forced to attend a group programme by the courts (e.g. substance misuse treatment) and may experience relief that help is finally available. Though 'forced' to attend, this involuntary member is a more than willing participant.

Recognizing that there are varying levels of voluntary and involuntary participation, in groups where attendance is a requirement, the groupworker needs to pay extra attention to the way authority is perceived and used, particularly in the *beginning* phase of work (Behroozi, 1992). Resistance is a common experience in working with involuntary groups and should be seen as a normal, even useful dynamic. Helping the group move beyond its resistance and perhaps anger is a crucial task for the groupworker.

Key *skills* to working with members who are resistant include acknowledging the hostility, whilst at the same time allowing the member to exercise as much choice as possible. Empathizing with these resistant feelings, the worker can focus on developing a common starting place for the work, a mutual *purpose*. This entails a skilful mix of giving support and making demands – not only allowing resistant members to feel genuinely heard but also understanding that the group has work to do.

For example, members ordered by the courts to attend a risk reduction programme for people charged with driving under the influence of alcohol are likely to be angry about having to join the group. Participants might not wish to change their drinking behaviour, but they will never again want to face the problems a conviction of this nature causes them. The group can be seen as a means to avoid such problems in the future and this provides an opening to develop a working agreement. The worker can acknowledge the hostility about attending and normalize the feelings (anger, etc.) while stating the purpose of the group. The groupworker might explicitly recognize that whilst some people might not see any problems with their alcohol intake, not at this stage anyway, all have had direct experience of the problems of going through the courts and being convicted. This kind of approach increases the probability that involuntary members will engage with the group.

The benefits of groupwork are especially strong in such groups as the worker does not have to manage this task alone. Frequently the group will have members who have moved beyond anger and resistance and can help challenge the resistant behaviour of members in ways that are more difficult for the worker to accomplish.

Implications for practice

- Members' willingness to participate in a group exists on a continuum from voluntary to involuntary. Groups for 'involuntary' members will likely have some members who are willing to attend. The converse is true as well;
- Acknowledging resistance and anger about being forced to attend an involuntary group while also giving as much choice as possible is a key strategy in working with involuntary groups.

FURTHER READING

- Kindred, M. (2011) *A Practical Guide to Working with Involuntary Clients in Health and Social Care* (London: Jessica Kingsley), Chapter 13
- Rooney, R.H. (2009) *Strategies for Work with Involuntary Clients.* 2nd edn (New York: Columbia University Press), Chapter 9 'Working with Involuntary Groups'
- Schimmel, C.J. and Jacobs, E.E. (2011) 'When Leaders Are Challenged: Dealing with Involuntary Members in Groups', *Journal for Specialists in Group Work,* 36 (2): pp. 144–158

j

joining and leaving

SEE ALSO **beginnings; middles and endings; open and closed groups; planning and preparation; process; selection; session**

From the perspective of group members, perhaps the two most significant points in time are joining the group and leaving it. We might think that the moment prospective group members come together for the first *session* of the group is the moment of joining, but the period of *planning and preparation* is just as much part of this process, especially if there has been an individual offer of groupwork to potential members prior to the group's start, as part of the *selection*. People have begun to join the group as soon as they have been introduced to its possibility.

Leaving, like joining, is as much a process as it is an event. Although the final goodbye is a point in time, the process of leaving should be anticipated from the start of the group, so that members are prepared for it.

There are different types of joining and leaving. In the 'classic' group, members join and leave together, recruited at the same time, all meeting at the first session and departing at the final session. However, there are alternative group templates. For example, ongoing groups might welcome new members and say farewell to existing members without the group itself closing. These *open* groups need to decide how to help new members feel part of the existing group (we all know how difficult it can be to join a group of people who already know one another well) and how to mark a member's departure from the group. This will depend on the reason for leaving – whether it is planned or sudden. In all cases, a member's leaving should never be swept under the carpet (Shulman, 2009).

Some groups are part of a bigger groupwork service, so that members join from other groups (perhaps they have moved from an intensive group to a less intensive one, as they have made progress and become more independent). So their leaving of one group has become a joining of another – a transition.

What are the difficulties associated with joining and leaving? Joining and leaving might be symbolized by, respectively, an aircraft's lift-off and landing. The lift-off is exciting; even when it is bumpy and scary there is exhilaration, and the acceleration into a journey to a new place usually compensates for the possible danger. Landing is a different matter. Deceleration is not so exciting and the knowledge that the trip is over can leave people with a sense of anti-climax. Even when the group has been successful, perhaps even more so, leavings can be difficult. In groups where emotions have been strong, perhaps with members transferring their feelings into a deep attachment to the group leader, the ending can seem regressive. However, usually it is better to avoid extending the leaving process and to resist extra sessions.

Joining and leaving are processes that are rehearsed throughout the life of the group, at the beginning and ending of each session. People who experience separation anxiety, particularly children, are likely to find it a challenge to join and particularly to leave each individual session.

Implications for practice

- The group and its members should be prepared for the leaving, seeing it as a transition rather than an ending, with appropriate individual follow-up where needed;
- Group leaders should prepare themselves for the possibility of a bitter–sweet ending, perhaps the more so when the group has been successful.

FURTHER READING

- Birnbaum, M.L. and Cicchetti, A. (2008) 'The Power of Purposeful Sessional Endings in Each Group Encounter', *Social Work with Groups*, 23 (3): pp. 37–52
- Corey, G. (2011) *Theory and Practice of Group Counseling*. 8th edn (Belmont, CA: Brooks/Cole, Cengage Learning), Chapter 4 'Early Stages in the Development of a Group', pp. 94–120
- Whitaker, D. S. (1985) *Using Groups to Help People* (London: Routledge and Kegan Paul), Chapter 12 'Problems, Opportunities, Comings and Goings During the Established Phase', pp. 317–360

l

leadership

SEE ALSO **co-working; democracy; difficulties in groups; membership; planning and preparation; process; power; resources; role; selection; self-help groups**

Leadership is a function and a process that might be exercised by a particular named person (the leader of a group) or might arise informally from within the group *membership*. Assertive leadership is the capacity to inspire or persuade others to follow a particular course of action or strategy; facilitative leadership is the capacity to direct the *process*, so that others are helped to decide on a course of action (Heap, 1988a). Effective leadership usually requires a combination of assertive and facilitative leadership. As we will see later, leadership can be exercised even in the absence of a formal leader.

Styles of leadership
The classic treatment of leadership styles comes from Kurt Lewin and colleagues (Lewin *et al.*, 1939). They suggested this typology:

> *Autocratic leaders* take decisions without consultation. This can be appropriate when decisions must be taken quickly, when the quality of the decision will not be impoverished by lack of input, and when the group's agreement is not necessary for a successful outcome.
>
> *Democratic leaders* enable the group to provide input before a decision is made, although the degree of input will vary from leader to leader. This style of leadership is important when group agreement matters, for instance, in achieving the best outcome or enabling the group's processes to develop, but it can be difficult to manage when there are lots of different views.
>
> *Laissez-faire leaders* do not interfere; they allow people within the group to make many of the decisions. This can work well when the group is highly capable and motivated, and when

there is no need for close monitoring. However, this style can be a result of laziness or lack of confidence on the part of the leader and might lead to members of the group assuming leadership functions inappropriately. Ironically, a laissez-faire style can lead to autocratic leadership developing within the group.

Lewin's experiments found that groups led by autocratic leaders were more productive than *democratic* styles which, in turn were more productive than laissez-faire. However, levels of hostility and resentment were highest in the autocratic groups. Thus there are advantages and disadvantages to all three styles. It is important to question the assumption that the democratic style is 'the best'; the most effective leadership is that which is capable of recognizing which style is most suitable at any point in the group and an ability to move between styles whilst not confusing the membership.

The leader of a group that is created anew has a number of responsibilities:

- **Selection** – Where the membership of the group is defined by a relatively broad criterion (such as 'women with severe and enduring mental health problems'), the leader is usually responsible for offering the group to potential members and making the final *selection*.
- **Planning and preparation** – The leader has responsibility for overall *planning* and the preparations necessary for each individual *session*.
- **Group process and task** – Leaders must attend to *process* in the group and ensure full participation wherever possible of all group members. If the group gets stuck, group leaders must help it to move on, to confront *taboo* topics and to attend to the group's *tasks*. A responsibility of leadership is to create a balance between focusing on group tasks and outcomes on the one hand, and group relations and processes on the other.
- **Evaluation and recording** – Group leaders must help the group to review its progress and *evaluate* the group process and outcomes. Leaders need to make sure that the group keeps an account of itself through some kind of *recording*.

Not infrequently the notion of leadership is strongly associated with the idea of control. The bottom line for any leader is that group members should be physically safe: this control is usually best exercised internally by the group itself, but if this is not possible or is not happening, the group leader is responsible for control. *Difficulties in groups* are best explored by the group as a whole, under the leadership of a skilled and experience group leader – but only when it is safe to do so.

Group leaders are members of the group, yet *not* members of the group at the same time. This ambivalent situation is illustrated every time group leaders face the dilemma as to whether they can truly begin the sentence with 'We ...'. In most cases the group leaders are not in the same boat as the group members (in terms of their personal circumstances), though they are sharing this particular boat (the group). This simultaneous closeness and distance has been referred to as the authority–intimacy dilemma and is closely associated with different stages of the group's *development*. Paradoxically, group leaders often dislike exercising authority yet fear losing control (Reid, 1988).

Sharing leadership

The responsibilities named earlier are those of *leadership*; this does not mean they have to be exercised by the person designated as *leader*. Indeed, empowered groups are those where these responsibilities are shared as best they can be with the membership as a whole. It is paradoxical that the group leaders will usually need to exercise and demonstrate leadership in order for the group itself to recognize leadership and begin to take it for itself.

The formal leaders are more likely to have the *resources* and the experience to exercise leadership, but they must exercise their *power* to transfer resources to the group membership, or certainly decisions about how resources can be used. When the group can see *itself* as a resource it is truly empowered and able to exercise leadership.

In some groups the formal leaders leave the group after an agreed length of time; their leadership *role* has been to help launch the group, but once the group is considered self-sustaining, leadership comes from within and the leaders might move on to create a new group.

Sometimes leadership is shared among two or more formal leaders. In the UK, co-leadership is quite common in social groupwork (less so in the US); in these circumstances it is necessary for the leaders to develop skills in *co-working*. Sharing leadership functions between the formal leaders can be a good model for how these functions can be shared among the group as a whole. If there are three or more leaders (not uncommon in groups where high physical demands are placed on the leadership, such as groups for people with dementia) the leadership itself can be considered to be a *sub-group*, a leadership group. This group needs to attend to its own processes, not least to ensure that it does not overwhelm the membership with its *size* and power.

Not all groups have formal leaders. Indeed, there is a well-developed model of self-directed groupwork in which the group's purposes and processes are decided and directed from within (Ward and Mullender, 1991). *Self-help groups* often meet without a designated leader. However, though there may not be a formal leader, all groups require attention to the leadership functions and the responsibilities we have outlined in this entry.

Implications for practice

- The leadership role comprises many different functions and responsibilities and these need not always be exercised by the person who is formally designated the leader;
- Failure to attend to leadership is likely to result in a group drifting or fragmenting.

FURTHER READING

- Caplan, T. (2005a) 'Active or Passive Intervention in Groups: The Group Leader's Dilemma', *Groupwork*, 15 (1): pp. 24–41
- Doel, M. (2006) *Using Groupwork* (London: Routledge/Community Care), Chapter 6 'Lead?', pp. 99–113
- Gitterman, A. and Salmon, R. (eds) (2009) *Encyclopaedia of Social Work with Groups* (New York: Routledge), 'Group Work Leadership', pp. 299–308

learning groups

SEE ALSO **activities; conflict; continuing professional development; difficulties in groups; groupthink; individuals; leadership; methods; models; outcomes; process; purpose; roles**

All groups involve some form of learning. Sometimes the group is guided by an overt learning theory, such as cognitive behavioural therapy. Even in groups using *methods* with different theoretical underpinnings, such as a psychodynamic approach, the development of insight and self-knowledge has, in the broadest sense, an educational impact (Bamber, 2004; Berry and Letendre, 2004; Brown, 1998; Holmes and Gahan, 2006). Some groupwork has a purpose that is *primarily* about learning or is educational in nature, such as parent education groups (O'Neal, 1999) or sex education groups for young people.

Classes in formal educational settings are one particular kind of group, though there is a wide range of teaching approaches. For example, in a didactic 'talk and chalk' class students do not engage with one another, rather communication is switchboarded through the class leader. However, in some methods of teaching, class members have a high degree of interaction through discussion, problem-solving and decision-making (Creswell, 1997). This kind of learning in student groups is based on andragogical (adult learning) techniques and is well researched. These techniques engage participants in their own learning and encourage them to use their own and others' experience rather than relying solely on the expertise of the teacher or leader. Andragogy and small group theory and practice have much in common and, at one end of the spectrum of educational groups, there is little to distinguish the classroom from social groupwork.

Learning in small groups is an increasingly common approach to teaching and learning in universities and colleges. There are numerous benefits to establishing learning groups; these range from improved performance and grades, and long-term retention of learning to softer outcomes such as improved attitudes towards learning and better engagement in the learning process. *Models* of active group learning include problem-based learning (PBL), enquiry in action learning (EAL), action learning sets, small group projects and small group presentations. These activities help students to learn the skills and tasks required to work with others in small teams (Burgess and Taylor, 1995; Davies, 1999: Hartley and Dawson, 2010). They are very transferable skills and highly desired by employers.

For students in the helping professions, learning in student groups is a good model for working with service users in groups (Berman-Rossi and Kelly, 2004; Lee *et al.*, 2009; O'Dee, 1995; Rose, 2008). There are opportunities for learning in groups on placements, where students learn about professional practice in agencies (Lindsay, 2005; Worden,

2000) and for learning from each other's experiences on placement (Maidment and Crisp, 2007). Positive experiences of learning in groups also lay a strong foundation for continuing professional development in learning groups, following professional qualification.

Some student groups are designed to model groups using experiential *methods* (Rose, 2008; Smith and Davis-Gage, 2008), but most student learning groups are *task* groups. These kinds of group function best when:

- **There is agreement and clarity about the shared task.** This shared agreement should be developed at the first meeting.
- **The tasks required to complete the overall goals are understood by all and assigned to appropriate members.** Tasks should be agreed during the first meeting(s) of the group and assigned to individuals. It is important that members are happy with the tasks assigned to them. New tasks may emerge later, and these should be agreed and assigned quickly.
- **The group members have clear, flexible and agreed roles.** Like most task groups, student learning groups need functional *roles*. The roles may include formal ones such as leader, secretary and timekeeper, but also informal roles – initiator, sceptic, gatekeeper, harmonizer, compromiser, devil's advocate, etc.
- **Transparent and effective communication strategies and patterns.** Given the wealth of electronic communication systems available, student learning groups have numerous options for keeping all members in the loop regarding task completion and progress. Personal relationships also need to be transparent and support the group progress.
- **The group stops to reflect on and evaluate progress and processes at regular points.** It is helpful if student learning groups reflect regularly on both the *process* and progress towards the *outcomes* of task completion. Such temperature checks can help identify and resolve any problems before they become entrenched (Kurland and Salmon, 1998; Muskat and Mesbur, 2011).

Even if all the tips outlined above are followed, learning groups may encounter difficulties in functioning. Group problems in a learning group should not necessarily be seen as problematic – what is important is the way they are resolved and the learning that is derived from them. *Difficulties in groups* might arise from disagreements or *conflict* about the balance of shared work or the ways in which group members are working (or not pulling their weight). Conflict allows for creative solutions and open and frank discussions about the direction of the group. As long as the conflict is not allowed to escalate, it is important for the group to confront the conflict and find ways to resolve it, usually using a combination of accommodation, competition, compromise, avoidance and collaboration. The natural inclination for many inexperienced groups experiencing disagreement is to use the democratic approach of voting. This type of conflict resolution results in a majority winning at the expense of a minority, and not necessarily the best outcome. An alternative is compromise, with everybody giving up something, but again not always achieving the optimum result. A collaborative approach requires dialogue and careful listening skills (sometimes called a dialectical process); it takes more time but, when successful, can achieve a better outcome for the group and improved communication patterns.

Implications for practice

- Learning groups benefit from having clear and agreed purposes, tasks, roles and communication;
- Regular 'temperature checks' can help identify problems in group functioning before they escalate.

FURTHER READING

- Ashmore, R., Carver, N., Clibbens, N. and Sheldon, J. (2012) 'Lecturers' Accounts of Facilitating Clinical Supervision Groups within a Pre-Registration Mental Health Nursing Curriculum', *Nurse Education Today*, 32 (2012): pp. 2224–2228
- Freire, P. (1972) *Pedagogy of the Oppressed* (Harmonsworth: Penguin)
- Hogan, B. (2012) 'Reflective Practise and Mutual Aid in Educational Groups: a Gateway to Constructed Knowledge' in G.J. Tully, K. Sweeney and S. Palombo (eds), *Gateways to Growth* (London: Whiting and Birch), pp. 25–38
- Johnson, D. W. and Johnson, R. T. (2005) 'Learning Groups' in S.A. Wheelan (ed), *The Handbook of Group Research and Practice*

(Thousand Oaks and London: Sage), pp. 441–461

- Reynolds, M. (1993) *Groupwork in Education and Training* (London: Kogan Page)
- Penn State University (2005) 'Building Blocks for Teams: Student Tips', http://tlt.its.psu.edu/suggestions/teams/student/index.html

m

manualized groups

SEE ALSO **activities; conflict; evidence-based; leadership; process; researching groups; session; skills; time; values**

Manualized groups are structured groups delivered around a manual or defined curriculum, with set topics and activities identified for each *session* (Middleman, 2005). The manuals are typically based on research as they have primarily grown in popularity over the past 20 years as an outgrowth of the *evidence-based* practice movement. They are found in most areas of groupwork, especially criminal justice, health, mental health and schools. They focus on a particular problem or identified need, such as, parenting skills, anger management, depression and social skills.

Group programmes that have been evaluated and shown to be effective with specific service user groups can help ensure that the groupworker is using best practice. If group programmes are delivered in the required order, there is some assurance for the groupworkers, funders and organizations that the desired skills are taught. If previous *research* suggests that the programme has been successful, there is some confidence that the programme will be successful with current and future groups. For busy workers, having a pre-developed curriculum can greatly ease the planning process, as there is a given set of *activities* and guidance.

One of the drawbacks to the curriculum-driven groups is, indeed, that it is driven by a curriculum, rather than by the needs of the group. As the programmes are evidence-based, there can be pressure on groupworkers to follow the curriculum exactly as it is written in order to preserve 'treatment fidelity' (i.e. it can be properly compared to other groups using this curriculum). On one level this makes good sense; if the programme has been found to be effective as written, then it should be delivered as it is, as changing the programme may interfere with its effectiveness. On the other hand, strict adherence to the curriculum may prevent the worker from using group *process* to engage the group members or addressing important problems in the group. If a group is in *conflict*, for instance, it would be folly to complete a prescribed exercise simply because the curriculum plan says it is the allotted *time* to do so.

A skilled groupworker can follow a manual or any planned activities in spirit rather than to the letter, blending group process and the curriculum into a meaningful and relevant experience for the particular group. However, if manualized group programmes are delivered by people without appropriate groupwork knowledge and skills, it is likely that the curriculum will be delivered didactically or at the expense of group process, thereby reducing the effectiveness of the programme. To be most effective, before using a manualized or curriculum-driven programme, the group *leadership* should be trained not just in the content of the programme but in the *skills* and knowledge base of groupwork.

Implications for practice

- Groupworkers should not neglect the needs of group members in favour of the demands of the curriculum;
- It is important to use group process in curriculum-driven groups.

FURTHER READING

- Comer, E., Meier, A. and Galinsky, M.J. (2004) 'Development of Innovative Group Work Practice Using the Intervention Research Paradigm', *Social Work*, 49 (2): pp. 250–260
- Galinsky, M., Terzian, M. and Fraser, M. (2006) 'The Art of Group Work Practice with Manualized Curricula', *Social Work with Groups*, 29 (1): pp. 11–26
- Letendre, J. (2009) 'Curricular-Based Approach' in A. Gitterman and R. Salmon (eds), *Encyclopeadia of Social Work with Groups* (New York: Routledge)

membership

SEE ALSO **differences and similarities; groundrules; joining and leaving; leadership; open and closed; planning and preparation; roles; size**

People new to groupwork often ask questions such as: What is the best *size* for a group? What kinds of people should you have in a group? What kind of mix of people is likely to work well? What if I have to have the same life experience as the members – is that good or bad? Should groups be open or closed? All these questions are ones about group *membership*. Though answers with certainty do not exist for these questions and others like them, there are practice principles and practice wisdom, *theories* of groups and groupwork and *research* evidence that can help us to respond to these questions. These responses will also be shaped by the purpose, setting and type of group (Brown, 1994; Gitterman, 2005b; Northen and Kurland, 2001).

Group composition refers to the characteristics of the members in a group, including the groupworkers. In the *planning and preparation* phase, there are decisions to be made about the approximate number of group members, whether membership should be *open* or *closed*, the number of groupworkers, the demographic mix of the group, any desired behavioural characteristics of the members and, overall, how much range or *difference* is possible or desirable in all of these areas. The *purpose* of the group will be the principal guiding factor in all of these decisions. These items are discussed below.

- **Size:** If the group is likely to require a good deal of personal interaction, intimate sharing, and the development of strong emotional bonds, then a group of eight or so is likely to be appropriate. Groups that are more about sharing information and *social action* benefit from larger numbers (Ward and Mullender, 1991). The characteristics of group members are also significant. For example, a group of older carers working on permanency planning for a seriously intellectually disabled adult child would likely be able to function very well with a group size of eight to twelve. However, a group of ten confused older people with mid-stage dementia or a group of ten very active 8 year olds with attention deficit hyperactivity disorder may be difficult to manage or, alternatively, require a large *leadership*.

  Group size in open groups might fluctuate. In residential *settings* a group may grow or shrink depending on the abilities of members and the changing population of residents. See the A–Z entry on *size* for more details.

- **Open or closed membership:** Closed groups encourage greater intimacy, open groups more diversity. The impact of new members in an open group can be quite considerable. See the A–Z entry on *open and closed* for more details.
- **Number of groupworkers:** The size of the leadership group is a matter of group composition, too. Co-working has many benefits, but the size of the leadership group must not overwhelm the rest of the membership. See the A–Z entries on *co-working* and *leadership* for more details.
- **Demographic mix of the group:** Demographic characteristics include *gender*, age, sexual orientation, *race*, ethnicity, nationality, language, class, religion, etc. Group purpose once again will influence the decision about the demographic make-up of group membership (Cox and Ephross, 1998). Many groups have a purpose that limits membership around a particular demographic characteristic. For example, a group to support non-custodial fathers who want support to re-establish relationships with estranged children would include only men as members. A group to support gay teenagers navigate the challenges of the coming out process would include only gay youth.

  Age is an important consideration, especially for groups for children and young people as children of the same age can inhabit very different developmental worlds. As such, groups for children and young people may need to have a narrow age range, or even grouped around developmental stages and transitions rather than ages. Mixing carers of early and late onset dementia would need careful consideration – are the experiences and needs of the two groups of carers too different to be met in the same group?

  So, the primary purpose of a group and shared experience usually override simple demographic differences. However, an important principle of composition of the group, sometimes called the Noah's Ark principle, is that – wherever possible – it is better not to have one member who is unique in one of the important demographic characteristics (e.g. having only one woman in a group of men or having one black person in a group of white people). It is not a hard and fast rule, but a useful guide. When the Noah's Ark principle is broken, perhaps for pragmatic reasons, the worker must be alert for issues of 'otherness' that may impact on the unique individual in the group. See the A–Z entry on *differences and similarities*.

Behavioural characteristics that would prevent interaction in the group might be criteria for excluding potential members. There is some evidence to suggest that some people's circumstances might make it very difficult for them to benefit from group life: if they are severely depressed, floridly psychotic, actively suicidal, suffering from acute dementia, extremely autistic, very narcissistic, acutely anxious or have severe communication difficulties. However, this is not a rule and merely guidance. There is evidence of successful groupwork with people in these circumstances (Kelly, 2005); for instance, groups for people who hear voices can be beneficial, and they will include people with psychotic symptoms. On the other hand, an actively psychotic member in a substance abuse treatment group, where all the other members are not psychotic, is likely to experience difficulties in the group.

Members need to have enough in common to be able to relate to each other, at the same time, enough that is different to give the group energy.

Once the criteria for the composition of a new group have been decided, there are many ways to recruit members. These are discussed in more details in the A–Z entry on *selection*.

Membership *roles* change with the group's *development*. This usually brings an increasing sense of belonging and awareness of *membership*. The members transform from a collection of individuals into a cohesive group. In a group that is functioning well, rates of attendance are typically high; however, if members are absent, it is important to find out the reasons for this. If the group is not meeting the needs of some of its members, they are likely to drop out and group leaders need to consider whether they will follow-up individually with people to see why they are not attending. In groups where membership is *involuntary*, absence is more significant and the group leaders will normally have to report the absence (e.g., to a court).

The group should pay attention to the *endings* with individual members who are leaving. In groups with an open membership this might be quite frequent; in a closed group, it means the member is leaving prematurely and this might be difficult for both the individual member and the rest of the group. It is important that these occasions are marked and that the *individual* and the group discuss the experience, positives and negatives, share the meaning of the ending for the worker and members, and identify any work to be continued outside and beyond the group.

A new member *joining* an ongoing group needs to be welcomed, perhaps by sharing the group's journey so far, a discussion of the group's *groundrules* and a discussion of the culture of the group (Kelly and Berman-Rossi, 1999). Groups develop a culture of their own, which can feel quite alien to newcomers.

Implications for practice

- The purpose of the group should determine decisions made about group membership: for instance, groups with purposes requiring intimate sharing should have smaller membership and social action groups may function better with larger membership;
- Group members need enough in common to develop relationships, but enough differences in order to bring energy to the group.

FURTHER READING

- Brown, A. and Mistry, T. (2005) 'Group Work with "Mixed Membership Groups": Issues of Race and Gender' in A. Malekoff and R. Kurland (eds), *A Quarter Century of Classics (1978–2004): Capturing the Theory, Practice and Spirit of Social Work with Groups* (Binghamton: The Haworth Press), pp. 133–148
- Douglas, T. (1994) *Survival in Groups: The Basics of Group Membership* (Buckingham: Open University Press)
- Lindsay, T. and Orton, T. (2011) *Groupwork Practice in Social Work.* 2nd edn (Exeter: Learning Matters),Chapter 2 'Planning Your Group: Initial Decisions', pp. 19–41
- Steinberg, D.M. (2004) *The Mutual-Aid Approach to Working with Groups: Helping People Help One Another.* 2nd edn (New York: Haworth Press), Chapter 3 'Pregroup Planning with Mutual Aid in Mind'

methods and models

SEE ALSO **context; individuals; manualized groups; problem-solving; process; social action; theories; therapy groups; values**

When one groupworker asks another 'which method do you use'? it can mean a number of things. The term 'method' is slippery and ill-defined and often confused with model. In this entry we aim to clarify these two notions and understand their implications in practice.

A method can be defined as the systematic process of groupwork when applied in practice. A model, on the other hand, is a simplified representation of something – this 'something' might be physical, psychological or social. In a physical sense one can think of a model airplane as a simplified representation of a real airplane. If the model airplane is sophisticated enough it could be used to explain how flight occurs or to test the lift of different wing configurations; such physical models can help us to understand the world in which we live. In a conceptual sense, a model is the representation of a system or a process. This conceptual representation serves to help understand and predict how different parts of a system or process will interact with one another. It can help with predictions and explanations about how things work.

In a groupwork context, methods explain *what* to do and models explain *how* the group process works or *why* certain methods should be used in particular contexts.

Groupwork *methods* and *methodologies* are closely linked, with the second providing the theoretical underpinning for the specific practices of the first. So, the task-centred method of groupwork has a methodology that draws from learning and systems theories as well as positive psychology. This methodology underpins the various methods that task-centred groupwork deploys.

The same *techniques* can be used in different methods, though some techniques are likely to be more closely associated with specific methods. For instance, the task planning and implementation sequence (TPIS) is unique to the task-centred groupwork method, but the elements within this sequence, the different techniques used, can also be employed with methods other than task-centred.

All practice methods need these following constituents:

- **A systematic way of working,** so one practitioner of practice method X can recognize the work of another practitioner of X.
- **A body of knowledge** that informs the practice method. The knowledge base might be organized into a particular theory.

- **A tested and researched** evidence base that continues to deepen knowledge and broaden practice. The evidence base should help to refine the practice method.
- **A value base** that is open and explicit and finds clear expression in the workings of the practice method.
- **A practice technology** that guides the use of the method. Some methods will develop associated techniques and *skills*, such as paradoxical injunction in family therapy methods.

Some groupwork methods adhere more than others to these components, and some are more explicit than others.

There is an enormous and growing range of groupwork methods and not space to consider them all in detail here. However, there is a bibliography of methods in an appendix at the back of this book. Some methods and approaches, such as *learning groups, self-help, social action, support groups, therapy groups* and *virtual groupwork* are considered in separate entries.

It is common for a group to use a variety of methods – an *eclectic* approach. Well-established group methods can be eclectic, in the sense that they use a variety of different methods – such as encounter groups that use a mix of problem-solving, insight development, emotion-sharing and activity methods to achieve their purposes.

The discussion concerning methods is complicated further by the fact that groupwork is, itself, often described as 'a method'. Groupwork sits as one method among others – individual casework, family work and community work. When groupwork itself is described as a method, it is likely that there are two possible meanings. One refers to the act of bringing people together into a grouping – the group as a *context* for groupwork; the other refers to specific methods that are linked to theories of groupwork (such as mutual aid) that can only occur in groups.

A brief overview of groupwork models

Much of the development of models to guide and explain groupwork began in the US in the mid-twentieth century. Subsequently, Papell and Rothman (1966) published a seminal article, presenting three models of groupwork, all of which continue to be relevant to modern groupwork:

1. **Social goals model:** The *purpose* of groups in the social goals model is to increase social consciousness, responsible citizenship and social action. The theoretical underpinnings of the model include humanistic, developmental and phenomenological psychology. *Democratic* ideals permeate the early writing. In addition, *problem-solving* approaches were developed in this model. The social goals model is best exemplified in the writings of Tropp (1976) and Klein (1953; 1972).

The critical assumption of the social goals model is the unity of social action and psychological health. Through participation in social causes and in the mainstream of society, groups and their members can affect social change and promote social health. In this model the worker is an 'influence person' with responsibility for developing social consciousness, functioning as a role model to inculcate democratic *values* and responsible citizenship.

2. **Remedial model:** This model encompasses those groups established to help people who are thought to be most in need, defined at the time as 'dysfunctional behaviour'. Help was defined as rehabilitation of the dysfunctional person through an improvement in coping skills. The theoretical underpinnings of the remedial model include role theory, social systems theory, cognitive and behavioural theories, social psychology and the scientific or 'medical' model.

The individual is the focus for change, with *individual* goals for change. These should be precise, realistic and measurable. The group is a means and a context for change; in other words, the worker uses the group to create an environment that will facilitate a change for the individual. There is a strong emphasis upon an empirical basis for practice. The groupworker in a remedial model is an expert *outside* the group who will assess, diagnose and treat the individual members of the group. Garvin (1996), Vinter (1959) and Rose (1977) were early authors associated with this model.

3. **Reciprocal model:** This model brings people together to work on common problems by forming a system of *mutual aid*. Adaptation, socialization and problem-solving are central components. The theoretical underpinnings of this model are

> systems theory, field theory and small group theory. Later, developmental psychology, ecological systems theory and resiliency theory were incorporated.
>
> The critical assumptions in this model are that people are capable of self-realization and that group members must participate fully with the helping process. The worker is an integral part of the group and there is a here and now, existential focus. The model reflects a belief in mutual relationships and the interdependency of societies and individuals. When there are tensions and strains in this symbiotic relationship, people experience problems. In this model the worker's role is that of a mediator between the needs of the members and those of the group and the larger society. Schwartz (1976) is the author most closely associated with the early development of the reciprocal model.
>
> Papell and Rothman's identification of three different models was a significant theoretical advance for groupwork. Subsequently a core of common themes was found in an overarching model of contemporary groupwork practice (Papell and Rothman, 1980). The core elements included the group as a mutual aid system; negotiating agreed goals; group *process* as a means to promote group purpose; an understanding of group *development*; the importance of internal *leadership* (i.e. group members exercising leadership); empowerment of group and group members; and the influence of group *contexts,* the systems in which the group exists.

The influence of these different models is evident in contemporary approaches to groupwork practice (Gitterman and Shulman, 2005); for example, empowerment models (Lee, 1991, 2001; Nosco and Breton, 1997) and the self-directed model (Ward and Mullender, 1991) are examples of both the reciprocal and the social goals models of groupwork.

Psychoanalytic models of groupwork are based on theories of personality development and of psychopathology (Radcliffe and Diamond, 2007; Roberts and Pines, 1991). The group process and the role of the worker are understood through a psychoanalytic lens; for example, group members' resistance might be understood as an unconscious defence mechanism. Person-centred models of groupwork are based on humanistic and existential psychology and theories of self-actualization. These groups focus on emotions, relationships, personal development and meaning in life. Behavioural groupwork models are based on experimental psychology and learning theories. Behavioural groups may use methods of systematic desensitization, practising and learning new behaviours and reducing. modifying or controlling problematic behaviours and beliefs.

Implications for practice

- It is important to be explicit about the theoretical underpinnings of a group – the group leaders' approach, the model of groupwork that influences their understanding of groups and groupwork and the methods that will be used;
- Confusion or neglect of model and method can lead to an unsystematic approach to groupwork, which makes it difficult to build the body of knowledge needed to develop groupwork theory and practice.

FURTHER READING

- Glassman, U. (2008) *Group Work: A Humanistic and Skills Building Approach*. 2nd edn (Thousand Oaks, CA: Sage)
- Manor, O. (1988) *Choosing a Groupwork Approach: An Inclusive Stance* (London/Philadelphia: Jessica Kingsley)
- Shaffer, J. and Galinsky, M.D. (1989) *Models of Group Therapy*. 2nd edn (Englewood Cliffs, NJ: Prentice-Hall)
- Steinberg, D.M. (2004) *The Mutual Aid Approach to Working with Groups Helping People Help One Another*. 2nd edn (Binghampton, NY: The Haworth Press)
- Wheelan, S.A. (ed) (2005) *The Handbook of Group Research and Practice* (Thousand Oaks/London: Sage)

O

open and closed groups

SEE ALSO **beginning; cohesion; ending; groupthink; joining and leaving; membership; purpose; resources; self-help groups; sessions; settings; support groups; time**

The terms 'open' and 'closed' refer to the nature of *membership* in groups. Closed groups have a defined membership and no new members are allowed to *join* the group once it has begun, sometimes called 'non-permeable boundaries'. Some open groups have new members entering and old members leaving on a very regular and frequent basis; others may only allow new members to enter at certain times. 'Open and closed' refers to the nature of group membership, whilst 'open-ended or close-ended' group refers to *time*. Close-ended groups are time limited, with a specific *beginning* and *ending*. Open-ended groups, on the other hand, can continue for an indefinite time. There is some confusion about these concepts, as frequently closed membership groups are also close-ended and open groups are more likely to be open-ended. Nevertheless, despite this close association, time limits and membership limits are independent of each other and can vary. There are benefits and drawbacks to both of group membership, depending on the nature and purpose of the group.

Why have a group with closed membership? Some difficulties that bring people to groups are sensitive, perhaps touching on cultural *taboos* and demanding high levels of privacy. Having a closed membership can increase the security and safety for the members, making it easier to engage as a group. Having a closed group may also help promote *cohesion*. Finally, the nature of some *settings* influences the decision to have a closed membership group, such as those with a captive audience.

Why have open membership groups? *Purpose* and *setting* are the most significant factors in open-ended groups. For example, a group in a hospital ward draws from a changing pool of patients, regularly discharged and admitted.

Some groups benefit from a membership that includes people at different stages in 'the journey'; for example, a group where members tend to be in initial denial about their situation (such as addiction, domestic violence and sexual offending) can be helped when there are novice and experienced group members. Older members can be reminded how far they have moved beyond denial to make positive changes, which helps to reinforce their own progress. Newer members can benefit from the experienced members as role models, and active challenges to their denial in ways that groupworkers cannot. New members can also be given a sense of hope by seeing that the experienced members have survived and even moved on. However, there are also dangers of destructive *groupthink* if incoming members have not moved on, for instance, if all the men in a group are in denial about their abusive behaviour (Preston-Shoot, 2007).

Why have close-ended groups? Time limits can provide the push for a group to achieve its goals and avoid a sense of drift. Ways must be found to distribute limited *resources* such as the group leaders' time, and time-limited groups allow groupworkers to move on to establish new groups. Finally, it can be easier for potential group members (and, indeed, group leaders) to commit to a group if it is within an agreed limit.

Why have open-ended groups? There are some problems and situations that are not amenable to short-term work and that require ongoing support. For example, carers who are providing care over many years benefit from a *support group*. Severe childhood sexual abuse may need longer periods of time for healing to occur (Northen and Kurland, 2001). In some models, the groupworkers commit to a certain period (say, the first eight *sessions*) with an understanding that the group can choose to transform to a *self-help* or self-led group after the groupworkers' departure.

Implications for practice

- The decision to establish a group with open or closed membership should be informed by the purpose of the group, the group setting and the likely characteristics of new members.

FURTHER READING

- Henry, M. (1988) 'Revisiting Open Groups', *Groupwork*, 1 (3): pp. 215–228
- Miller, R. and Mason, S.E. (2012) 'Open-Ended and Open-Door Treatment Groups for Young People with Mental Illness', *Social Work with Groups*, 35 (1): pp. 50–67
- Schopler, J. and Galinsky, M. (1984) 'Meeting Practice Needs: Conceptualizing the Open-Ended Group', *Social Work with Groups*, 7 (2): pp. 3–19

organizations as groups

SEE ALSO **cohesion; conflict; group development; groupthink; joining and leaving; power; research using groups; roles; size; skills; sub-groups; taboo; teamwork**

The established definition of a group is three or more people who are connected and interdependent, usually to accomplish a shared purpose. This definition helps to distinguish a group from other collective nouns for people, such as a crowd. If we apply this same reasoning to the question of whether or not an organization can be a group, the answer is a conditional yes. In small organizations a collection of people will know each other, share a purpose and be interdependent on one another to accomplish their work. Large organizations, however, cannot technically be classified as a group because the criterion for members knowing each other is unlikely to be satisfied. However, these large organizations are usually composed of *teams* and other smaller groupings that constitute a group. It can be useful, then, to see the 'groupness' in small and large organizations (Longres, 2000).

Organizations, like groups, develop their own cultures. Organizational culture is a composite of its norms, values, beliefs, customs and traditions. It may not be 'visible' but its impact and presence is noticeable. The culture can be constructive and supportive of the work the organization does or it can inhibit and even prevent its mission; or, most likely, there are elements that promote the work and some that do not. Sometimes, individuals in the organization assume *role* behaviours just as they do in small groups (Carson and Dennison, 2008).

Although a degree of *cohesion* is important to good working relationships, if this develops into *groupthink*, there can be a failure to consider alternative strategies and options close. *Sub-groups* are built into most organizations; because of their overall *size* it is important to create smaller units where there is more possibility for coordination and specialization in certain tasks. However, if there are tensions with the organization as a whole and members of a sub-group hold more allegiance to it than the wider organization, this can pose a threat to the greater mission of the agency.

It is useful to view organizations though a groupwork lens and to have groupwork *skills* and techniques in the organizational toolkit (Goodman, 2006). In fact, groupwork abilities are the 'soft skills' that are valuable to employers, regardless of the field or sector. Examples are understanding and working with feelings, clarifying purpose and role, eliciting feedback, managing *conflict* and working with *taboo* areas. Some quite specific groupwork techniques are useful in organizational life, such as brainstorming with a group to generate a wide range of creative ideas before applying more rational, linear criteria.

Focus groups can be used in organizations to gather and inform opinion. *Research using groups* in the organization can provide invaluable feedback about how the agency is functioning.

Committee work is a common group forum in organizations. Roles are generally more formalized than those in social groupwork, but attention to group process and the use of creative groupwork techniques can help committees to develop and work well.

Communities of practice are increasingly being used within and across organizations. These learning groups are established by people who share common interests and provide a forum to share good practice and innovations. They have become a central plank in organizational knowledge management and practice development (Gray, Parker and Immins, 2008; Tolson *et al.*, 2006; Wenger, 1998). Organizational change also requires groupwork skill, often to shift the organizational culture (Berman-Rossi, 2001; Ward, 2008).

Implications for practice

- Understanding the organization as a collection of smaller groupings can help influence organizational culture and bring about organizational change;

- Group specific skills such as brainstorming, eliciting group feedback, attending to group process and developing group cohesion can enhance the work of an organization and improve the functioning of committees and teamwork.

FURTHER READING

- Douglas, T. (1983) *Groups: Understanding People Gathered Together* (London: Tavistock), Chapter 6 'Work Organizations', pp. 111–137
- Pullen-Sansfaçon, A. and Ward, D. (2012) 'Making Interprofessional Working Work: Introducing a Groupwork Perspective', *British Journal of Social Work,* doi: 10.1093/bjsw/bcs194.
- Toseland, R.W. and Rivas, R.F. (2001) *An Introduction to Group Work Practice,* 4th edn (Boston: Allyn and Bacon), Chapter 12 'Task Groups: Specialized Methods'

outcomes

SEE ALSO **beginnings; evaluation; evidence base; middles and endings; process; purpose; researching groups**

Outcomes have become increasingly important in all branches of the human services; yet, despite this near obsession, outcomes are often confused with processes, inputs, outputs and impact.

In the group context, an outcome is the effect, change, benefit or learning that occurs as a result of group participation. The outcome can be for the individuals, the group or both. Outputs, on the other hand, are the products or services that result from a group's activities, such as a booklet that promotes the group's work and outlines recommendations for community changes. An organization as a whole might have an output of, say, ten 'desistance' groups in criminal justice work. Outcomes in such groups could be an increased desire to desist in crime, better social behaviour and improved family relationships or a cessation of criminal activity. An input refers to the *resources* required to carry out activities, such as staff *time* to deliver group sessions. Impacts relate to longer-term effects of a programme or service and they are broader than outcomes for individual member outcomes (IRISS, 2012).

Organizations that sponsor groups will no doubt be seeking specific outcomes, but the group members are unlikely to be concerned about the difference between outcomes, outputs or inputs. For groups to be meaningful to members they must meet the needs of those members and help them provide results that are of importance to *them*. Part of the 'result' is the *process* as well as the outcome.

The potential outcomes are not always clear at the *beginning* of a group, though groupworkers should nevertheless present provisional *purposes* and modify these if it becomes clear that the group needs or wants to change direction. In *manualized* groups (those that have a very directive programme) this repositioning might not be possible. In self-directed groups, the members are encouraged to take increasing control.

Desired outcomes should be expressed without jargon and using members' own words. Once a general shared sense of the group purpose is developed, more specific and personalized outcomes can be developed. Many members begin groups feeling overwhelmed and unfocused. The groupworker can help break these large problems into smaller steps that are more manageable and help the desired outcomes to become clearer – specific, measureable, achievable, realistic and timely (SMART).

How are outcomes to be measured? Satisfaction surveys can help to measure group process, but additional methods are needed to measure outcomes, especially if 'independent' *evidence* is required of the group's effectiveness (Buckingham and Parsons, 2005). In self-directed and *self-help* groups the decisions about how effectiveness is to be demonstrated can lie entirely with the group; with groups that are *accountable* to agencies, it is likely that a pre-designed format will be a requirement.

The advantages of this latter format are that the group does not have to design its own and that it makes comparison with other groups possible, by using the same data collection methods. An *evaluation* instrument that has been tried and tested will satisfy independent requirements for reliability and validity and can build the *research* base for groupwork knowledge. The disadvantages are that it can be experienced as an imposition and not have a good 'fit' with this particular group. Evaluations that are designed outside the group too frequently focus on individual outcomes and forget to evaluate the *group as a whole*.

Implications for practice

- The notion of outcomes should be discussed with the group from the outset, and the group should take increasing control of how outcomes are to be defined and measured;
- Any focus on group outcome should not neglect group process – the latter is important to the achievement of the former.

FURTHER READING

- Fischer, J. and Corcoran, K. (2007) *Measures for Clinical Practice.* 4th edn (New York: Free Press). There are two volumes. Volume 1 contains standardized measures for practice with couples, families and children. Volume 2 contains measures for adults. Most areas of practice are covered
- Marsh, P. and Doel, M. (2005) *The Task-Centred Book* (London: Routledge)
- Preston-Shoot, M. (1989) 'Using Contracts in Groupwork', *Groupwork,* 2 (1): pp. 36–47
- IRISS (2012) `Leading for Outcomes. Guidance on Leading Teams Towards an Outcomes-Focused Approach`, http://www.iriss.org.uk/project/leading-outcomes

p

personal development groups

SEE ALSO **counselling groups; encounter groups; therapy groups**

There are many types of personal development group, such as training (T-groups) and *encounter groups* (Jones, 1972). The sensitivity training group movements are not as prominent and this has led to a narrower definition of personal development groups; they are groups with the explicit purpose of increasing self-knowledge through interactions with others in a small group. The emphasis is on giving and receiving honest and empathic feedback with a focus on the here and now and group processes (Berg, Landreth and Fall, 2013; Young *et al.*, 2013). These groups are frequently used in educational programmes for the helping professions, especially in counselling and psychotherapy, with the recognition that the professional (counsellor, psychologist, social worker, etc.) is a *person* first. Who the *person* is within the professional has a profound impact on the helping relationship; good practice, therefore, requires the development of in-depth personal understanding through personal development groups that are integrated into the curricula of professional training programmes.

Personal development groups may have different theoretical underpinnings and practice models (e.g. person-centred, Gestalt, existential, humanistic).

However, they share a common purpose, to develop deeper self-awareness. Moreover, personal development groups are *not* therapy groups or counselling groups.

Implications for practice

- Developing insight and self-awareness are important for human service professionals and can be facilitated by personal development groups;
- Personal development groups can be used to learn about groupwork practice and process.

FURTHER READING

- Rose, C. (2008) *The Personal Development Group: The Students' Guide* (London: Karnac Books)
- Rose, C. (2003) 'The Personal Development Group', *Counselling and Psychotherapy Journal*, 14 (5): pp. 13–15

planning and preparation

SEE ALSO **beginnings; co-working; evaluation; involuntary groups; leadership; manualized groups; membership;middles and endings; purpose; reflection; resources; selection; session**

There are some well-established models for planning and preparation, such as the FAAST model (Focus, Aim, Activities, Structure and Techniques), which provides a chronology for planning group sessions (Westergaard, 2009). In this entry, we will consider the general principles of planning and preparing for groups and offer some advice regarding the practicalities.

There are several stages to planning a new group from scratch:

- **Researching the need for a group**. Why is this group needed and what are its essential *purposes* likely to be? These are the fundamental questions that all would-be group leaders must ask themselves if they are proposing to create a new group. Usually the need for a group has been identified through their own experience, or perhaps from requests from colleagues or people who are likely to be future members of the group. The groupworker's own beliefs need to be backed up with evidence, especially if an agency is expected to sponsor the group. A case needs to be built that shows what gap in current provision the group is expected to fill, alongside the likelihood that there will be sufficient people interested to attend the group and the identification of the *resources* that will be required for it to be successful.
- **Getting others on board.** In most cases, the success of the group is likely to depend not just on what happens *inside* the group, but on external circumstances and *context* for the group – especially the support of colleagues. The *leadership* of the group is likely to consist of the person who proposes the group (though not always); but will the group benefit from

other leaders, too? There are often good reasons to consider *co-working*. Even if the group is planned to be sole-led, the co-operation of colleagues is important to ensure that there is ample support for the leader to spend the time needed for the group to be successful.

A small planning group should be considered. This group is charged with supporting and managing the group (as opposed to leading it) and should constitute people who have an interest in the potential group: ideally, a team colleague, a manager, an experienced groupworker and someone who can speak for the client group that will constitute the group's membership. Although the existence of a small planning group might feel like some of the decision-making power is being removed from the group leadership, the opposite can be true: the planning group can provide the weight needed to support the proposal for the group, especially if there is opposition from other parts of the organization. As long as planning groups do not become bureaucratic, they can ensure that the group is fully embedded in the agency, with interested parties who will argue for the development of a *groupwork service*, not just occasional groups here and there.

The planning group can help with any criteria that might be developed for the *selection* of group members, and it can provide feedback as a critical friend and independent *evaluation* of the group, too.

- **Finding the resources.** Time is undoubtedly the largest resource that most groups require. Team members need to be on board with the idea that some of the time of one or more of its members will be taken up with the group – planning, leading and debriefing. However, other necessary *resources* should be identified in the planning stage, with reasonable confidence that they can be secured.
- **Methods to recruit potential group members.** The planning stage should identify the means that will be used to recruit members to the group. In some cases the 'target group' might be obvious and very accessible, at other times the constituency for the group might be widespread or hard to reach. Publicity for the group needs to reflect these different realities.

The same kind of group, for instance a group for women with eating disorders, would require very different recruitment approaches depending on whether it was a group for women who are already in close touch (e.g. using a daycare facility regularly), a group for women who do not know one another but are known to the professional services, or a group drawing from anyone who meets the criteria for group membership and are not known to the formal services.

Group leaders have a wide range of recruitment tools available and the skill is to decide which ones are likely to be the most effective and efficient. So, how will people find out about the group? By invitation (an interview, a letter, email, text or phone call), through posters, ads and fliers, by word of mouth through the community, via direct referral from professionals, through local news media and social networking groups – any or all of these methods should be considered.

- **Individual offer of groupwork**. Once a person has signalled an interest in the group it is important to make individual contact with them prior to the group beginning. Sometimes called an individual offer of groupwork, this is an occasion for group leader and potential member to meet and ask questions of each other. The potential member can get a feel of the group and whether its preliminary purposes are fitting; it means that, if they do come to the group, they will at least know the group leader. For the leader, it is a chance to test out the suggested aims of the group and refine them through discussions with would-be members; and, if the selection decision is going to be the leader's, to decide whether the person meets the criteria for *membership*.

  The group leaders need to have thought what to do if more people wish to attend the group than it is possible to accommodate. Are there other community groups or internet resources that can assist? Is a further group of this nature planned, so they might join a waiting list?

Much of the preparation for a new group is bound up with the planning discussed above. For instance, a competent and thorough system of offering the group to prospective members on an individual basis is part of the process of preparation and *beginnings*.

- **Practicalities.** This is an area that can be underestimated, but the practicalities of groupwork require careful preparation. The *time* and timing of the group (how long for each session, how frequent and at what time of day and which day of the week) can all make or break a group. The venue is hugely important, both in terms of its suitability (comfort, privacy, places to keep things from one session to the next and facilities for refreshments) and access (on a bus route, not too far for all the different members to get there). Is the venue somewhere that members will feel comfortable to enter; for instance, an old school might bring back difficult memories of early education or seem a bit infantilizing for adults; a clinic might be too medicalized. The health and safety of all the group members is an important consideration for the groupworker when making practical arrangements for the group. Will group leaders and any volunteers need police checks from the Criminal Records Bureau and how long will these take?

  It might not seem like a 'practicality' as such, but part of the preparation is the *recording* of the group's life – how will this be documented? The group leader might wish this decision to be taken by the group as a whole, but that requires preparation, in terms of offering the group alternatives or, at the least, preparing a way for the group to make these choices in an informed way.

So far we have been considering those newly created groups where selection is more or less voluntary – a group is proposed and its potential membership either self-selects or is selected by the group leader. However, there are groups where membership is *involuntary* – people are required to attend the group, perhaps as a result of a court order.

In fact, the planning and preparation of these groups is surprisingly similar to the elements that we have described so far. The individual offer of groupwork is better named an individual preparatory contact, but even in those cases where individuals have no choice about attending a group, it is better to have one-to-one contact with them prior to the group beginning. It is an opportunity to discuss feelings about being required to attend the group. The consequences of failure to attend are different when the group is mandated and these consequences must be made explicit; but the necessary planning is similar to groups that are entirely voluntary.

The planning needed for *existing groups* (those not planned from scratch) is similar to the preparation needed for each individual *session* of an existing group, so we have grouped these topics together in this section.

- **Preparation and endings.** Preparation for each individual session of a group should begin at the end of the *previous* session. This might seem paradoxical, but the *endings* of sessions should look forward to the next session as well as backwards over the session just completed. Group members can be asked to complete some homework that they will bring to the beginning of the next session to start it off; or group members might be asked to bring an object or some materials that will be needed next time.
- **Tuning in.** In addition to the environmental preparations that might be needed (unlocking and opening up the group room, setting out the chairs and any equipment or materials that are required), group leaders should make sure that they have some time as near to the beginning of the session as possible to 'tune in' to the likely feelings of group members. This has sometimes been likened to tuning in to a radio station as the group leaders 'search for the frequency' of the group based on their understanding and knowledge of the group from previous sessions.

  Group leaders should tune in to their own feelings about the forthcoming group session, too, so they are self-aware and best prepared for it. They might try to find ways in which group members 'tune in' together at the beginning of the session as a way of dealing with any baggage that they are bringing with them, either from the previous session of the group or from their lives outside the group.

There is an increasing use of *manualized* groups that use ready prepared materials in which the structure of the group is directed by a tested curriculum. In these groups, the leader's role is to execute the curriculum as skilfully as possible. The tendency to use preparatory time to focus on the materials that will be used in the next session should not overshadow the need to tune in to the dynamics of this particular group, as manuals are written at a generic level. Groupworkers know that each group is unique and responds in its own ways to the materials that have been readymade.

The question of How much planning and preparation is required is not a straight forward one to answer. This is a 'how long is a piece of string?' question, so it needs much reflection. The irony is that it is essential to plan and prepare in order to depart from those plans and preparations. Failure to plan and prepare might be dressed up as going with the group's flow and 'emancipatory' in purpose, but frequently it is laziness or the leaders' failure with time management and comes across in the group as drift and carelessness. However, there are dangers with a tightly planned session, too: group leaders might feel so wedded to their carefully crafted preparations (or the manual) that they cannot leave them behind when necessary.

It is important not to cut off a significant discussion just because the manual or prepared schedule says that 20 minutes into the session the group is supposed to start a new exercise. However, the group also usually benefits from a leader who is able to give direction and bring closure to a topic that is becoming exhausted. Leaders should always review with group members how the membership is experiencing the preparations – overly directive, too non-directive or just about right?

Finally, it is worth considering how group members might be involved in the planning of future similar groups, perhaps as volunteers. Their experience is invaluable and, if they have the time and interest, they are in a good position to plan and publicize a new group if it will include people in similar circumstances to their own.

Implications for practice

- Group leaders must ensure that they have the necessary resources for the group to run successfully – to do otherwise is to be irresponsible and to risk the group's collapse;
- Plans, structures and materials that have been developed at a general level need to be adapted to the dynamics of *this* particular group in *this* particular session; group leaders should

not stick rigidly to their plans and group members should increasingly be involved in the planning process.

FURTHER READING

- Doel, M. (2005) *Using Groupwork* (Abingdon: Routledge/Community Care), Chapter 3 'Prepare', pp. 39–55
- Kurland, R. (2005) 'Planning: The Neglected Component of Group Development' in A. Malekoff and R. Kurland (eds), *A Quarter Century of Classics (1978–2004): Capturing the Theory, Practice and Spirit of Social Work with Groups* (Binghamton: The Haworth Press), pp. 9–16
- Manor, O. (1988b) 'Preparing the Client for Social Groupwork: An Illustrated Framework', *Groupwork*, 1 (2): pp. 100–114
- Popplestone-Helm, S.V. and Helm, D.P. (2009) 'Setting Up a Support Group for Children and Their Well Carers Who Have a Significant Adult with a Life-Threatening Illness', *International Journal of Palliative Nursing*, 15 (5): pp. 214–221
- Shulman, L. (2009) *The Skills of Helping Individuals, Families, Groups, and Communities*. 6th edn (Belmont, CA: Brooks/Cole), Chapter 3 'The Preliminary Phase of Work'
- Westergaard, J. (2009) *Effective Groupwork with Young People* (Maidenhead: Open University Press)

populations

SEE ALSO **co-working; gender; power; process; race; skills; and the Appendix for further detailed reading**

A population is yet another word for a group of people – in this case, a group defined by a category of specific characteristics. This might be geographical (the Scottish population) or along lines that are socially constructed, such as class, *race, gender* and sexuality (the working-class population, the black and gay communities). In social groupwork, 'populations' are generally defined at another level of detail. For example, a group created for women with severe and enduring mental health problems is at the intersection of two populations: women and people with certain kinds of mental health problems. Most of the populations served by social groupwork are marginalized and in vulnerable situations, experiencing some form of oppression and discrimination and generally less *powerful* than the majority populations. Groupwork frequently exposes and develops the resilience of these populations.

We could pose questions such as *'How do you work with older people in groups?' 'How do you do groupwork with young immigrants from Somalia?'* etc., but the really interesting question is *'How important is it to know your population group – weighed against your knowledge of groupwork?'* In other words, could a skilled groupworker work with *any* group of people?

Let us take the example of a group created to help gay teenagers manage the process of coming out. Relevant background knowledge might include:

- how identity is formed;
- denial, ambivalence, acceptance and the coming out process;
- coping with possible family rejection;
- social pressures on young people regarding sexuality;
- overt and subtle oppression and stigma that gay youth faces;
- signs and symptoms of bullying behaviour;
- increased risk of self-harming behaviours and suicide;
- safer sex practices;
- community resources for gay youth;
- knowledge of adolescent developmental stages common to gay and straight teenagers.

The above list constitutes knowledge specific to the population group (in this case, gay teenagers) rather than knowledge or skill in groupwork. There is no clear research *evidence* to tell us what is the best balance between groupwork skill and knowledge specific to the population group; suffice it to say that it helps if the groupworker can blend both. *Co-working* models of group leadership can help to square this circle, with one of the co-workers more experienced in groupwork and the other in working with the particular population.

Background knowledge of a population group must always adjust to individual characteristics, which are frequently more diverse than the use of general categories suggests. This is where the *skills* of groupwork are pre-eminent.

Groupworkers need to remember that some members will strongly identify with their population group, proudly so in some cases, whilst others will be much less attached or aware. They might be in denial or possibly they cross the borders of population groups, such as people of mixed heritage, bisexual people and those who are transgender. In reality, people have multiple identities. Rather than the group merely recreating the closeted social constructions of the world outside, it is important that it encourages the expression of these many identities. The group should be emancipating.

Implications for practice

- A groupworker needs sound background knowledge and understanding of the population(s) being served by the group;
- Though members may belong to a specific population group, variation exists in any one category (older people, women with enduring mental health problems, etc.) – as such, groupworkers should be alert to individual and group differences.

FURTHER READING

- Berman-Rossi, T. and Kelly, T.B. (2003) 'Teaching Students the Link Between Group Composition, Diversity, and Group Development', Paper presented at Council of Social Work Education, Annual Program Meeting, February 2003, Atlanta, GA, USA
- Doel, M. (2006) *Using Groupwork* (London: Routledge). This book presents rich examples of nine groups, each with a different population, seen through the lens of the portfolio notes of the various groupworkers
- Gitterman, A. and Shulman, L. (2005) *Mutual Aid Groups, Vulnerable and Resilient Populations, and the Life Cycle* (New York: Columbia University Press)

power

SEE ALSO **democracy; development; involuntary groups; leadership; models; populations; process; roles; taboo; theories; values**

Power is the ability to control and influence ideas, resources and, indeed, other people. It is also a quality that people possess in relation to themselves, the ability to control their own lives and actions. As every group is, in some respects, a microcosm of its wider society, the social constructions of power in that society are present in the group. In addition to these broader social meanings, group dynamics can be understood through a framework of power. *Theories* of group *development* suggest that groups encounter issues of authority, between group members and also between the members and the group *leadership*. In some groups, for example *involuntary* groups where members are required to attend the group (perhaps via a court order), the authority theme is explicit and usually present from the start of the group; in other groups, questions about who is in control of the group's *processes* and group direction might be much more implicit and suppressed and require the group's leader to bring into the open. Sometimes this power hierarchy is referred to as the 'pecking order' in groups (Bennis and Sheppard, 1956; Bion, 1959).

Social groupwork has *democratic values*, encouraging participation by all group members, celebration of diversity and respect for individual autonomy. This is hard to square with the power differential between the groupworkers and the group members – not just in their role, but also often in differences in educational attainments, economic status and professional power. 'We are all in the same boat' except that the groupworker is usually a temporary visitor to this particular boat, able to disembark to their own very different world at the close of the group. Group members take 'the boat' home with them.

Some *models* of groupwork embrace the group leadership role as central person, using this power to present as a powerful expert. Other models conceptualize the groupworker as a group member, but one with a particular and unique role (facilitation of the group), albeit one that bestows a certain power on that member. The mathematics of groups (there are a lot more group members than professional leaders) also helps to democratize them.

Most groupwork aims to empower the group by enabling it to take increasing control. However, groups of people who are marginalized in the wider society can find this process a difficult one, perhaps responding initially with confusion, distrust or compliance rather than participation. Power might be the *taboo* topic that the groupworker needs to find ways to help the group confront.

There is power in collective action. Groupwork has a long *history* of empowerment (Berg, Landreth and Fall, 2013; Gutiérrez *et al.*, 1989) both within the group, as a process of self-discovery and increasing confidence and control, and outside the group, through social action to make changes in people's neighbourhoods and lives. One example is self-directed groupwork (Mullender, Ward and Fleming, 2013). This model critiqued those empowerment models that had become consumerist (i.e. conferred the power to choose between products and services rather than the power to create and shape them). Self-directed groupwork is built on these principles:

- refusal to accept negative labels and stereotypes;
- establishment of rights (including the right to not participate and to choose the direction for the group);
- analysis of power and oppression is an integral part of the groupwork;
- individual troubles are understood in the context of social and economic policies.

Self-directed groupwork has five stages of practice, initiated by work on three questions: what problems should we tackle? why do these problems exist? how can we bring about change? Once the group understands the problems and their causes, it agrees on a course of action and embarks on it. In the final stages the group membership takes over and the worker increasingly moves into the background, perhaps leaving the group altogether. By this time group members are taking control of their lives and believe they have a right to this power.

Implications for practice

- Group leaders need to help members to take increasing control of the group as part of the process of empowerment;
- The *authority theme* in groups is an expression of power – groups must work with power and authority honestly and to the benefit of group process, which in turn aids group purpose.

FURTHER READING

- Adams, R. (2008) *Empowerment, Participation and Social Work*, 4th edn (Basingstoke: Palgrave Macmillan)
- Lee, J.A.B. (2001) *The Empowerment Approach to Social Work Practice: Building the Beloved Community*. 2nd edn (New York: Columbia University Press)
- Thompson, N. (2007) *Power and Empowerment* (Lyme Regis: Russell House Publishing)

problem-solving

SEE ALSO **activities; differences and similarities; groundrules; individuals; methods and models; purpose**

Problem-solving is a method by which problems are carefully identified and analysed, and strategies are developed to address the problem, with the intention of solving it or, at least, alleviating it. This method can be used with individuals, with groups or with individuals in groups (Marsh and Doel, 2005). As a *group-work method* it goes further than working with a set of individuals in a group. Sometimes the problem will be one that is shared by everybody in the group and experienced by them in the same way (such as a group formed to combat the problem of a neglectful landlord); at other times the problem will have a common name (such as alcoholism) though it might be experienced as a problem in different ways by each *individual* in the group and each might take a different course of action to overcome it, using the group as a source of strength.

The offer of the groupwork service made to each prospective group member in the *planning and preparation* of the group is the opportunity for group members and group leaders to begin to explore the nature of the problems that bring people to the group, if only in a brief and provisional way. These individual meetings enable the leaders to describe how the problem-solving process works in a group setting so that the members can anticipate the likely feel of the group and the kinds of activity the group will undertake.

The group will not usually leap straight into a discussion of problems. It is important that people feel comfortable in the group and start to trust one another, perhaps using warm-up *activities*, developing *groundrules* and conducting an exercise to elicit hopes, fears and expectations. Then the group can be invited to share its problems. This might be conducted as a 'round robin', where each member in turn talks about the problem or problems that bring them to the group, or it might be a group affair, for instance using flipchart paper to record a group brainstorm focused on 'problems that bring me to this group'. Group leaders search for commonalities and *differences* among the group members' responses, making links and helping the individual members to feel they belong as a group.

Next steps vary depending on the particular problem-solving *model*. However, it is common for the group to consider what they have done to work on the problem so far, what has worked and what has not worked and why. All the time, group members are encouraged to learn from one another – to gain support from others who have been through similar experiences and to be stimulated by hearing others with different stories and strategies. The group might go on to develop individual or group goals and a strategy to achieve them, usually with a timescale that includes deadlines. Group and individual tasks can be developed that are designed, step by step, to achieve the goals and the group is used as a source of creative ideas, support and review.

A common technique is to suggest homework, i.e. activities that build on the work undertaken in the group by asking members to take this work back into their everyday lives. This is referred to as an incubation period, when new ideas introduced in the group that might have been quite challenging and difficult to accept at the time are allowed time to take root, so that their relevance or usefulness becomes more apparent. Often, this happens when the person leaves the spotlight of the group, where they may have found themselves 'taking a position' that they felt they had to defend; once out of the spotlight, they can try out related exercises and activities in their own time and reflect on the group experience. The group members report back on their homework and their experiences towards the beginning of the next *session*.

When is problem-solving not an appropriate method? Problem-solving techniques rely on the use of reasoning. Group members may not be in the right place to use their reasoning – perhaps they are overwhelmed by strong feelings (grief, anger, guilt, etc.) or their capacity for reasoning is impaired. Children's understanding of reasoning is different from adults' and this needs to be accommodated in groupwork with children. Problem-solving methods do not have to be strictly linear; they can be very creative and employ lateral thinking and they must acknowledge and welcome the impact of feelings and emotions on thought processes. It is also important not to *problematise* people's lives and to emphasize the groups' strengths, so that problems do not overshadow achievements, solutions and goals.

Implications for practice

- Although individual group members might come to the group with similar problems, it is important to recognize that they may develop different solutions for these problems;

- The problem-solving process should aim to combine linear thinking (problem – tasks – goals) with lateral thinking (sometimes called 'outside the box') to provide the best combination for groups.

FURTHER READING

- Delbecq, A.L. and Van de Ven, A.H. (1971) 'A Group Process Model for Problem Identification and Program Planning', *Journal of Applied Behavioural Science*, 7 (4): pp. 466–492
- Grey, S.J. (2007) 'A Structured Problem-Solving Group for Psychiatric Inpatients', *Groupwork*, 17 (1): pp. 20–33
- Robson, M. (2002) *Problem-Solving in Groups*. 3rd edn (Aldershot: Gower)

process

SEE ALSO **beginnings; contexts; development; endings; group as a whole; groupthink; middles; power; purposes; roles; silence; social action; taboos**

Group process and *group dynamics* are often used interchangeably. However, process is a slightly broader term that includes group dynamics. Its meaning, as defined in the *Oxford English Dictionary*, has over ten variations. These definitions include: concepts such as a succession or order of things (e.g. stages or steps); everything that occurs during those stages (e.g. the patterns of behaviour); a series of actions occurring in a purposeful way (e.g. actions that can be mapped using a flow chart); and the interactions between groups and the wider society. In groupwork, process includes some of all these definitions, perhaps best summed up as all the interactions, procedures and forces that have an impact on the *individuals* and the *group as a whole* (Theodoratou-Bekou, 2008).

Group process can be seen as a succession or order of things. For example, process includes the influence of the stages of group *development*. The meaning of the group changes for group members as the group develops, as does the behaviour of the group as a whole.

Group process includes a series of actions occurring in a defined and purposeful way. For example, most groupwork considers the work of the group as a series of phases: e.g. tuning-in, *beginnings*, *middles* and *endings;* alternatively, as the worker taking stock, the group taking off, the group taking action and the group taking over. These planned steps bring order to the group's work and *purposes.*

Finally, group process can be seen as all that occurs in a group and the patterns that emerge. All that happens within the group's space *becomes* the group. If we consider a group as a *system,* all the verbal and non-verbal interactions, the activities and actions influence this system. For example, if the groupworker challenges a sexist comment early in the group, all its members watch and learn that such comments are not allowed in the group. The manner in which the challenge is conducted, and the response by individuals and the group as a whole become part of the group's process and have an impact on subsequent developments in this process. Quite quickly, patterns of group behaviour emerge and they become a powerful part of the process, too. They can become energetic drivers that help the group move forward, or obstacles that interfere with achieving the group's purpose.

An example of a communication pattern in a group is *wheel and spoke,* when all interaction goes through one member (often the leader) and back out to other members. Patterns of communication, or lack of it, may emerge around *taboo* subjects or *silence.* People may assume or be given certain *roles* within the group, some with greater status and *power* than others. Established ways of decision-making may emerge such as consensus building, compromise or majority rules – this process can sometimes harden into a *group-think* that finds it hard to tolerate differences of opinion. All of these patterns of behaviour and belief influence the group culture and how the group as a whole develops.

The groupworker's role is to aid these group processes and to help the group deal with problematic group dynamics (Henchman and Walton, 1997; Szymkiewicz-Kowalska, 1999; Toseland and Rivas, 2001). Groups have the potential to develop the dynamics of mutual aid or 'curative factors' and it is these forces that make groupwork such a powerful approach to working with people.

The *context* for a group has a significant impact on group process. For example, the racism, sexism and oppression within the larger society can be replicated within the group. People with higher status in the world outside the group are often given higher status within the group. Some groupwork approaches, such as *social action* and mutual aid, focus explicitly on this relationship between the group and society. Every approach needs to take account of the broader context if the dynamics within the group are to be properly understood and worked through.

Implications for practice

- A central role for the groupworker is to help the group develop positive group process;
- Everything that occurs in a group affects the group and becomes part of its group process.

FURTHER READING

- Cole, M.B. (2012) *Group Dynamics in Occupational Therapy: The Theoretical Basis and Practice Application of Group Intervention* (Thorofare, NJ: Slack Books)
- Lewin, K. (1947) 'Frontiers in Group Dynamics: Concept, Method and Reality in Social Science: Social Equilibria and Social Change', *Human Relations*, 1 (1): pp. 5–41
- Toseland, R.W., Jones, L.V. and Gellis, Z.D. (2006) 'Group Dynamics' in C.D. Garvin, L.M. Gutiérrez and M.J. Galinsky (eds), *Handbook of Social Work with Groups* (New York: The Guilford Press), pp. 13–31

purpose

SEE ALSO **evaluation; group as a whole; individuals; outcomes**

The notion of purpose is linked closely to that of *accountability*. Knowing the purpose of a group helps everybody involved to account for the group. These purposes might be 'soft' or 'hard': an example of the former is a support group for displaced persons where there is no expected outcome at the end of the group, just the hope that they have felt comforted by the group; an example of the latter is a group for young offenders with the express purpose of preventing re-offending.

Purpose refers to the reason the group was formed and it includes the aims, objectives and the hoped-for result of the *individual* members as well as the *group as a whole*. Clarity of purpose is essential in most groupwork practice because of the collective nature of the groupwork endeavour, though the clarity might arise out of group processes rather than be clear from the start. A large part of the power of groups rests on the mutuality of either problems and/or desired outcomes or both. Shared group purpose is key (Kurland, 1978).

Before purpose can be clearly formulated, groupworkers must first identify a 'felt need' (a want) for which a group might offer a means of help, support and achievement. A common mistake is to identify a need that potential members do not recognize. For example, some school children are fighting in school and a professional decides that they need an anger management group. Do the children feel they need an anger management group? Unlikely, and this will explain why it is difficult to get their participation and engagement in such a group – even though they might indeed need help with controlling anger.

Once a want is identified by the groupworker a *tentative* group purpose can be formulated as a starting point to develop a purpose that is shared by group members. There are several principles for developing a clear group purpose (Doel, 2006). These include:

- **No jargon.** The purpose of a group should be stated in plain language, understood by all and easily shared with others.
- **No hidden agendas.** The worker must be working towards the same purposes as the members. For instance, a play group should not be an attempt to teach anger management by 'the back door'. This is unethical practice. If the group members themselves arrive at a point where they identify their anger as a problem, and one they want help with, that is a different matter. So, if the group purpose cannot be shared with potential members, the group should not be started.
- **Outcomes are related to needs and wants.** Stated simply, group members benefit from knowing why they are in the group, where the group is going and how one relates to the other.
- **Specific enough to be achievable.** The purposes of the group need to be realistic and the outcomes achievable. For example, in the anger management example, the worker's purpose might be to help the group's members to control their temper so that fights do not break out and the children are not excluded from playtime. The children may see the purpose as learning how to keep the teachers off their back by not getting mad and fighting so they can go to playtime. These are shared purposes

and potentially achievable, even though the group leader and members come from different perspectives.

Implications for practice

- The initial purposes for a group can be tentative and 'soft', but they must be clear enough for members to feel that the group is capable of meeting some of their needs;
- A successful group is one where individual purposes can meld into a group purpose, even if individuals' solutions are different and varied.

FURTHER READING

- Doel, M. (2006) *Using Groupwork* (London: Routledge/Community Care)
- Gitterman, A. (2005b) 'Group Formation: Tasks, Methods, and Skills' in A. Gitterman and L. Shulman (eds), *Mutual Aid Groups, Vulnerable and Resilient Populations, and the Life Cycle*. 3rd edn (New York: Columbia University Press)
- Kurland, R. and Salmon, R. (2006) 'Purpose: a Misunderstood and Misused Keystone of Group Work Practice' in A. Malekoff, R. Salmon and D.M. Steinberg (eds), *Making Joyful Noise: The Art, Science and Soul of Group Work* (Binghamton: The Haworth Press), pp. 105–120

race

SEE ALSO **conflict; democracy; development; gender; ground rules; leadership; models; planning and preparation; power; process; selection; social action; sub-groups; values**

Race is a socially constructed and culturally transmitted concept, and one that is highly contested. It is beyond the scope of this A–Z entry to explore the nuances of this social construction and cultural transmission (please follow up citations in the text and further reading), suffice to note that individuals are quickly socialized into a particular racial grouping, depending on the particular social constructions in use in their time and place. People quickly understand their 'place' in society, as racial classifications in particular have a profound impact on access to goods, services and resources. These social stratifications also greatly influence the formation of individual and group identity, as well as relationships among people in any society (Germain and Bloom, 1999; Longres, 2000; Machery and Faucher, 2005).

What is the potential influence of race on groups? As conceptions of race have a profound impact in the wider society, these forces will find themselves in groups of people, too. As such, race has significance to groupwork in a similar way to *gender*, groups being a microcosm of society (Brown, 1994). Group members and workers will bring with them the broader social constructions of race alongside their personal experiences of race and beliefs about it (Cox and Ephross, 1998).

It might be argued that race is possibly the primary determinant of roles taken by *subgroups* (Bilides, 1991). Some black and minority ethic (BME) groups perceive themselves as having less power in groups than white members and some white members may have a sense of privilege that those from BME communities may not share, even when the white members are not conscious of it (Northen and Kurland, 2001). The differential expectations of power and status can influence, among other things, leadership roles within groups (Garvin and Reed, 1994).

Members from different racial groupings may have different understandings and expectations of authorities. This can greatly influence communication in groups, especially the relationship between the members and the group *leadership*. For example, the degree of deference shown is likely to vary as well as the nature and amount of acceptable challenge and *conflict*. Self-expression and *democratic* process may not be equally valued by all groups, which can make communication in mixed group settings complex. There may be differences across groups regarding their views of competitiveness and intimacy. All of these differences can have an impact on the group's *development* and *process*. There are many other potential influences of race on a group (see Berger, 2009; Chau, 1990; Francis-Spence, 1994; Mistry and Brown, 1997; O'Neal, 2006; Singh, 2007). The key factor to understand is the potential replication of structural racism and oppression within groupwork practice (Kurland, 2003; Lee and Berman-Rossi, 1999; Mullender, 1988). At the same time, whilst recognizing the strength of racial influences, it is important to avoid racial stereotyping and to understand that there are influences on the socialization of individuals in the group other than race, too.

Groupwork principles have strong anti-oppressive *values*, especially those approaches that identify *power* as a critical concept, such as the *social action* and empowerment *models*. When using other approaches, ones that perhaps focus less on social and structural models of practice, it is important that the groupwork practice should, nevertheless, incorporate explicitly anti-oppressive principles of groupwork practice. For instance:

- attend to race and ethnicity during the *planning and preparation* and *selection* for group composition;
- negotiate a working agreement with the group that is congruent with members' cultures;
- develop *groundrules* to promote beliefs and behaviours that are not oppressive;
- be alert to oppressive behaviour and reflections in the group of structural inequalities in society (e.g. sub-grouping and status differentiation along racial divisions);

- reflect on your own racial background and its impact on your behaviour and communication with the group and the impact of racial differences and similarities between you and group members.

It is a mistake to assume that race is unimportant or 'not present' in groups that are not mixed; frequently it is all-white groups where race is forgotten, hidden or denied. The dynamics of race will differ between mixed race and single race groups (and the same is true of gender), but 'race' does not disappear in a single race group.

Implications for practice

- Consider issues of race when forming groups – the potential impact of same-race and mixed race groups;
- Be open about issues of race in the group, promote transparent discussion and relate issues of race to wider, structural issues of power and discrimination.

FURTHER READING

- Marsiglia, F.F. and Kulis, S. (2009) *Diversity, Oppression, and Change: Culturally Grounded Social Work* (Chicago: Lyceum Books)
- Phillips, J. (2001) *Groupwork in Social Care* (London: Jessica Kingsley Publishers), Chapter 3 'Power, Race, and Gender'
- Stark-Rose, R.M., Livingston-Sacin, T.M., Merchant, N. and Finley, A.C. (2012) 'Group Counselling with United States Racial Minority Groups: A 25-Year Content Analysis', *Journal for Specialists in Group Work*, 27 (4): pp. 277–296

recording and documentation

SEE ALSO **accountability; confidentiality; evaluation; reflection; researching groups; sessions; supervision of groupwork; see the Appendix (page 200) for an example of a Groupwork Log.**

Recording is rarely seen as a glamorous activity, but it is an important and potentially rewarding aspect of groupwork. It should be a feature from the start of the group, not an afterthought. The methods that will be used to record the group need to be decided early and agreed with group members. Group *sessions* should be documented as soon as possible after their conclusion.

There are many reasons groups should be recorded:

- To *describe* what is happening in the group – snapshots of group sessions;
- To *analyse* group *processes* and dynamics;
- To *measure* change in respect of *individuals* and the *group as a whole*;
- To *evaluate* the impact of the groupwork: what works well, what less so;
- To *reflect* on the continuing professional development of the group leaders;
- To *account* for the work of the group to others such as the sponsor;
- To *capture data* to build knowledge of groups and groupwork, perhaps for *research* purposes.

The purpose of the recording will influence the methods used and different documentation might be necessary to suit different purposes.

The methods and style of recording should reflect the group itself and be agreed with group members so issues of *confidentiality* are clarified. A distinction is necessary between the group's record and individual personal folders that can be reflective accounts that are private to each member.

A group should feel empowered by the way in which its life is documented. Usually, the group can be involved in much of the recording. Questionnaires and flipcharts (photographed to make them more accessible) can record participants' levels of satisfaction and their views about whether and how the group is helping them. The group's portfolio could contain photos and any artifacts from the group's activities.

Some methods might not seem like 'recording' but could be used for these purposes. At the beginning of a group, for example, members might be asked to write a letter to themselves about how they hope to see themselves at the end of the group. These are sealed and opened in the final group session. Copies of these letters, properly anonymized, with the subsequent *reflections* of group members, would provide a good record of the group's impact.

It is important for group facilitators to reflect immediately after the group on what happened and how this influences their planning for the next session. Although the primary purpose of recording should suit the needs of the group and its members, the leaders should consider their own developmental needs. A reflective diary is one way that groupworkers can capture their own learning and these notes and reflections can be used as an aid to *supervision*. They can be shared with a *co-worker* as part of a process of peer supervision.

If the group is sponsored by an organization or agency, there is a responsibility to account to the sponsor for this support. An agency is more likely to access succinct summaries and, thereby, to make use of the intelligence gained from the experience of the group. Attracting the attention of senior managers in the agency is one way in which best practices can be broadcast. This relies on clear, accurate and perhaps audio-visual documentation so that others who have not directly experienced the group can understand what happened and why, and the implications for policy and future practice.

Groupworkers should also consider the needs of the wider professional community. It is important that groupwork knowledge is enhanced and broadcast, perhaps by publication in a journal.

The Groupwork Log in Appendix 2 is an example of how a brief record of each group session can help groupworkers to recognize patterns in the group and also develop their own skills.

Implications for practice

- Discuss and decide what purposes the group record has, and this will help to determine the methods of documentation;
- Include group members in recording group process and individual outcomes and aim to be creative in the methods used.

FURTHER READING

- Coyle, G.L. (1930) *Social Process in Organized Groups* (New York: Richard R. Smith)
- Doel, M. and Sawdon C. (1999) *The Essential Groupworker*(London: Jessica Kingsley), Chapter 12 'Recording and Evaluating Groupwork', pp. 229–249
- Finley, R. and Payne, M. (2010) 'A Retrospective Records Audit of Bereaved Carers' Groups', *Groupwork*, 20 (2): pp. 65–84

recreation groups

SEE ALSO **activities; endings; history of groupwork; leadership; middles; process; skills**

The influence of recreation on the development of groupwork has a long *history*. The settlements, camping movement, scouts, YMCA, YWCA and adult progressive education all saw the small group as a vehicle for growth and change through recreation, among other *activities*. Growth and change were not just the domain of 'talking therapies', rather active doing was seen as important, both as a means and as an end. Recreation continues to be a significant methodology in groupwork practice today.

Recreation groups include a wide range of activities such as sports, arts and crafts, music, hobbies and many other leisure pursuits. These activities can be used just for the enjoyment of the participants. On the other hand, they can be deployed in recreation groups to encourage socialization, to learn life skills, decrease isolation, teach positive social values and increase confidence. A useful distinction is that between an activity and *action technique*. A recreational activity can be done for its own intrinsic value as an activity or with a further purpose that transforms it into an action technique.

Recreational techniques in groupwork can 'pepper' a group that generally relies on discussion, helping to change the tempo and liven the pace of the group. This is especially important where group members might have short attention spans or find verbalization difficult. For example, in a homeless hostel for women, a cooking group taught the women to cook or to resume their cooking and this group also served as the weekly residents' meeting which, before the cooking initiative, had been poorly attended. Through cooking together the women developed relationships, practised new skills and began to address the concerns for residents (Berman-Rossi and Cohen, 1988).

Recreation activities can serve as icebreakers in initial group meetings, or as opportunities to address group problems in group *middles*, or as a means to help a group *ending*.

Group sports and other recreational activities provide opportunities to learn what it is to be part of a group (Brown, Garvey and Harden, 2011). Children can learn about cooperation, inclusion and respect, mutual aid, managing conflict and solving problems.

To get the best from recreational groups, leaders need good groupwork *skills* and proficiency with the recreational activity helps, though it is not always necessary. It is possible, for instance, to lead a quilting and crocheting group for older people with chronic mental illnesses without the skills to sew or crochet, assuming the *leadership* role is not a teaching one. Indeed, it is the opportunity for group members to teach one another and share their expertise that is important: the groupworker aids this *process* rather than leads it.

Implications for practice

- Recreational groups can be provided solely for the purpose of enjoyment and recreation and they can also be used for therapeutic, educational or socialization reasons;
- The purposeful use of recreational activities can further the aims of many 'talking' groups.

FURTHER READING

- Brown, S, Garvey, T. and Harden, T. (2011) 'A Sporting Chance: Exploring the Connection between Social Work with Groups and Sports for at-Risk Urban Youth', *Groupwork*, 21 (3), 62–77
- Doel, M. and Sawdon, C. (1999) *The Essential Groupworker: Teaching and Learning Creative Groupwork* (London: Jessica Kingsley), Chapter 7 'Action Techniques in Groups', pp. 130–159
- Moxley, D.P. *et al.* (2011) 'Quilting in Self-Efficacy Group Work with Older African American Women Leaving Homelessness', *Art Therapy: Journal of the American Art Therapy Association*, 28 (3): pp. 113–122

reflection and groupwork

The idea of reflection was popularized by Donald Schön in the 1980s. He theorized that the kinds of rules that might help engineers build a bridge (technical and rational) are less useful in more complex social situations, such as groupwork. Schön differentiated between reflection-on-action and reflection-in-action. In groupwork terms, the former is central to the debriefing that is important after a group session, and the latter is characterized by the internal dialogue a facilitator has during a group session. The difficulties of reflecting whilst in the midst of the action is one of the potential benefits of *co-working*, when one of the leaders can attend to the here and now and the other can reflect on how to explain what is happening at a *process* level (for instance, that there is *sub-grouping*, and reflection on whether this is beneficial or harmful to the group.

Another aspect of reflection is the possibility that a groupworker might reflect the behaviour in the group in their own behaviour to their supervisor. This can be a diagnostic tool in the supervision of groupwork. However, there is also concern that the notion of reflection has been advanced uncritically (Ixer, 1999) and that evidence for its existence or impact is sketchy.

The *reflective cycle* is when groupworkers make observations in their work with groups (a concrete experience), these experiences evoke thoughts and feelings to be explored, followed by an *evaluation* and analysis of whether these were good or bad, helpful or hindering to the group; and from all of this an action plan is formulated to not only guide the next encounter with that group in particular, but is also generalized to other groups.

This cycle of experience, thoughts and feelings, evaluation, analysis and action is loosely based on Kolb's learning cycle (1984). It is more of a 'loop' than a perfect cycle, but it helps to illustrate the reflective cycle in groupwork which, it is hoped, improves the groupwork experience.

Reflection is a technique that can be used with group members as part of the group process. Inviting the group to reflect back over a session is not the same as asking them to fill out an evaluation questionnaire. It is a more open-ended process inviting discussion, so it is important to allow time for it. During the session itself, the group can be invited to reflect on what is happening, perhaps by the group leader making a reflective comment to the group as a whole, such as 'it seems to me that what is happening here is that the discussion between Raj and Sally is reflecting the difficulties the group is having in confronting this topic.... ' The group leader aims to be a mirror, reflecting the group back to itself and inviting the group to comment.

Implications for practice

- Reflection takes time, whether it is within the group session itself or following on from the group's meeting;
- Reflection is not just for group leaders; the group as a whole should be given opportunities for reflection.

FURTHER READING

- Hogan, B. (2012) 'Reflective Practise and Mutual Aid in Educational Groups: A Gateway to Constructed Knowledge' in G.J. Tully, K. Sweeney and S. Palombo (eds), *Gateways to Growth* (London: Whiting and Birch), pp. 25–38
- McDermott, F. (2002) *Inside Group Work: A Guide to Reflective Practice* (St Leonard's NSW: Allen and Unwin)
- Schön, D. (1983) *The Reflective Practitioner: How Professionals Think in Action* (London: Temple Smith)

research using groups

SEE ALSO **confidentiality; groupthink; populations; recording; virtual**

Group life is a common feature of human existence so it is reasonable to consider the group as a possible context for activities such as research (Swift, 1996). Research might best be conducted in groups for these reasons:

- The *population* being researched feels most natural in a group (Walmsley, 1990); for instance, the teenage tendency to spend time in small groups suggests that a more accurate picture will be drawn if teenagers are studied in their groups rather than (or as well as) individually (France, 1996).
- The people under study are living in groups, such as people in residential institutions, so research conducted at the group level is congruent with their everyday experience.
- A group is an opportunity to bring people together with a wide range of experience, in the hope that this will provide richer data than individual research interviews. In a group setting, techniques such as brainstorming can generate more ideas more quickly.
- A group is an opportunity for researchers to test out hypotheses with different people and to observe how people respond to other people's views and reactions through group discussion.

There are potential difficulties with group-based research strategies, too. One is the phenomenon of *groupthink*, in which a dominant member or *sub-group* enforces a false consensus around a particular topic, so the findings from the group's experience are misleading and unrepresentative. Individuals may not be so candid in the semi-public arena of a group as they would one-to-one. Observing and *recording* a group is more complex than an individual research interview and the analysis of data more time-consuming. Group-based research requires researchers with groupwork skills in addition to their research skills and even clearer lines of *confidentiality* and privacy (Taylor, 1996).

There are many group-based research methods (Adams, 2004; Casstevens and Cohen, 2011; Home, 1996; Walton, 1996). We briefly outline three that are commonly used:

- **Focus group.** A focus group usually consists of 8 to 12 people whose discussion of a topic is facilitated by a moderator who helps to keep the group focused on the topic in question (Krueger and Casey, 2009). The process is very similar to directive groupwork, except that in the focus group the purpose is to accomplish the goals of the researcher not the group members, though these can be congruent with one another. For instance, a focus group to discover what kind of advertising campaign is likely to help reduce smoking might help group members' self-awareness at the same time as meeting the research aims.
- **Nominal groupwork.** There are variants of the nominal groupwork technique but essentially it provides a structure whereby a potentially large number of people can generate views and opinions, then prioritize them within groups of common interest and finally come to a consensus or an agreed set of priorities. Initially people are asked to respond individually to a specific question. They might brainstorm a number of responses on post-it notes, which are collected together by the researcher/facilitator and grouped into common themes. This same process can be undertaken with a number of related questions (e.g. What is best about X? What is worst about X? How would you like to see X develop?). These clusters are then discussed, culminating in a scoring system through which the top priorities survive and the others are eliminated. If this same process has been occurring in a number of parallel small groups, these groups merge into large groupings to share their priorities, discuss them and culminate in another round of

scoring and elimination of the least favoured positions. This can continue until the whole group has reached a final position on its priorities.
- **Delphi method.** Named for the Delphic oracle, this method is a *virtual* group method in that participants (who are experts in their field) do not meet one another but their responses, usually to a survey, are made available to other respondents in feedback summaries, so that they influence subsequent rounds of response.

Implications for practice
- Decisions about whether to use individual or group arrangements (or a combination of the two) in research enquiries is the same as the decision whether to use individual, group or both in professional practice;
- Ensure follow-up with group members, either individually or in the group, so that participants can learn what contribution the group has made to the research question, how the findings will be used and how their privacy will be respected when the research findings are disseminated.

FURTHER READING

- Abu-Samah, A. (1996) 'Empowering Research Process: Using Groups in Research to Empower the People', *Groupwork*, 9 (2): pp. 221–252
- Van de Ven, A.H. and Delbecq, A.L. (1974) 'The Effectiveness of Nominal, Delphi and Interacting Group Decision-Making Processes', *Anatomy of Management Journal*, 17: pp. 605–621
- Wheelan, S. A. (ed) (2005) *The Handbook of Group Research and Practice* (Thousand Oaks/London: Sage)

researching groups

SEE ALSO **evaluation; evidence; group as a whole; groupthink; history of groupwork; individuals; outcome; process**

The notion that human beings are not solitary beings and are attracted to group life was advanced long ago by Plato and Aristotle; however, methods of scientific enquiry to understand and theorize about groups began only a century or so ago with the development of the social sciences. The *history* of the study of groups and groupwork (both social groupwork and large group behaviour in mobs, crowds and mass movements) is relatively modern.

At a formal level scholarship in groupwork combines researching groups with writing scholarly accounts of groupwork for publication. Scholarly accounts are those that are based on groupwork research, perhaps through doctoral study or a research grant. Scholarship increases the stock of reliable knowledge about groups and how they work; it also helps to theorize about groupwork – corroborating or challenging existing *theories* and developing new ones.

Models for researching groups

Early researchers of groups turned to the natural sciences as a model, looking to emulate scientific rigour. One of the greatest challenges of the scientific method in complex group situations was, and remains, the development of measuring instruments. What are the equivalents of telescopes and microscopes when measuring, say, notions of intimacy and authority in groups? *Sociometrics*, developed first in the 1930s, was seen as a response to this challenge and scaling procedures such as Likert's continue to be used to measure changes in attitude and perception, though they tend to focus on the impact of the group on the *individual* rather than a measurement of the *group as a whole*.

Observational methods generally require trained observers and involve the sampling of data across time and setting so that comparisons can be made. However, the vast range of variables in groupwork make it difficult to establish firm causal relationships and meaningful generalizations. The limitations of laboratory settings for group experiments is better understood now, with the findings of some of the classic group experiments called into question; for instance, the convergence of group members' judgements in the clinical setting (*groupthink*) might be *a result* of the clinical setting and not endure outside it.

The case study is a method associated with the study of naturally forming groups such as families, gangs and communities, describing in depth the workings of these groups. Experimental designs such as randomized control trials are rare because of the complexity of groups, the difficulties of controlling variables and the cost. As the physical sciences have embraced chaos theory and notions of complexity, the social sciences, too, have retreated from a hard, empirical position, with fundamental questions asked about the nature of *evidence* (MacGowan, 2008). There is an acceptance that information is incomplete, often contradictory and fast changing, and that work to alleviate one problem might create others, all summed up in the notion of 'wicked problems'. So, the group is conceptualized not so much as a set of mechanical functions and more as an ever-changing phenomenon with different meanings for different people.

Many aspects of groups and groupwork can be the focus of research to generate scholarly groupwork. Loosely, these are sometimes characterized as *process*-oriented and *outcome*-oriented. The former research concerns itself with group dynamics and the internal workings of the group – affiliation, authority and intimacy, *cohesion*, *conflict*, *leadership*, belonging and the like. The latter research focuses on the group's product, its impact and whether it achieved its goals. Agencies that sponsor groups usually want an *evaluation* of their outcome and are not especially concerned with how this was achieved; groupwork professionals tend to be most interested in research that throws light on the dynamics of groups to help them improve their skills. The two are mutually compatible, though the relationship between them is too infrequently researched (Kelly *et al.*, 2011).

Who conducts the research? The model of a professional researcher subjecting a group to independent scrutiny is sometimes referred to as outsider research, whilst the model of professional groupworkers researching their own practice is insider research (McDermott, 2005). Those who believe that research is concerned with a search for objective truths are likely to be drawn to the first model and those who see truths and meanings as socially constructed are likely to favour the latter. The former tend to focus on quantifiable outcomes, the latter on meaningful processes. Outsiders can bring rigour and independence, whilst insiders can unlock the subtext and the hidden meanings in group life.

As research is a moral activity as well as a scientific one, the impact of the researcher on the group is an important consideration. Different kinds of knowledge are recognized – not just objective knowledge gained through empirical research, but the expert knowledge that group members bring as 'experts in their own lives'.

Increasingly, research teams are ensuring that these voices are included in the initial research design so that the research process is not experienced passively and that 'research subjects' are actively engaged.

Implications for practice

- Groupworkers should make best use of the existing knowledge by regularly reading research related to their groupwork practice;
- Groupworkers should also see themselves as *generators* of knowledge, making their groupwork findings known to the wider community by publishing in relevant journals.

FURTHER READING

- Brower, A.M., Arndt, R.G. and Ketterhagen, A. (2004) 'Very Good Solutions Really Do Exist for Group Work Research Design Problems' in C.D. Garvin, L.M. Gutiérrez and M.J. Galinsky (eds) *Handbook of Social Work with Groups* (New York: The Guilford Press), pp. 435–446
- Doel, M. and Orchard, K. (2007) 'Participant Observation and Groupwork: Researchers as Temporary Insiders', *Groupwork*, 16 (3): pp. 46–70
- Johnson, P., Beckerman, A. and Auerbach, C. (2001) 'Researching Our Own Practice: Single System Design for Groupwork', *Groupwork*, 13 (1): pp. 57–72
- Wheelan, S.A. (ed) (2005) *The Handbook of Group Research and Practice* (Thousand Oaks/London: Sage), Part III, 'Methods in Group Research and Practice', pp. 221–282

residential groups

SEE ALSO **activities; beginnings; collective; community; contexts; groundrules; joining and leaving; leadership; membership; recreation groups; settings; skills; taboo**

Residential services can be considered as 'twenty-four hour groups' – the residential milieu as a special type of group. Young people in a group home for young people who are 'looked after' are likely to share many experiences, such as having biological parents whose rights were terminated, experiences perhaps of foster care placements that broke down, problems with broken education, and uncertainty about the coming transition to life beyond care. They will need to learn to live together as a surrogate family, to develop life skills, prepare for the world of work or further education, cope with the emotional hurts and damage caused by their chaotic upbringings, as well as managing a care system that has possibly failed them at key points in their lives.

A residential facility has many of the characteristics of an open-ended group, with members *joining and leaving* at different times. This can affect group *development* adversely if the leadership does not address the dynamics of fluctuating *membership*. Strategies include welcoming new members into the home and helping them connect with existing members, negotiating a working agreement, perhaps revisiting *groundrules* and using *activities* that accelerate the relationships with the residents and workers. This all aids the development of a culture for living and being together.

Group *conflicts*, scapegoating, communication difficulties and *power* struggles are not uncommon in group living, and viewing these as a group phenomenon enables the residential workers to see themselves as groupworkers needing groupwork *skills* to work with the situation. The problems of group living should not obscure the fact that the residential context is also a great opportunity for problem-solving, mutual aid, personal growth and social learning – if the residential workers have the groupwork knowhow to facilitate this.

In addition to viewing the residence itself as a group, formal groups are a common practice in residential settings (Lewis, 1992; Mullender, 1990). Establishing regular *community* meetings can allow a group to set aside time to consider residents' concerns, individual or collective (Ward, 1995; Duffy and McCarthy, 1993). In therapeutic group homes, a range of treatment groups are likely to be available as well as *recreation* groups, socialization and study groups, homework clubs and groups for supporting life transitions. The *taboo* of death is too frequently ignored in residential care, yet groupwork is well placed to help residents with others' deaths or to prepare for their own.

Groups in residential settings operate within a larger, ongoing group, unlike those in community settings. What happens within a formalized group is, therefore, strongly influenced by the dynamics of the 'outer' residential group, and vice versa.

Implications for practice

- Thinking of the residential facility as a type of open-ended group can help guide professional practice;

- Group processes occur within the residential milieu and groupwork skills can be utilized to facilitate positive *group dynamics*.

FURTHER READING

- Fulcher, L.C. and Ainsworth, F. (eds), (2006) *Group Care Practice with Children and Young People* (New York: Haworth Press)
- Martin, R. and Harrington, M. (2001) 'Group Work in a Residential Setting: The Twenty-Four Hour Group' in T.B. Kelly, T. Berman-Rossi and S. Palombo (eds), *Strengthening Resiliency through Groupwork* (New York: Haworth Press)
- Ward, A. (1993) 'The Large Group: The Heart of the System in Group Care' *Groupwork*, 6 (1): pp. 64–77

resources

SEE ALSO **activities; group as a whole; planning and preparation; setting; skills; time**

There are two kinds of resources, those external to the group and those internal to it. The external resources needed for successful groupwork are:

Skills and *time* are probably the most significant resources. Groupwork skill is a valuable resource that agencies should cultivate – it transfers to skills in *teamwork*. Individual practitioners who undertake groupwork training as part of their continuing professional development are a resource to help develop a groupwork *service* for the agency, not just to lead individual groups.

The practicalities of groupwork should be considered during the *planning and preparation* for any group. Briefly, the resources that might be necessary are:

- **Venue.** The *setting* for the group should be appropriate for the purpose. For instance, space for any physical *activities*, secure cupboards to store the group's materials from week to week and a kitchen area to make refreshments. The venue needs to feel welcoming, with comfortable chairs and a private space and accessible for people with special needs, such as any wheelchair users. Transport to the venue should be considered.

- **Experts.** Is there a need for specialized expertise – art specialists, sexual health counsellors, legal advisors, etc.? Will outside help come at a cost?
- **Funds.** These might be needed in a small way for refreshments and travel costs, if these are not to be met by members themselves. Larger funds would be needed if the group has more ambitious plans and it might be that fundraising will be part of the group's work.

In addition to all the resources that are brought into the group, the group is potentially its own biggest resource. It is the groupworker's role to convert this into a reality, to help the group see itself as a resource and to use these resources for the benefit of all the group members and any others who are in some way touched by the group.

- **Group members' experience.** The most significant of the group's resources are the experiences that members bring with them. Stories that have proved painful, problematic and traumatic are, in the group, valuable and respected. This can be very empowering for group members, realizing that experiences that are devalued outside the group are recast as a kind of expertise within the group.
- **Sounding boards, rehearsal rooms and the like.** A group can be used to try new ways of thinking and behaving and to reflect on issues and concerns that might be *taboo* outside the group. This makes the group a *unique* resource to its members.
- **More than the sum of its parts.** The collection of individuals who arrive at the start of a group only realize their potential as a resource when the chemistry of groupwork fuses their singular experiences into a *group as a whole*. By pulling together as one, the group is able to feel its *collective* strength.
- **Advocacy.** In addition to providing advocacy within the group, some groups go on to become a resource to other people in similar circumstances in the *community*, or to advocate for their own cause (such as better facilities for children with learning disabilities). The group can advise other services and become known as a community resource.

Implications for practice

- The external resources necessary to underpin a successful group must be in place before the group starts, so that it is has solid foundations;
- The leaders' role is primarily to release the potential of the group's own internal resources, largely derived from the experiences of the individuals who come to the group.

FURTHER READING

- Douglas, T. (1993) *A Theory of Groupwork Practice* (Houndmills: Macmillan) Chapter 3 'Resources', pp. 49–62 and Chapter 7 'Resource Theory', pp. 96–109
- O'Neal, G.S. (2006) 'Using Multicultural Resources in Groups', *Groupwork*, 16 (1): pp. 48–68
- Phillips, J. (2001) *Groupwork in Social Care* (London: Jessica Kingsley), Chapter 5 'Physical Environments', pp. 75–86

roles

SEE ALSO **group as a whole; leadership; problem-solving; silence; supervision; taboo**

Role is defined as a 'person's allotted share, part, or duty in life and society; the character, place or status assigned to or assumed by a person' or a 'function performed by someone or something in a particular situation or process' (Oxford English Dictionary). These definitions provide several important insights into the meaning of 'role' in group dynamics.

In formal groups, roles are often named and assigned, such as 'chair', 'secretary', etc. However, in most social groupwork, roles are implicit, fluctuating and not assigned as such, with the exception of the *leadership* role of the groupworkers.

The groupwork literature is fond of naming individual roles. These are usually a cluster of characteristics gathered together and assigned a title, the most famous being *the scapegoat*. Other common examples are: the clown; the gatekeeper; the gossip; the monopolizer (dominant member); the teacher's pet; the *silent* member.

It is important to avoid identifying *the person* with *the role* (sometimes called personification); for instance, the person using humour in the group being labelled 'the clown'. This stereotyping is liable to prevent the groupworker from seeing the behaviour in its many facets; for example, that humour can sometimes be used to ease a difficult situation and at other times to block the group from confronting a *taboo*. It can also block the worker from understanding the individual as a rounded person for whom the use of humour is just one aspect of their group personality.

Role theory is very helpful if we avoid personification. So, once we develop a view of roles as a collection of behaviours or attributes, we can reframe individual roles as group behavioural characteristics. For example, we can reframe 'the energiser' into energizing characteristics, 'the intellectualiser' into intellectualizing, 'the timekeeper' into timekeeping, etc.

Some role types are associated with task and purpose in the group, such as timekeeping, recording and reminding of procedures; yet others are concerned with feelings and the emotional climate in the group, such as self-disclosing, encouraging, joking and welcoming.

These roles are important in the context of the group: they are group roles, then, and are wrongly conceptualized as individual roles. What sometimes happens in groups is that one particular member becomes closely identified with a particular behaviour pattern, and becomes stuck in that particular pattern, such as monopolizing the discussion. It is useful to understand the meaning of this behaviour for the *group as a whole* rather than to give a label such as The Monopolizer.

Roles perform a function in the group and this function can have a negative, positive or mixed impact (Shulman, 1967, 2009). Roles become problematic when an individual member becomes stuck in one. Let us take the example of a group to help people arrested for driving over the alcohol limit. At the initial group sessions, most members did not want to speak; some feared their comments might get them assigned to a treatment programme rather than just a risk reduction programme; others were angry at having to attend such a programme; yet others were too embarrassed. Steve noticed this reluctance but was not afraid to speak so he shared his story. The groupworker and other members were quietly relieved that Steve was speaking and he was encouraged to continue.

At the next session, this pattern of encouraging Steve to do most of the talking continued, as it did for several weeks until some of the members got tired of hearing Steve 'monopolise the conversation'. Steve too, tried to get other people to speak. Yet as soon as there was a lull in the conversation, the group encouraged Steve to talk. In this instance, Steve was not the Monopolizer, rather the group became stuck in a pattern of communication in which one of its members was given a role, one that helped the group in its early stages but that became dysfunctional.

Problem-solving approaches are useful in unfreezing a group where a role or roles have become stuck (Kurland and Salmon, 1998). Recognition of the problem is the first critical step, and this is where regular *supervision* can be critical. The way in which the problem is framed is also crucial – do the groupworkers personify the behaviour or do they understand the transactional nature of the problem? In other words, it is a problem in the transactions between an individual (or sub-group) and the group as a whole.

Once a problem is identified it needs to be named and the groupworker should consider how to help the group gain this same insight – either by directly bringing it into the group or, usually preferably, by finding ways to help the group come to its own understanding. The key is to help the group really explore and understand the problem, before jumping to solutions. It is always best to consider many options before landing on a solution. Taking the example above there are many steps that Steve and the group could take to help unstick the group's reliance on Steve's talking, including a decision to be comfortable with its own silence.

Implications for practice

- Group roles belong to the group not an individual;
- If a group gets stuck because roles are too fixed and inflexible, the groupworker can use problem-solving processes to help the group break free.

FURTHER READING

- Brown, A. (1994) *Groupwork*. 3rd edn (Aldershot: Arena Ashgate Publishing), pp. 122–128

- Douglas, T. (1991) *A Handbook of Common Groupwork Problems* (London and New York: Tavistock/Routledge), Chapter 3 'Problems Relating to the Members of a Group'
- Northen, H. and Kurland, R. (2001) *Social Work with Groups*. 3rd edn (New York: Columbia University Press), Chapter 8 'The Problem-Solving Process' and Chapter 10 'Group Member Roles'

S

selection

SEE ALSO **differences and similarities; gender; group as a whole; involuntary groups; joining and leaving; leadership; process; purpose; race; social action; task; work group**

The first step in selecting for group membership is to ask what are the *purposes* for which a group is appropriate, as opposed to individual or family work. Once the idea of a group has been justified, the next step is to reach out to an appropriate membership and possibly offer the groupwork service individually (Doel and Sawdon, 1999).

The type of group will influence the likely criteria for selection – even the very question as to whether there should be 'selection'. In much groupwork where a new group is created, selection criteria are designed to try to ensure that the needs or competencies of group members match the purposes of the group. For a *task* or *work group*, these competencies might be self-evident. For a community-based group with *social action* at its core, group members are more likely to select themselves. For many support, educational and therapy groups, the groupworkers are likely to be making choices about membership in concert with potential members. In *involuntary groups*, members are 'selected in' by others (often a court).

Selection is a common word in groupwork, though it does have unhappy associations with school memories of not being selected for a team. It should be seen as, usually, a process by which a potential group member and the group *leadership* are able to decide whether the group is right for the individual: a transaction, then, rather than a judgement.

Groupworkers use a variety of strategies to recruit members. For instance, a voluntary bereavement organization advertises a group for widows in the local paper or church bulletins; a centre for older people displays flyers about a falls prevention programme; a youth centre has information on its bulletin board about a sexual health group. These approaches allow people to self-select.

Other groups may be formed by directly approaching and inviting known service users. For example, in a local authority team a social worker has seven or eight older people who are caring for an adult child with a learning disability and are concerned about what will happen to their child when they die. The older carers could be approached and invited to form a group to support each other and consider possible plans for their children. It is reasonable to suppose that the people approached would come to their own understanding about whether the group will suit their needs. Some agencies will have formal assessment processes that are used to access group services, such as the intake worker suggesting a group, or more formal criteria.

Orchestrating the selection of a good mix of members for groups can be challenging. The balance of *differences and similarities* in the circumstances of group members is difficult to judge. Moreover, it can be difficult to predict an individual's behaviour when they move into a group, and the chemistry of that particular group. We have all experienced how different groups can bring out contrasting responses – cooperative in some and uncooperative in others. So, selection is far from a science (Brown, 1994).

This lack of precision does not mean that pre-group screening should be abandoned (Caplan, 2005b). There are times when either the groupworker or the potential member decides the group is not appropriate and it is better that these choices are made before the group begins rather than *leaving* a group once joined. Though group process can help break through a person's denial of a problem, the opposite can happen and an individual's denial can inhibit other members' openness. Some potential members may decide that discussing their situation in a group would be too threatening and decide not to join.

Group leaders have responsibility for the composition of the *group as a whole* and not just the 'fit' for individuals. In general, a group needs to have enough homogeneity that its members can relate to one another's situations, with sufficient heterogeneity for diversity and creative tensions. The attributes of members, for example *gender* and *race*, should be considered in recruitment and selection and the possible mix in the final group.

Implications for practice

- The purpose of the group should inform decisions about how to select the membership;
- A pre-group interview (*individual offer of groupwork*) can help potential members and groupworkers come to a decision about the fit between the member's needs and the group's purposes.

FURTHER READING

- Northen, H. and Kurland, R. (2001) *Social Work with Groups*. 3rd edn (New York: Columbia University Press), Chapter 6 'Pregroup Contact: Selection and Preparation of Members'
- Phillips, J. (2001) *Groupwork in Social Care: Planning and Setting up Groups* (London: Jessica Kingsley Publishers), Chapter 7 'Group Structure'
- Preston-Shoot, M. (2007) *Effective Groupwork*. 2nd edn (Houndmills: Palgrave Macmillan), Chapter 4 'Planning the Group', pp. 69–88

self-help groups

SEE ALSO **collective; leadership; power; process; support groups; therapy groups**

Self-help groups are widespread and popular. They include groups set up for a very wide range of life conditions or stressful transitions – from micro-credit to consciousness rising to pain support groups. The best-known self-help groups are the 12-step programmes such as Alcoholics Anonymous, Al-Anon, Narcotics Anonymous and Overeaters Anonymous. Despite this widespread popularity, there is still confusion between self-help groups, *support groups, therapy groups* and self-directed groupwork.

A self-help group is a collection of people who come together around a single shared concern in order to bring about a needed or wanted change. This concern often has an individual rather than a societal focus (e.g. stopping drinking, recovering from mental illness), though these individual troubles are related to broader social realities, like the promotion of alcohol. Even so, some self-help groups do form around social and environmental issues, such as the micro-credit movement.

Self-help groups do not have professionals in *leadership* roles, though they may be members of these groups in their own right.

Sometimes, professionals help people to establish their own self-help groups and support from behind the scenes (Lavoie, Borkman and Gidron, 1994). Such groups are typically free of charge, though members may give small donations to support the work of the group. Many self-help groups develop a programme for working together on the members' shared concern.

Self-help groups have the potential to develop mutual aid, particularly from a sense of being 'all in the same boat', not alone. In addition, members can gain a sense of strength by gathering together around a common purpose, experiencing *collective power*. Self-help groups share information, provide mutual support, engage in individual problem-solving and give members a place to rehearse new behaviours. They can also place implicit, and sometimes explicit, expectations or demands for change, using peer pressure and exposure to diverse opinions and experiences. A self-help group can be a safe place for members to speak about *taboo* areas (Yip, 2002).

In professionally facilitated groups, one of the primary roles of the workers is to facilitate the group *process* and help group members remove any barriers to the development of mutual aid. In self-help groups, these processes may occur naturally, with the group establishing its own norms and rituals.

Although professionals typically do not have a formal role in the running of self-help groups, they can play an important supporting role (Habermann, 1990; Matzat, 1989, 1993). This may include referring service users to an existing self-help group, helping service users to establish their own self-help group or providing and organizing space for meetings. If a self-help group finds itself 'stuck', input from professional groupwork can help to move it on.

Implications for practice

- Professionals should know about local self-help groups and refer to these groups when appropriate;
- Consider how a professionally led group might transform into a self-help group.

FURTHER READING

- Kurtz, L.F. (1997) *Self-help and Support Groups: A Handbook for Practitioners* (Thousand Oaks, California: Sage)

- Lavoie, F., Borkman, T. and Gidron, B. (1994) *Self-Help and Mutual Aid Groups* (New York: The Haworth Press)
- Nylund, M. (2000) 'The mixed-based nature of self-help groups in Finland', *Groupwork*, 12 (2): pp. 64–85
- http://www.selfhelp.org.uk/
- http://www.selfhelpgroups.org/

sessions

SEE ALSO **activities; beginnings; context; flash groups; manualized groups; middles and endings; planning and preparation; settings; structure; time**

Session is the term usually given to each individual meeting of a group. In the *planning and preparation* stage one of the decisions to be made is the number of group sessions. In off-the-shelf packages, sometimes called *manualized groups*, this number is almost always fixed (according to the curriculum for the group), whilst in groups where the groupworkers are creating the group *structure* themselves, the decision rests with them. In many groups, the number of sessions might be provisional and a final decision is taken by the group itself. Groups that are open-ended do not have a predetermined final session, but they nevertheless have sessions, i.e. times when the group comes together.

With the caveat that there are no 'typical' sessions in groupwork, almost all sessions of all groups, no matter how large or small or how diverse their *purpose*, will have characteristics that we can sum up as *beginnings, middles and endings*, just like the whole course of the group. To a certain extent, then, each session mirrors the group as a whole.

Many groups are *semi-structured*, i.e. where the group leaders have a rough plan for each session that outlines how the *time* will be used. Within each item there are often sub-items, not necessarily providing detailed content, as this content is meant to be liberated by the general structure provided by the leaders, who aim to encourage maximum participation by the group members. To use a travel metaphor, the group leaders provide the vehicle and the fuel but the group members decide where to drive and how.

More often than not the group will develop a recognizable *pattern*, a similar one for every session. This familiar pattern can provide the security that is needed to take risks (emotional ones, risks of disclosure, the development of intimacy in the group) that help the group to grow. If the sessional pattern is likely to change it is usually better to signal this with the group – and to consider why the pattern will be broken. First and last sessions are likely to have their own distinct patterns.

Groupworkers need to consider what kind of contact, if any, will occur between themselves and group members from one session to another – and possibly between group members. Do any of the group leaders work individually with any of the members and, if so, how is this likely to affect the dynamic of the next group session? Are group members living in the same community, members of the same families, etc. and, if so, how should all the communication that is likely to take place outside the group be incorporated within the group? The group's *context* – its external world – can be just as significant, more so, than the internal world of each session.

Do all groups have sessions? There are some kinds of group that do not have sessions as such. Spontaneous groups – *flash groups* – may consist of only one 'session'. Work in informal *settings*, such as with street kids, has to be spontaneous, with little opportunity for more than the barest of plans, sometimes referred to as 'guerrilla groupwork'. So, a group is not defined by the fact that it is composed of sessions, even though this is the most common form of group in social and therapeutic groupwork.

Implications for practice

- Plan each session but be prepared to adapt and even abandon these plans if the group requires it;
- Establish a pattern for each session of the group as this will provide the security for group members to take emotional and other kinds of necessary risk.

FURTHER READING

- Doel, M. (2005) *Using Groupwork* (London: Routledge/Community Care), Chapter 5 'Do', pp. 75–98
- Manor, O. (2010) 'The Single Session Format: Common Features of Groupwork in Acute Psychiatric Wards' in J. Radcliffe *et al.* *Psychological Groupwork with Acute Psychiatric Inpatients* (London: Whiting and Birch), pp. 132–155
- Sharry, J. (2008) *Solution-Focused Groupwork.* 2nd edn (London: Sage), Chapter 5 'The Stages of Solution-Focused Groupwork', pp. 89–106

setting

SEE ALSO **activities; community; purpose; values; also see the Appendix for further detailed reading**

The setting in which any experience occurs shapes and influences that experience. Space has cultural meanings and expresses more than just a physical location. A school building, its classroom and the children's chairs hold associations for adults (pleasant or not) that would inevitably colour any group that met there. The space and setting tells group members about the *values* of the group and how the group is valued by the larger community. The physical context for a group – whether it is in the *community*, outdoors, in an institution or a medical or educational setting – has a profound impact on the group.

These are some of the key components when considering settings for groupwork (adapted from Gitterman and Germain, 2008; Doel and Sawdon, 1999; Lindsay and Orton, 2011; Northen and Kurland, 2001).

- **Agency context.** Some of the constraints of groups in an agency setting are that they must fit within the mandate of the agency and that the agency culture may not be congruent with the groupwork *purposes*. Moreover, group members who are service users will have a history that might colour their response to the group – and they might not see the offer of groupwork as entirely voluntary.
- **Relationship of the host setting to the rest of community.** Agencies vary in the degree to which they are seen as part of their communities; in the best circumstances, groups can help marginalized groups to gain access to the agency. For example, support groups for older Chinese carers were possible if provided through a local Chinese community centre. On the other hand, agencies that are stigmatized can act as a barrier. For example, in the early days of the AIDS epidemic, support groups for black HIV positive men were difficult to run in agencies that initially had served gay HIV positive men.
- **Physical space.** The group's space must be inviting – and 'inviting' might mean different things to the group members

that to the groupworkers. The group sense of belonging might be increased if there is some room for the group to shape the space itself – sometimes, for instance, decorating the space it occupies. The building in which the group is held can convey the sense of worth (or not) that the larger population has for the communities who compose the group (Seabury, 1981).

- **Physical accessibility.** The group should be best placed for the community that it serves – this includes ease of access in terms of transportation as well as people's physical abilities.
- **Emotional accessibility.** Does the setting present any emotional barriers to its members? In sectarian cultures, holding groups in certain buildings automatically excludes some parts of the community. Having groups in a familiar place can increase emotional accessibility. However, familiarity can have complications. For example, young people asked a youth worker to set up a sexual health group for them at a local community centre, until the youth worker reminded them that their grandmothers frequented the centre. They decided a more private venue was preferable.
- **Seating arrangements.** Groupworkers are known for their penchant of rearranging the furniture. It stems from an understanding that seating arrangements greatly influence communication patterns. Group shapes that encourage the maximum participation are favoured (usually but not always a variation on a circle). Space to easily break out of the whole group formation into small groups or standing *activities* is important.

Implications for practice

- The location and appearance of the physical space of a group are important considerations when planning a group or group session;
- Groupworkers should attend to the meaning and unspoken messages that are implicit in the space and setting of groups.

FURTHER READING

- Gitterman, A. (2005b) 'Group Formation: Tasks, Methods and Skills' in A. Gitterman and L. Shulman (eds), *Mutual Aid Groups, Vulnerable and Resilient Populations, and the Life Cycle.* 3rd edn (New York: Columbia University Press), pp. 73–110

- Manor, O. (2001) *Ripples: Groupwork in Different Settings* (London: Whiting and Birch)
- Mason, K. and Adler, J.R. (2012) 'Group-Work Therapeutic Engagement in a High Secure Hospital: Male Service User Perspectives', *British Journal of Forensic Practice,* 14 (2): pp. 92–102

silence

SEE ALSO **activities; context; co-working; individuals; process; reflection; roles; skills**

Perhaps no single topic grips the groupwork literature more than silence. There is no bad fantasy (other than violent *conflict*) that haunts the groupworker more than silence when anticipating a group *session*. Why is this the case?

In part we must look outside the group to the broader social *context* to understand that silence is often viewed as uncomfortable, more particularly in western societies. The French might mark a conversational hiatus as *'un ange passe'* (an angel passes by) but this is more a device to break the silence than to laud it. We describe silences as awkward and, increasingly, silence in public spaces is filled with background music lest we fall into a pit of solace. The group is a semi-public forum in which silence can be felt as acute embarrassment.

One of the challenges for a group is to understand what is meant by a silence. It is a sudden loss of a form of communication that most people rely on heavily. However, though it represents a lack of verbal communication, it is not an absence of communication. At an existential level, perhaps silence reminds us of our stark individuality, only able to be certain of our 'own' existence and this reminder is more striking when it occurs in a group.

The quality of the silence is what is most significant. Is it the silence of a group in quiet *reflection* on what has been said and happy to be at peace with itself, or the silence of repressed anger, even rage, emotions so strong that no one dares to lift the lid? Is it somewhere in the middle, a group that can't really think what to say or is not certain what is going on or what is expected, fearful of saying something that makes them ashamed?

One of the *skills* of groupwork is to be able to make the judgement about what the silence is conveying or, even better, to find ways to help the group itself make that judgement.

Just as interesting (or challenging, depending on your point of view) is a group where there is just one member who keeps silent. Whilst the rest of the group is busy exchanging histories and opinions and making connections, one corner of the group is silent. This person is often termed 'the silent member' in the groupwork literature; indeed, there was a vogue in *role* theory for ascribing all kinds of labels to *individual* members: the dominant member, the scapegoat, the clown, the gatekeeper, etc. This tendency to personify the role with the individual is unhelpful as role behaviours can change with context and over *time*, so it is better to look at the behaviour rather than identify the person *as* the behaviour.

Someone who is quiet in a group might be reflective, sleepy, distracted, out of their depth, aggrieved, on medication, worried about something outside the group ... the list goes on. Groupworkers need to try to help the individual to voice their concerns, preferably in the group, but sometimes it is necessary to check this out one-to-one, perhaps during the refreshment break or after the group. Other group members will be wondering why this person is silent, too, so it is important to prevent inaccurate stories being constructed. *Activities* that break the group into small groupings ('introduce your neighbour') can help ease diffident members into the group.

The big question for the groupworker is whether to break a silence. Often, a group member will do so because of their own discomfort, but sometimes the group is resolute, in an unspoken pact, that the decision lies with the group leader. The vogue for long periods of silence (indeed, silent group leaders) in some kinds of *therapy group* (such as T-groups and encounter groups) has generally passed. Does the discomfort that these silences provoke the group to new levels of disclosure and honesty, or is the sustaining of long silences so very counter-cultural that it is really an aggressive act by the group leader? The answer is that it depends on the group and the group leader; it can be both.

Unless the group has been quite clearly badged as an *encounter group*, in which participants expect to use the group *process* introspectively and experimentally, the group leader has a duty of care to break a silence once it is no longer reflective. This can be done divertingly by suggesting that the group now moves on, or reflectively by specifically alluding to the silence. *Co-working* is valuable, as there is an opportunity (usually later when debriefing, but sometimes there and then in the group) for the co-leaders to discuss the options and to learn from the choices that they and the group make.

Implications for practice

- Silence is always a communication, albeit non-verbal; it can only be understood in the context of the particular group and group session where it occurs;
- There is always a choice as to whether the group should be invited to discuss the silence or just to note it. These choices are dependent on the specific nature of both the silence and the group.

FURTHER READING

- Batsleer, J. (1994) 'Silence in Working across Difference', *Groupwork*, 7 (3): pp. 197–209
- Doel, M. and Sawdon C. (1999) *The Essential Groupworker: Teaching and Learning Creative Groupwork* (London: Jessica Kingsley), Chapter 9 'Individual Behaviours in the Group', pp. 179–193
- Heap, K. (1985) *The Practice of Social Work with Groups: A Systematic Approach* (London: Unwin Hyman), pp. 87–93

size

SEE ALSO **leadership; membership; planning and preparation; residential groups; sub-groups; values**

Does size matter? Definitional boundaries are far from straightforward; anything from a threesome to a large crowd can be described as a group. So, what is the 'groupness' that connects them all and does the number in the group affect the properties of that group?

The biggest impact of size is thought to be intimacy; the smaller the group, the more intimate the relations within the group are likely to be. Viewed mathematically, the sum of possible dyadic relationships grows from 3 between three people (A/B; B/C; A/C) to 28 for eight people. So, if one person speaks to another in the group, there are just 3 variations in the group of three, 6 in a group of four and 28 in a group of eight. In addition to the 28 dyads in a group of eight, there are numerous other possible groupings (threes, fours, etc.) which add to the complexity and richness, but which also dilute the intensity.

There is a point at which the variety of relationships within a group becomes so great that there is a tendency for *sub-groups* to form in order to create the desired levels of intimacy. This point varies from person to person and group to group; the definition of a large group is said to be one where you are out of your comfort zone. For some people this is four or five whilst others are OK in groups of sixteen or more. Some people who regularly experience very large groups, such as politicians, might feel more comfortable with the relative anonymity of hundreds than under the intimate scrutiny of eight.

Size matters to groupworkers who are *planning* a group. If they want to increase the privacy and intimacy of the group (e.g., for people who will be talking about childhood sexual abuse) they will want to keep the size relatively small; if the group is outward-looking and will benefit from many points of view, such as group to take action over a matter of local concern, a large membership is appropriate. Perhaps the most challenging situation for groupworkers is not necessarily small or large *membership*, but one that *fluctuates*.

Large group dynamics

The classic template for groupwork is around eight participants – often termed 'small groupwork' (Omsted and Hare, 1978). The large group is normally associated with purposes that are more social, even political. However, large group dynamics have been seen increasingly as a milieu for therapeutic work. Large group experiences (say 40 to 100 people) alter our states of mind, with a suggestion that the lessening of intimacy actually increases our disinhibition and allows more primitive behaviours and passions to emerge. If properly harnessed, these can be therapeutic. Indeed, the dynamics of group life in *residential* homes benefit if they are understood in large group terms (Ward, 1993).

Most people have some experience of large *gatherings* such as rallies, concerts, conferences and sports events, but when do these gatherings become 'large groups'? The answer is when they are experienced as a group by the participants. In a gathering that has been called together explicitly as a large group experience (such as a large group training conference), this consciousness is likely to be present from the outset; in a political rally the consciousness might develop with the skill of the orator. Certainly, *leadership* is crucial to the development of large group consciousness; though it might be argued that a gathering of people who strongly share a *value* base, such as the Wall Street Occupation of 2011, might develop large group consciousness without formal leadership.

Large group consciousness might not be shared by everyone in the group. This is no different from small group consciousness, where some group members feel themselves belonging to something they experience as a group where other members do not; and this consciousness can come and go – a Mexican wave at a large sports event is a coordinated expression of large group consciousness, but the crowd just becomes a crowd once the wave has run its course.

The size of the *leadership* group is often overlooked but it is significant for the group. In high maintenance groups where there is a need for much one-to-one work (such as a group for people with advanced dementia), it is not unusual to have a leadership group of up to four, or perhaps one leader and several assistants. It is important that the size of the leadership group does not overwhelm the group as whole.

Some large groupwork practice techniques deploy a number of groupworkers within the large group. It might be argued that this is small groupwork with a number of small groups at the same time – valuable but not necessarily the same as unleashing the potential of large group dynamics.

Implications for practice

- Small groups tend to promote greater intimacy; large groups might split into sub-groups in order to find this level of intimacy;
- The disinhibition that may arise in large groups can allow primal emotions to be released, but this usually requires inspirational leadership.

FURTHER READING

- Boyd, R.D. (1991) *Personal Transformation in Small Groups* (London: Routledge)
- Kreeger, L. (ed) (1994) *The Large Group: Dynamics and Therapy* (London: Karnac Books)
- Turkie, A. (1995) 'Dialogue and Reparation in the Large, Whole Group', *Groupwork*, 8 (2): pp. 152–165

skills

SEE ALSO **development; group as a whole; individuals; leadership; process; roles; session; taboo**

A skill can be defined as knowledge in action. By this we mean doing something specific based on explicit knowledge. Skills are actions that can be learned and rehearsed through practice and these actions might be verbal or non-verbal. In a groupwork context, a skill is a purposive action by the groupworker with the intention of influencing group *process* or the behaviour of *individuals* in the group. For example, a group member is asked to repeat a question to the group rather than to the groupworker (the skill of *redirecting*). This action may be based on the groupworker's knowledge that member-to-member interaction builds and strengthens relationships, or it might stem from their experience of this effect or be an intuitive understanding that this helps group process.

Many of the helping skills are generic ones that apply not just to groups but to individual and family work, too; others are specific to groupwork (Gitterman and Germain, 2008; Northen and Kurland, 2001; Trevithick, 2012). First let us consider some of the relevant generic skills.

- **Advice** giving – suggesting a course of action;
- **Attending** to behaviour, verbal and non-verbal, including eye contact, body posture and gestures;
- **Challenging** obstacles, for instance that might impede group process;
- **Clarifying purpose** and *roles*;
- **Confronting**, by pointing to discrepancies between words and actions; confronting *taboo* topics that are being avoided;
- **Empathizing**, for example by verbalizing what people are likely to be feeling;
- **Encouraging**, by supporting people to talk or act in new ways;
- **Expectations** – helping to describe outcomes that are achievable;
- **Feeding back** – asking people to share their opinion and thoughts, for instance about the way that the group is working;
- **Feelings** – exploring feelings and inviting people to share them; helping to put feelings into words and responding to these feelings accurately;

- **Focusing** – in the case of a group, bringing it back to its purpose;
- **Humour** – using humour to create a positive working culture and lighten the mood when needed;
- **Information** management – asking for and giving information;
- **Listening** accurately and attentively;
- **Modelling** particular behaviours, *values* and beliefs that help personal an group growth;
- **Negotiating** a working agreement, often involving *groundrules*;
- **Paraphrasing,** thereby demonstrating an understanding of people's meanings and checking for accurate understanding;
- **Partializing** – breaking problems and goals into smaller, manageable parts;
- **Questioning,** especially open questioning as demonstrated by questions that ask who, what, when, where and why;
- **Reframing** – offering a different point of view about a person's situation; in a group this can help to move the perception of a 'problem' from an individual member to the *group as a whole*;
- **Rewarding** – giving positive reinforcement;
- **Silence** – understanding *silence* and working with it, perhaps by allowing silence to aid reflection;
- **Summarizing** a story or process, thereby checking for accurate understanding;
- **Supporting** people, for instance to talk about difficult and painful subjects;
- **Tuning-in** – getting in touch with the likely feelings that a person brings to an encounter, and that members might be experiencing before a group or *session* begins.

Here is a brief A–Z of skills that are specific to groupwork practice In many ways they constitute the complex skills of group *leadership*.

- **Adapting** and **creating activities** and action techniques, deploying them to suit group purpose and process;
- Promoting **collaboration** and *cohesion*, for example by helping members to work together on a task and pointing out similarities of experience and feeling;
- **Connecting** group members to one another, for example by helping them see parallels in their thought processes and beliefs;

- **Consensus building**, perhaps through activities that help group decision-making;
- **Differences** – encouraging members to share and respect differences in biographies and outlooks;
- **Gatekeeping** to achieve balanced participation between more verbal and less verbal participants and encourage full participation of all members;
- **Guiding** the group, for example through a problem-solving programme;
- **Mediating**, for example by helping *sub-groups* to hear each other's messages and to come together;
- **Naming** (sometimes called voicing) group processes that members are not conscious of; also naming the group's achievements and putting into words the unstated group norms and ways of working that have developed;
- **Parking** topics that are important and need to be returned to, but that are deflecting the group process and task just now;
- **Redirecting** the focus of communication towards the member or members for which a message is intended and deflecting too much routing through the group leader;
- **Reflecting** communication patterns by sharing with the group the ways in which members are communicating (or not);
- **Scanning** – actively looking around the group to read how the group as a whole and the individual members are responding;
- **Softening** strong messages by reframing or rephrasing difficult-to-hear messages in ways that are easier;
- **Starting and ending skills** – specific to the dynamics of group (and session) *beginnings* and *endings*;
- **Stacking** – when several people want to speak at the same time, suggesting an order so that they all get a chance to speak;
- **Task development** – helping the group to shape tasks that will help it progress towards its goals;
- **'Thinking group'** – it is a broad skill that entails the groupworker is always thinking and seeing the group, even when the spotlight is heavily on one individual in the group. Remembering that all actions and interactions are occurring within a *group* context – there is a group 'audience' even when two people are talking to one another in a group. Two people talking to each other is more than just the two people talking.

There is a difference between skill and being skillful. Skill refers to the action or the doing of something. Skillful, on the other hand, is an evaluation of the use of a skill – 'was this a good or bad use of a particular skill?' Skills can be deployed unskillfully; for example, a group member in a group for survivors of childhood sexual abuse may begin to share with the group a painful memory. The groupworker may 'ask for information' (a groupwork skill), but if this enquiry were about the person's journey to the group we would judge this to be an unskillful question and a poor use of the asking for information skill. We might also judge that the best intervention was not to use the requesting information skill, but empathizing or scanning to see how other members were responding, or – indeed – a combination of these skills.

It is not always clear whether an intervention was skillful or not. Immediate and longer-term outcomes are one part of this *evaluation*, but reflective time is also important. Groupworkers need to make time to reflect on their practice, perhaps via debriefing with *co-workers*, through formal *supervision* and in courses of *continuing professional development*.

Implications for practice

- Groupworkers should be aware of the range of their skills and always aim to extend their repertoire;
- Skills are not 'neutral' – they can be used skillfully or unskillfully.

FURTHER READING

- Bertcher, H. J. (1994) *Group Participation: Techniques for Leaders and Members* (Thousand Oaks, CA: Sage)
- Doel, M. and Sawdon, C. (1999) 'Interactional Techniques in Groups', Chapter 8 in *The Essential Groupworker: Teaching and Learning Creative Groupwork* (London: Jessica Kingsley Publishers)
- Middleman, R. and Wood, G.G. (1990) *Skills for Direct Practice in Social Work* (New York: Columbia University Press), Part III, 'Skills for Working with Groups'
- Preston-Shoot, M. (2007) *Effective Groupwork*. 2nd edn (New York: Palgrave Macmillan), Chapter 7 'Working with Groups'
- Shulman, L. (2009) *The Skills of Helping Individuals, Families, Groups, and Communities*. 6th edn (Belmont, CA: Brookes Cole), Chapter 1 'An Interaction Approach To Helping', and Part IV, 'Social Work With Groups'

social action

SEE ALSO **collective; community; leadership; outcome; process; support groups**

Social action emerged in the 1970s, especially in the field of juvenile justice and work with young offenders, though it has shown its transferability to other fields of groupwork practice, such as *health, education* and active citizenship. Social action challenged the orthodox view that juvenile crime is attributable to individual pathology or the breakdown of social norms and developed an action-centred *community* work approach in contrast to the prevalent social education approach.

The philosophical underpinnings of social action come from Freire (1972), a South American adult educator who saw education as a potential liberation and emphasized the need for an equal dialogue between teacher and student and between students themselves, with an emphasis on the importance of students' own experiences in this process. The disability movement, black activism and feminism have also been strong influences on the development of the social action model.

As a model of groupwork, the core principle of social action is *collective* strength through working in groups. This approach is best articulated in the self-directed groupwork model (Ward and Mullender, 1991). This focuses on social and community issues rather than private troubles, though it does seek to foster people's understanding of how the latter are grounded in the former. Rather than starting with the groupworker's definition of what the problems are, self-directed groupwork asks people what their problems are and roots these in a broader understanding of social forces. The groupworker's role is to lend support to the group rather than to lead it.

In outline, the stages of self-directed groupwork are:

Stage 1: Pre-planning
Stage 2: Open planning – makes planning empowering
Stage 3: Skills and techniques of self-directed groupwork – what, why and how?
Stage 4: Taking action
Stage 5: The group takes over

Are there circumstances when a directive *leadership* style is appropriate? For example, when a person's own resources are so depleted by their life circumstances it might be unrealistic to expect them to turn their focus from their traumatized self to the wider social forces that are contributing to this trauma. Social action groupwork should be seen as a valuable approach, but only as part of a spectrum of groupwork provision, starting with very basic *support groups*. Once a person has experienced the healing of a support group, they might be in a better place to draw on their own resources to take social action.

Another critique of social action is that it minimizes the experience and expertise of the groupworker. Is the exercise of leadership by groupworkers necessarily experienced as oppressive? Of course, within the social action model, groupworkers *do* exercise their power and they use it to ask the group to ask itself 'why?' questions. The issue is not the exercise of leadership itself but the way it is experienced. Paradoxically, the desire ultimately to play a supporting role requires considerable leadership skills to get to that point.

Implications for practice

- The group needs to develop a *critical consciousness* – only by a careful interrogation of the 'why' can the 'how' be successfully decided and achieved;
- Social action is *process*-oriented rather than *outcome*-focused; the group is not working towards a fixed result, but engages in a process that helps it understand the underlying causes, to take action based on these conclusions and to reflect on these actions.

FURTHER READING

- Keenan, E. and Pinkerton, J. (1988) 'Social Action Groupwork as Negotiation: Contradictions in the Process of Empowerment', *Groupwork* 1 (3): pp. 229–238
- Mullender, A., Ward, D. and Fleming, J. (2013) *Self-Directed Groupwork Revisited: A Model for Service User Empowerment* (Basingstoke: Palgrave Macmillan)
- Ward, D. (ed) (2004) 'Groupwork and Social Action', *Groupwork,* 14 (2): pp. 96 (special issue)

structure

SEE ALSO **cohesion; co-working; joining and leaving; manualized groups; open and closed; planning and preparation; purpose; resources; session; setting; size; support groups; tasks; time**

In engineering, structure refers to physical objects assembled in such a way as to be able to carry a load. Similarly, in groupwork, structure refers to the elements that need to come together in order to support the group. Many of these are described in detail in separate A–Z entries, but here we collect them together in a brief overview. Decisions about the structure of the group should be made during the *planning and preparation* phase of work. However, issues of structure continue to influence the functioning of the group across its course, and need to be reviewed and adapted to best support the group.

The structure of the group is a powerful influence on group functioning and dynamics. As such, it is important to build a solid structure at the beginning of a group, yet remain flexible enough to change elements if they become a barrier to positive group functioning. The following elements are key areas to consider (Doel and Sawdon, 1999; Gitterman and Germain, 2008; Heap, 1985; Kurland, 1978/2005):

- **Venue** – Decisions about venue should be based on member needs and ease of access, not on a default setting. (e.g. in the agency because that is where groups always take place).
- **Group room** – The room *setting* for the group needs to be comfortable and conducive to group interaction.
- **Duration** – Groups can last for just one session or continue for many years. Decisions regarding durations should be based on group *purpose* and member need, as well as available *resources* to service it.
- **Frequency** – The default setting for frequency of group sessions is weekly, but there are groups where a more intense pattern is appropriate (for instance, groups in inpatient settings) and others that might need only meet once a fortnight or even monthly, such as some *support groups* and groups where time is needed between sessions for complex *tasks* to be completed. Some groups meet once, and only once (e.g. groups run in a

hospital waiting room to address concerns regarding medical procedures).

- **Timing** – The *time* a group meets must fit the members' lives and needs as well as the working patterns of any host agency. A group meeting in a hospital probably needs to avoid shift changes and meal times. Similarly, a group for parents is best planned outside times when children are returning home from school. Daily rhythms are a consideration; people with dementia may become more agitated towards the end of the working day, so a time earlier in the day may be better.
- **Length of sessions** – The length of each individual *session* needs to fit with the abilities of the members and the purposes of the group, as well as the schedule of groupworkers and any host agencies. If group members have problems with attention span or prolonged social interaction, shorter sessions are indicated – or frequent breaks. In schools, group sessions are likely to have to fit to an allotted period in the timetable.
- **Size – Size** influences the possibilities for interaction and the individual's experience of the group. Smaller groups allow for greater intimacy and larger groups allow for the possibility of more points of view and ideas.
- **Constancy of membership** – An *open* structure allows members to *join and leave* the group at different times, and closed structures do not. The former enables a group to expand, which can be purposeful to, say, campaigning groups; the latter promote intimacy, *cohesion* and trust.
- **Leadership** – The decision to facilitate the group as a sole worker or with a co-worker is a structural one that affects the way the group is experienced. *Co-working* can safeguard continuity, for instance a group session need not be cancelled if one of the groupworkers is unwell.
- **Pattern of working or running order** – Most groups develop some patterns for each individual session. This is probably the most visible expression of *structure* that group members experience. Group rituals can help to focus the work of the group, such as 'check in' time at the beginning of each session. Some groups might be relatively 'free-wheeling' whilst others, such as *manualized* groups, have a high degree of internal structure, with a fixed running order for the items in each session.

Implications for practice

- In order to function effectively, groups require appropriate structures in place;
- A key leader task is to ensure the appropriate structures exist to support the work of the group and to decide whether the purposes of the group suggest relatively loose or tight structures.

FURTHER READING

- Gitterman, A. and Germain, C. (2008) *The Life Model of Social Work Practice: Advances in Theory and Practice.* 3rd edn (New York: Columbia University Press)
- Lindsay, T. and Orton, S. (2011) *Groupwork Practice in Social Work.* 2nd edn (Exeter: Learning Matters), Chapter 2 'Planning Your Group: Initial Decisions', pp. 19–41
- Northen, H. and Kurland, R. (2001) *Social Work with Groups.* 3rd edn (New York: Columbia University Press), Chapter 6 'Pregroup Contact: Selection and Preparation of Members'
- Preston-Shoot, M. (2007) *Effective Groupwork.* 2nd edn (Basingstoke: Palgrave Macmillan), Chapter 5 'Planning Group Operation'

sub-groups

SEE ALSO **activities; differences; group as a whole; individuals; leadership; power; process; size; skills**

A sub-group is a group within a group. Usually it is a small grouping of people whose loyalties, interests and sense of belonging are strong, and sometimes stronger than their commitment to the *group as a whole.* Members of a sub-group might share characteristics that are notably different from the rest of the group, such as a sub-group of men in a group where the majority are women, a minority ethnic sub-group, or a sub-group of shy, *silent* people. A sub-group might consist of just a pairing or a trio, but it might be larger. The group might be constituted of readymade sub-groups, such as a group for sibling or family groups.

Members of a sub-group will often sit together on a regular basis, marking their own space within, or to the side of the main group. If the group's interactions were mapped, the lines of interaction around a sub-group would be stronger within the sub-group than between the sub-group and the rest of the group.

The impact of the sub-group depends on a number of factors, one of the most significant being *size*. In a large group such as a school class, it is inevitable that sub-groups will form to create a degree of intimacy that might be difficult or impossible to achieve in the full class. Sub-groups provide a safe shell from which *individuals* can explore group life, and within which the individual can make more impact – 'a big fish in a small pond'. In these circumstances sub-groups can seem very natural and might help the larger group to manage itself.

In a smaller group of, say, eight to twelve, the impact of a sub-group is likely to be felt more strongly. Much depends on the dynamics of the two systems, sub-group and group as a whole. A sub-group might be seen as an energetic, constructive power house *within* the main group and, therefore, largely positively. In this case the sub-group still maintains it chief allegiance to the main group, which willingly devolves some of its functions to the sub-group for the greater good. However, sub-groups are just as likely to form in opposition to the main group and to be seen as counter-cultural, perhaps as undermining the group as a whole. For instance, suggestions from members of the main group members are met with giggling and inaudible put-downs from the sub-group.

It is easy for groupworkers to see a sub-group as a problem to be managed and to feel angry with it for 'spoiling the group', which leads to a collusion with the scapegoating of the sub-group ('there they go again'). However, the formation of a sub-group is a message and, like all communication patterns in groups, it needs to be read for its meaning rather than suppressed. The formation of a sub-group might be an indication that the members of the sub-group are not ready to join the full group, do not know how to join it, feel themselves excluded, or possibly have been excluded by the full group. There are many interpretations, each depending on the specific set of dynamics in the particular group. The groupworker's *skill* is first to recognize the sub-grouping as a message and then to help both systems, group and sub-group, to begin to unpick what this communication means. Note that this is not an opportunity for the groupworker to show off their amazing powers of deduction, but to use their *power* and *leadership* to guide the group to do this. The group, the sub-group and the leadership are in this together.

Although sub-grouping is regularly seen as a problematic dynamic, in fact groupworkers regularly create sub-groups to help group *process*. Particularly in the early stages of a group when individuals might find it difficult to address the whole group, *activities* that break the group into twos, threes and fours (such as 'introduce your neighbour') are ways in which individual members can find their voice in the relative safety of a paired partnership, so that they explore the larger group from the safety of a sub-group. If all of the group is going through this similar, planned process, it feels supportive, because each sub-group is at the same stage. Spontaneous, enduring sub-groups – especially those that emphasize the *differences* between the sub-group and the group as a whole – have a wholly different quality and must be explored to discover their meaning and, in the light of this understanding, the best way to respond.

Implications for practice

- Sub-groups can be both helpful and harmful to the group process;
- Leaders need to see sub-groups as a form of communication and to try to help the group as a whole understand what the formation of the sub-group means.

FURTHER READING

- Gitterman, A. and Salmon, R. (eds) (2009) *Encyclopaedia of Social Work with Groups*, 'Group Work Phases of Helping' (New York: Routledge), pp. 109–121
- Norton, K. (2003) 'Henderson Hospital: Greater Than the Sum of Its Sub-Groups', *Groupwork*, 13 (3): pp. 65–100
- Regan, S. and Young, J. (1990) 'Siblings in Groups: Children of Separated/Divorced Parents', *Groupwork*, 3 (1): pp. 22–35

supervision of groupwork

SEE ALSO **accountability; confidentiality; difficulties in groups; evaluation; group supervision; leadership; organizations as groups; planning and preparation; recording**

Supervision is an essential element in continuing professional development and is made up of four different but related functions: support, education, management and, in some cases, assessment. It is an opportunity to discuss any *difficulties in groups* so that the groupworker can be supported through these and guided towards appropriate action. Supervision sessions are also opportunities to celebrate good practice and the group's achievements (Turkie, 1992).

A group's *accountability* to a sponsoring agency is generally exercised via the supervision and management of staff who are leading the group. This enhances the agency's knowledge of the group and the way it is helping the people who use its services.

However, the administrative and managerial functions of agency supervision can too readily eclipse the educative and supportive elements. In these circumstances, supervision is experienced as a report back rather than a reflective space that develops learning, encourages innovation and provides support for taking risks.

So, an important decision is whether supervision should be provided as part of the groupworker's line management arrangements or through independent professional consultation. It might be that the line manager is not versed in groupwork. A consultant can provide supervision to a group of staff who have different line managers, thereby saving time and spreading expertise. Of course, *resources* may limit the choices; but appropriate supervision should be reckoned as a necessary resource in the *planning and preparation* stage, with a recognition that supervision must be developmental, stretching the groupworker's *skills* and not just a place where formal accounts of work are given.

The agency sponsoring the group has much to benefit from understanding itself as a group, a large group in this case. The knowledge derived from the experience of the agency's groupworkers is, therefore, of direct relevance to the functioning of the organization and to the quality of its *teamwork*. Good *recording* systems for the agency's groupwork will ensure that there is adequate *evaluation* and that the knowledge is not lost. In this way, it can be used by the agency as a whole to benefit its services.

Implications for practice

- The planning for a group should always include the arrangements by which the groupworker(s) will receive supervision;
- Groups often involve *co-working* with colleagues, often one of the few occasions when practitioners have the opportunity to

observe and experience one another's practice and to be a part of each others' development – this should be seen as valuable, informal co-supervision.

FURTHER READING

- Doel, M. (2009a) 'Assessing Skills in Groupwork: A Program of Continuing Professional Development' in C.S. Cohen, M.H. Phillips and M. Hanson (eds), *Strength and Diversity in Social Work with Groups* (New York and London: Routledge), pp. 69–80
- Hawkins, P. and Shohet, R. (2007), *Supervision in the Helping Professions* (Maidenhead: Open University Press)
- Paul, R. (2012) 'Reflective Insights on Group Clinical Supervision; Understanding Transference in the Nursing Context', *Reflective Practice*, 13 (5): pp. 679–691

support groups

SEE ALSO **differences and similarities; joining and leaving; session; therapy groups**

In general, support groups provide social assistance for people who are isolated and, for whatever reason, do not have access to their own personal support systems. Support groups can provide professional support, too, such as workers in various multi-professional *teams* who join together in a same-profession support group.

There are two main kinds of support group. The first, 'soft support', describes a situation where the group itself is helping to provide what is missing in someone's life. People who are isolated because of their social, physical or mental circumstances come together in the group to experience social interaction and the company of others. Relatively large, informal groups in a day centre can provide this kind of social contact. Often these support groups are *open*, perhaps 'drop in', where people can come and go, join and leave, as they wish. *Activities* are very informal and the group is open-ended (no fixed number of *sessions*) without any specific *outcomes* or group goals. There may be access to the group several times a week, maybe daily.

The second type of support group, 'hard support' depicts those groups that meet to combat a common adversary or problem

(Bollmann, 1989; Geirdal, 1989). A black workers' support group might be providing support to professionals who are experiencing racism in their organization, or certainly white ethnocentric policies and practices. In cancer support groups the common 'adversary' is ill health and participants gain strength from one another. These support groups are likely to be ongoing, with new people joining as and when, but unlike the soft support groups, they often have a tighter internal *structure*. Sessions might be more formally programmed with some emphasis on outcome as well as *process*. This is particularly true if the support group is used as a springboard for a campaigning group.

In the balance of *differences and similarities* among group members, support groups tend to draw most heavily on the importance of similarities. Their similar circumstances help members to understand one another in ways that are hard to find outside the group. All groupwork is intended to be supportive to some degree, but it is the profound level of *acceptance* that is fundamental to support groups (Rimmer, 1993; Thompson, 1995).

Support can be experienced in many different ways. A group for refugee women in the Balkans became aware that one of its members spent the sessions in *silence*. It was discovered that she did not speak the language of the other women in the group but, through translation, she was able to let them know that she wanted to continue to come to the group because she found it just being there and belonging was supportive.

Implications for practice

- All groups have a supportive function, but some groups' primary focus is supporting people who are otherwise isolated in their communities or work organizations;
- Support groups tend to work better when their members have a great degree of similarity and can experience the 'all in the same boat' phenomenon.

FURTHER READING

- Popplestone-Helm, S.V. and Helm, D.P. (2009) 'Setting Up a Support Group for Children and Their Well Carers Who Have a Significant Adult with a Life-Threatening Illness', *International Journal of Palliative Nursing*, 15 (5): pp. 214–221

- Simpson, I. (2010) 'Containing the Uncontainable: A Role for Staff Support Groups' in J. Radcliffe *et al.* (eds), *Psychological Groupwork with Acute Psychiatric Inpatien* (London: Whiting and Birch), pp. 87–105
- Westergaard, J. (2010) 'Providing Support to Young People through Groupwork: Delivering Personalised Learning and Development in the Group Context', *Groupwork,* 20 (1): pp. 87–102

t

taboos

SEE ALSO **differences and similarities; group as a whole; skills; values**

A taboo is a topic, activity or behaviour that is prohibited by custom, rule or social pressure. Taboo subjects in many cultures include sexuality, death, certain illnesses, discussion of topics such as religion, open expression of feelings, challenging authority or seeming to act above your station. Group members bring the *values*, norms and customs (including taboos) of their family and social groups with them, and sometimes a taboo can strongly interfere with the work of a group. For example, many groups are formed to help members deal with difficulties that are taboo in the wider society, and this makes them very difficult to broach. The strength of the taboo might even prevent some people from joining groups that could help them. For example, taboos around sex, drug use and HIV/AIDS can make it difficult for HIV positive people to join a support group; once joined, the taboo inhibits the group from discussion of the very topic that brings them together.

The first step is for the groupworker to identify the communication patterns that are blocking the group from discussion of a taboo subject. The groupworker might be prepared for some taboos to arise (such as death in a hospice group) but others may be more subtle, such as an avoidance of discussing loss and, therefore, need naming. Perhaps the groupworker notices that members are changing the subject as discussion gets too close to a certain area. Simply pointing out the pattern and asking the group what makes it difficult to discuss the topic can often be enough to help the group break through into the taboo. They may not have been aware that the loss, in our example, has been something they are all feeling but have been unable to name or face. From a psychodynamic approach, resistance or other defence mechanisms may underlie the avoidance of certain taboo topics. Exploring and understanding such resistance with the group may be a central piece of work for group members.

One of the benefits of working with groups is that members are rarely ever at the same place, so workers can use these *differences* to help members shift communication patterns. Whereas some members find it impossible to discuss taboo subjects, others are ready and able to broach it. These members can plough a furrow for other group members and encourage them by example to approach difficult subjects and to voice unspoken feelings. The groupworkers use their *skills* to guide these developments and help slow or quicken the pace depending on the needs and abilities of the *group as a whole.*

Implications for practice

- Identification of communication patterns blocking discussion of certain topics is the first step in helping group members remove barriers to taboo subjects;
- Exploring what makes talking about a taboo difficult helps the group then to move closer to the taboo subject.

FURTHER READING

- Gitterman, A. and Germain, C. (2008) *The Life Model of Social Work Practice: Advances in Theory and Practice.* 3rd edn (New York: Columbia University Press), Chapter 10 'Helping with Dysfunctional Group Processes', pp. 338–377
- Shulman, L. (2002) 'Learning to Talk about Taboo Subjects: A Lifelong Professional Challenge', *Social Work with Groups,* 25 (1–2): pp. 139–150
- Williams, A. (1991) *Forbidden Agendas: Strategic Action in Groups* (London: Routledge)

tasks

SEE ALSO **activities; beginnings; confidentiality; conflicts; endings; groundrules; group as a whole; middles; power; purpose; session; structure; taboo; work groups**

In groupwork, tasks refer to the actions, *activities* or work that must be accomplished by the worker and members so the group can develop and achieve its *purposes.* Some tasks are primarily the responsibility of the groupworker, others are that of the members, and yet others are shared. Though the tasks are important across the life of a group, some of the tasks take greater importance at different phases of work (Berman-Rossi, 1993).

The tasks that members collectively should accomplish in the *beginning* phase of work include:

- Gaining an understanding of the common purpose for the group (and one that is synonymous with agency purposes if there is a sponsoring agency).
- Establishing how the group will work together, perhaps by agreeing *groundrules* and limits to *confidentiality* (in *work groups* this is likely to mean the distribution of formal roles).
- Establishing a pattern for each *session* of the group and adapting this to suit the group's needs

In the *middle* phase of work, tasks change the focus to a strengthening of the *group as a whole*, such as:

- Activities that promote a sense of belonging and mutuality (sometimes referred to as a 'system of mutual aid').
- Resolving the group's relationship with the groupworker – tasks that shift *power* increasingly to the group members.
- Achieving a balance between individual members' need for privacy and the demands of the group for self-disclosure and openness.
- Identifying obstacles to the group's functioning and helping the group to grapple with any *taboo* topics or *conflicts*.
- Reviewing and strengthening *structures* to help the group's work, such as the *groundrules* and the group's communication patterns.

In the *ending* phase, tasks will include:

- Evaluating the work of the group as a whole and the progress for individual members.
- Preparing for transitions – especially how group members take the learning and experience of the group beyond its close.
- Dissolving the ties to the group and group members without damaging what the group has meant.

The nature of tasks in groups that are ongoing are more likely to concern group maintenance – helping the group to sustain itself and to review its purposes in the light of there being no formal process of ending.

Implications for practice

- The balance between focus on task and focus on process is not easily achieved, but even in task groups it is important to understand and work with the group process;
- The nature of group tasks changes as the group progresses.

FURTHER READING

- Corey, G. (2011) 'Early Stages in the Development of a Group' and 'Later Stages in the Development of a Group', *Theory and Practice of Group Counseling*. 8th edn (Belmont, CA: Brooks/Cole, Cengage Learning), pp. 94–141
- Frank, M.D. (2011) 'Community Social Service Projects: Working in Task Groups to Create Change' in C.F. Kuechler (ed), *Group Work: Building Bridges of Hope* (London: Whiting and Birch), pp. 67–80

theories

SEE ALSO **evidence; methods and models; reflection in groupwork; research; structure; values**

The main purpose of a theory, certainly in groupwork, is that it should be useful. It should organize knowledge and experience in ways that increase our understanding of what to do. As Kurt Lewin puts it so neatly, 'There is nothing so practical as a good theory'.

What is a theory? A theory is a set of concepts that are systematically associated with one another and that form a cohesive framework that can be used to explain or predict phenomena; *'-ism'* theories, such as Marxism, feminism and postmodernism, are used to explain the bigger picture. (Paradoxically, in the case of postmodernism, this is to debunk the very idea that there is a bigger picture.)

Contrasting with these grand theories are the pet theories that individuals hold to help them explain their experiences. These personal hypotheses are not subjected to the scrutiny and critical analysis that accompany grand theory, but there is evidence to

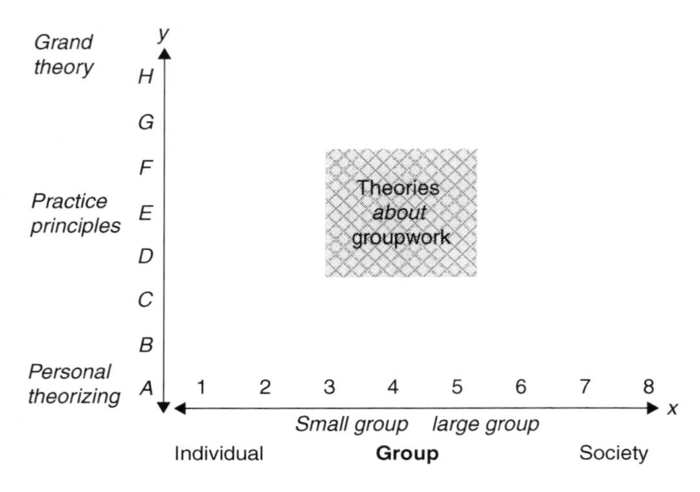

FIGURE 2 *Theories and groupwork*

suggest that they hold a much greater sway over an individual's actions. Personal theories are summed up occasionally in aphorisms such as 'blood is thicker than water'. When they are accepted as general truths by a group of people such as a profession, they acquire the status of *practice wisdom.* Personal hypotheses and a profession's practice wisdom are not theories as such, but they are examples of *theorizing* and their impact on practice means they should not be ignored.

Figure 2 illustrates the location of the scope and focus of different kinds of theory. The *x* axis (1 to 8) shades from a focus on the individual through groups to the wider society and the *y* axis (A to H) from the notion of personal 'pet' theories to grand theory, as described earlier. Of course, this is a simplification, as many theories cannot be located at just one point on the grid, especially those that aim to provide holistic or comprehensive explanations, such as systems theories. The shaded area, theories *about* groupwork, will be explained in the next section.

Theories for groupwork and theories about groupwork

In addition to the contrast between grand theory and pet theory, there are differences between theories from which groupwork borrows and theories that are about groupwork itself.

Groupwork borrows from other disciplines, such as those general theories that purport to explain human behaviour, social experience and the meaning of life. These are often called theoretical *perspectives* or approaches. Almost the whole of human knowledge can be seen to have some relevance to groupwork; not just the obvious discipline of social psychology, but – to name a handful of others – systems theories, learning theories, community and organizational development, theories derived from psychoanalytical traditions and theories of social identity.

Indeed, broad fields of study such as philosophy, anthropology and even physics can contribute to our knowledge of groupwork. Existentialism has much to teach groups about their meaning and sense of belonging, notions that are central to group formation. Learning about group bonds and identities in other societies, past and present, can teach us much about contemporary ideas of group identity. The study of flow and movement in physics can throw light on large group behaviours, as well as the potential for nonlinear dynamics to teach us about chaos and complexity and their relationship to small groupwork.

The usefulness of this borrowed knowledge varies from case to case and depends on the fit with the groupworker's own beliefs and *values*. A groupworker who believes that the here and now is paramount and that, for instance, you can learn how to untangle a ball of wool and keep it untangled, without knowing how it got tangled in the first place, will likely be drawn to perspectives drawn from learning theory. A groupworker, who believes in the significance of the there and then and that you can untangle the ball of wool but until you know why it was tangled in the first place it will keep on becoming tangled again, is likely to draw from psychodynamic theories.

The dispassionate observer might ask, surely we have some *research evidence* that tells us which of the perspectives is correct? In fact, the complexity and number of the factors involved make it difficult to come to a judgement that is not related to each specific instance; and even then, there is strong evidence to suggest that the theoretical orientation of the groupworker is less significant than their personal qualities.

In addition to theories *for* groupwork there are theories *about* groupwork. The former is borrowed knowledge that may or may not have application to groups and the group context. The latter are theories about groups, group *process*, *structure* and dynamics. These *homegrown* theories are located in the shaded area of the Figure 2 and they concern themselves with theorizing about the practice of groupwork.

Models are built on the basis of theories of groupwork and three of the best known are the remedial, reciprocal and social goals models. On the basis of models, groupwork *methods* are devised. Thus, in the case of task-centred groupwork, it borrows from general theories, such as systems theory and learning theory, but it has developed its own practice theory, based on the testing of the task-centred model in practice. It has a methodology, i.e. a systematic range of practice sequences that distinguish it as 'task-centred' and that have been evidenced through trial and error.

A practice theory is concerned with the practical consequences of its application. A practice theory of groupwork does not attempt to explain human behaviour at a general level, rather to theorize from the experience of practical groupwork and to theorize about what happens when people join together in groups. Practice theories need to be dynamic to respond to the ever-changing experience of practice, so they tend to be constructed through trial and error. Practice theory is in constant transit, which tends to weaken its theoretical reliability and verification, but strengthen its practicality and usefulness.

Theories can be considered according to their purpose. Some theories aim to give meaning to observable phenomena and are therefore *descriptive* of these phenomena. However, knowledge that is derived from practice frequently transforms into statements of principle and these morph into prescriptions for practice. *Prescriptive* theories determine what action *ought* to be taken. For example, a prescriptive theory derived from groupwork would seek to explain *difficult behaviour in groups* and prescribe practice methods that should be used to work with this behaviour. As a practice theory, this would derive not from abstract reasoning but from observed experience in groups. The major difficulty with these theories is their lack of comparability – that the relative 'weight' of one theory as compared to another is so difficult (and perhaps not possible) to measure.

Some theories that are descriptive, such as theories of group *development*, are extrapolated to be *predictive*. So, if group development can be described as norming, forming, storming and performing, might we predict that a group which has successfully normed will move on to a forming phase? However, the practical testing of group development theories suggests that they have severe limitations even as descriptions – with groups stalling or moving back and forth between these supposed phases and even showing characteristics of all the stages within one session. It is, then, all the more unreliable as a predictive theory.

Is it possible to develop a theory of practice about what groupworkers do whilst respecting the different theoretical approaches that groupworkers use? This was the question posed by Douglas in the 1980s when he attempted to develop a general theory of groupwork practice. If what happens in a self-directed *social action* group and a cognitive behavioural group for young offenders and a psychoanalytically oriented *therapy group* are all to be considered *groupwork,* what theory can unite these hugely disparate theoretical perspectives?

A general practice theory of groupwork remains a work in progress and is more often expressed as a set of principles of practice. These principles encompass most of the entry titles and cross-references in this book, such as group composition, membership and leadership; cohesion, intimacy, authority, sub-grouping and size; power, role, gender and race, etc. A general theory of groupwork practice eludes us and will probably continue to do so.

Implications for practice

- Even when groupworkers do not adhere to a formal 'espoused' theory, they use working hypotheses in their groupwork and it is important that these are made explicit so they can be challenged or replicated;
- Theoretical perspectives can help groupworkers to make sense of group process and behaviours in the group, but only if they make time for *reflection*.

FURTHER READING

- Doel, M. and Sawdon, C. (1999) *The Essential Groupworker* (London/ Philadelphia: Jessica Kingsley), Chapter 1 'Why Groupwork?', pp. 11–32
- Douglas, T. (1993) *A Theory of Groupwork Practice* (Houndmills: Macmillan)
- Preston-Shoot, M. (2007) *Effective Groupwork*. 2nd edn (Basingstoke: Palgrave Macmillan)

- Roberts, R.W. and Northen, H. (eds) (1976) *Theories of Social Work with Groups* (New York: Columbia University Press)
- Trevithick, P. (2005) 'The Knowledge Base of Groupwork and Its Importance within Social Work', *Groupwork*, 15 (2): pp. 80–107

therapy groups

SEE ALSO **educational groups; group as a whole; methods; model; process; purpose; recreational groups; self-help groups; social action; support groups; theories**

Groups are formed for many purposes. In this entry we consider the type known as therapy or psychotherapy groups (Corey, 2011; Zastrow, 2001). Therapy groups do not have a monopoly on therapeutic outcomes. Self-help groups, for example, can be very therapeutic for their members. Indeed, there is a sense in which any coming together of people around shared purposes or concerns has the potential for a therapeutic outcome – improved psychological well-being. However, these other types of groups do not have therapeutic outcomes as their primary purpose (Kurtz, 1997).

Providing a definition of group therapy or group psychotherapy that has consensus across the helping professions would be impossible (Burlingame, Kapetanovic and Ross, 2005). However, if we examine the word *therapy* we see that it relates to the curing or remediation of an illness or disease. Though an agreed definition may not be possible, focusing on the *therapy* in group therapy points to an assumption that group therapy's focus is to help members *remediate* or *treat* their psychological problems, mental health issues, maladjustment or other personal problems (Craig, 1990; Hajek, 2007; Neary and Brandon, 1997). The Association of Specialist in Group Work (2000) recognizes the difficulties in developing a conceptually discrete definition, but it does provide a useful description of group psychotherapy. It states that group psychotherapy can be characterized by the application of principles of normal and abnormal human development. It has group intervention strategies at the cognitive, affective, behaviour and/or systemic levels, which are implemented in the context of members' negative emotional arousal. The purpose of group psychotherapy is threefold. Psychotherapy groups work on personal and interpersonal problems of living, remediate perceptual and cognitive distortions or dysfunctional patterns of behaviour, as well as promote personal/interpersonal development. It is practised with people experiencing severe and/or chronic maladjustment (ASGW, 2000; Corey 2011). The focus can be on the conscious and unconscious and focus on the past as well as the present. Therapy group leaders work to engender an emotional experience (sometimes called a corrective emotional experience) that will bring about some desired change in functioning or way of being.

Different kinds of therapy groups
Burlingame and colleagues (2005) suggest that one of the reasons it is difficult to develop a universally agreed definition of group psychotherapy is that there are many different theoretical frameworks that underpin different models and methods of group psychotherapy. These same models of group psychotherapy can also underpin counselling groups and psychoeducational groups. They may also underpin the groupwork practice of various professions practising groupwork (e.g. counsellors, nurses, occupational therapists, psychologists, social workers). Though a complete discussion of each model of group therapy is outside the scope of this entry, it is useful to briefly examine the main approaches in group therapy.

Psychoanalytic therapy groups
The theoretical underpinnings of psychoanalytic therapy groups begin with an extension of Freud's individual psychoanalytic theory and have evolved to include later psychoanalytic theories. The goal of the psychoanalytic group is to restructure the personality systems of members through bringing unconscious conflicts into the conscious awareness. Family of origin issues become symbolically re-enacted within the group. Key concepts include free association, resistance, transference, countertransference, acting out, ego defence mechanisms and interpretation. Though initially drawn from individual theories, these concepts are applied within a group context.

Existential–experiential groups
The theoretical underpinnings of existential–experiential group therapy begin with the philosophical writings of existential philosophers of the 19th and 20th centuries and the existential psychology

movement, which originated in Switzerland. There is an emphasis on being, experience and meaning – central to a core groupwork concept of 'belonging' – and the group helps its members to move from inauthentic to authentic existence. Key concepts include self-awareness, freedom, self-determination, personal responsibility, existential anxiety, death and nonbeing and the search for meaning and relatedness. Existential group therapists facilitate group interaction and help members to develop self-awareness. The group therapist is engaged and spontaneous with group members.

Behavioural therapy groups

The theoretical underpinnings come from behavioural and experimental psychology, though there are various behavioural therapy approaches. In addition to the very fashionable cognitive behavioural therapy there is rational emotive therapy, systematic desensitization and skill practice therapy. They all have several common features: behaviour is seen as learned, and therefore old behaviours can be unlearned and new behaviours can be learned. Key concepts include a focus on specific and observable behaviour, creating measurable treatment goals and an emphasis on evaluating the change in identified behaviours. Some forms of group therapy are based on individual models of treatment, which are then applied to groups. Some behavioural approaches, on the other hand, are based on educational or learning theories, which easily translate into individual and group based applications. Rational emotive behaviour group therapy as an example 'fits' with the theory underpinning it.

Non-directive or person centred group therapy

Non-directive group therapy was developed by Carl Rogers and based on a humanistic psychological belief that people naturally moved towards wholeness, well-being and self-actualization. Through being present, empathic, genuine and accepting of others the group therapist creates an environment where self-actualization, growth and acceptance can occur. Key concepts in person centred group therapy include trusting in the group process and developing the therapeutic conditions for growth (genuineness, unconditional positive regard, empathy). For group therapy from a person centred perspective, the qualities of the group therapist are more important than specific techniques used. Rather than focusing on *doing* specific things to the group, the focus is on *being* genuine, empathic and accepting so that an accepting and therapeutic climate is created within the group.

Group analytic therapy

Group therapy, and particularly group analysis, in the UK was heavily influenced by S. H. Foulkes who is credited as the founder of the group analytic movement. Educated as a psychoanalyst and psychiatrist, he was influenced by sociological, psychological and neurobiological theories of early to mid-twentieth century. Foulkes' thinking on the development of the person represented a shift away from earlier psychoanalytic understandings of the personality developing from individual drives and crises. Instead, group analytic thinking saw humans as born into a social group with interconnected communication networks. The social group is the context in which personality develops and underpins the therapeutic effect of group analytic therapy.

In group analytic therapy there are no prearranged procedures, plans or topics. Instead, members are encouraged to spontaneously discuss what they wish, similar to free association in individual psychoanalytic traditions. Though the content of what is discussed is important, the facilitator or conductor pays more attention to the structure and processes of the group. The conductor facilitates an interpretive culture within the analytic group and therapeutic factors emerge. These are: socialization or moving from isolation into belonging; mirror phenomena or being able to see oneself in the other members of the group; condenser phenomena which describe the release of deep and primitive material due to the loosening of resistance through pooling of group ideas and interactions; and, exchange or the discussion and interchange of ideas, feedback, communication.

Implications for practice

- Different models of group therapy provide varied understandings of therapeutic groupwork – the group and the role of the groupworker;
- Be transparent about your therapeutic orientation and remain open to evidence about its effectiveness, whether this is supportive or challenging.

FURTHER READING

- Bieling, P.J., McCabe, R.E. and Antony, M.M. (2009) *Cognitive–Behavioral Therapy in Groups* (New York: Guilford Press)
- Ellis, A. and Dryden, W. (2007) *The Practice of Rational Emotive Behavior Therapy*. Kindle edn (New York: Springer Publishing)
- Pines, M. (2000) *The Evolution of Group Analysis* (London: Jessica Kingsley Publishers)
- Rutan, J.S., Stone, W.N. and Shay, J.J. (2007) *Psychodynamic Group Psychotherapy*. 4th edn (New York: Guilford Press)
- Shaffer, J. and Galinsky, M.D. (1989) *Models of Group Therapy*. 2nd edn (Englewood Cliffs, NJ: Prentice-Hall)

time

SEE ALSO **activities; flash groups; manualized groups; planning and preparation; process; purpose; session; structure**

Time is a significant element of groups and groupwork. It is a seemingly simple concept with a surprisingly complex number of applications, which we will explore in this entry.

The length of a group's life varies substantially from the kinds of *flash groups* that arise spontaneously, usually just one session long, to open-ended groups that can continue for as long as there is a need and the support of the membership (Liles and Wahlquist, 2006).

For a group established from new ('created groups'), a decision has to be made about whether it will be short term, long term on open-ended (Heap, 1988b; Schopler and Galinsky, 2005). Unless the group is *manualized* (it has a pre-determined programme), the initial decision about the duration of the group should be provisional, with the group itself making the final choice when possible. The *purposes* of the group and the likely time to achieve these purposes should determine its duration.

Timing of group sessions

One of the practical challenges of *planning and preparation* is when to hold each group *session* and how often. Finding a time of day and a regular day of the week that suits all the prospective group members and the groupworkers can be a struggle. The groupworkers need to tune in to the likely daily rhythm of members as they make their way to the group and adjust the *activities* accordingly. For example, a group meeting in the late afternoon or early evening in order to accommodate participants who work during the day, might do well to provide generous snacks to help raise blood sugar levels at the end of a tiring day.

The classic template for the frequency of group meetings is once a week. There are good reasons for this: it follows a natural rhythm in the calendar and helps everybody to remember when the group is meeting ('Tuesdays at 2:00'); it sets a pattern and this implicitly resonates with the pattern-making that groupworkers seek to achieve within the group sessions, a stable *structure* that provides the security to take risks in the group; it gives time for homework to be completed and for many of the ideas and experiences of one session to be reflected on and to take root, in time for the next session.

There are circumstances when a group might meet more frequently, for instance when there is urgent work to be done, or the group *process* needs accelerating. Similarly, a group might meet less frequently – fortnightly or monthly – where the group is task-focused and more time is needed between sessions in order to complete *tasks*. In general, the more frequently the group meets, the more intimate and intense the relationships between its members will be.

Skilful groupwork is a blend of art and science. Knowledge derived from the systematic study of groups is important, but a talented groupworker also uses their artistry to inspire the best in groups. One aspect of this artistry is the groupworker's ability to keep time – like a gifted musician. 'Keeping time' is different from 'keeping to time' (the latter is an important rule but, like all rules, sometimes needs to be broken). It is the ability to know how to pace a topic or when to open up a *taboo* and when to let it lie. A groupworker in touch with the pulse of the group knows when it is ready for physical activity and when it needs to pause, even resting in *silence*; when the group should stick to its agreed plan and when it should spend time off-piste. In the group context the way that time is paced is critical, though it does not lend itself easily to empirical study.

Finally, the timing of a groupwork intervention itself can be critical. Using groups for early intervention in people's troubles can be very effective (Moe, 1989).

Implications for practice

- Groupworkers need to match the frequency of group sessions with the group's purpose;
- Timing in groupwork is critical; skilled groupwork helps the group to find its own pace.

FURTHER READING

- Cwikel, J. and Oron, A. (1991) 'A Long-Term Support Group for Chronic Schizophrenic Outpatients: A Quantitative and Qualitative Evaluation', *Groupwork*, 4 (2): pp. 163–177
- Daste, B. (1995) 'Creative Short-Term Group Therapy in a Managed Care Environment', *Groupwork*, 8 (3): pp. 302–312
- Steinberg, D.M. (2005) 'She's Doing All the Talking, So What's in It for Me? (the Use of Time in Groups)' in A. Malekoff and R. Kurland (eds), *A Quarter Century of Classics (1978–2004): Capturing the Theory, Practice and Spirit of Social Work with Groups* (Binghamton: The Haworth Press), pp. 173–186

values

SEE ALSO **collective; democracy; history of groupwork; individuals; methods; models; roles; social action**

Groupwork is a method practised by many different professions, encompassing many different beliefs about how and why groups can and should be used. Moreover, there are numerous *models* and *methods* of groupwork. It is, then, a very broad church and any attempt to define *the* groupwork values is challenging but not impossible.

The *historical* and geographical contexts influence the values of groupwork (Smith, 2004). In the late 19th and early 20th centuries, groupwork emerged out of the settlement house movement, progressive adult education, boys and girls clubs, ragged schools, the camp movement and recreation. Shortly after the development of this social groupwork, the first treatment groups emerged within the medical profession from a physician treating people with tuberculosis. From these diverse roots, groupwork incorporated a range of values, including – perhaps ironically – a respect for autonomous *individuals* and a sense of personal dignity and equality. However, in most models of groupwork, individuals are seen in the context of their relationships to one another and their environment. Mutual interdependence is, then, a core groupwork value, alongside the value of *democratic* participation and social justice. In societies that are highly individualized, such as western ones, the group is a place to find one's *collective* voice, but in more collectivized societies, a group can be a place to find one's individual voice.

Values are often expressed in practice principles or embedded within methods for working with groups (Glassman, 2008). For example, the value of interdependence is expressed through methods and techniques designed to strengthen the bonds among members. The value of participation is embodied within the contracting techniques and group negotiation common to many groupwork methods; members shape the decisions that will affect their group, such as developing a shared group purpose and experience an authority figure (in the shape of the groupworker) who is facilitative and promotes equality, acceptance and mutual respect by ensuring all members have a voice in the group and that no one, leader included, has a privileged place there.

Although groups bring people together with common problems or concerns, differences in groups are valued, too and group members have different *roles* in the group, leader included. Groupwork values are made explicit in the *Standards for Social Work Practice with Groups* (AASWG, 2010), *Ethical Guidelines for Group counsellors* (ASGW, 1990).

Implications for practice

- Values have corresponding behaviours in practice – for example, the value of respecting privacy is expressed through efforts to ensure the confidentiality of group members;
- Be aware of groupwork values and how you put those values into action.

FURTHER READING

- Association for Specialists in Group Work (ASGW) (1990) 'Ethical Guidelines for Group Counsellors: ASGW 1989 Revision', *The Journal for Specialist in Group Work,* 15 (2): pp. 119–126
- Corey, G. (2011) 'Ethical and Professional Issues in Group Practice' in *Theory and Practice of Group Counseling.* 8th edn (Belmont, CA: Brooks/ Cole, Cengage Learning), pp. 71–93
- Preston-Shoot, M. (2007) *Effective Groupwork.* 2nd edn (Houndmills: Palgrave Macmillan), Chapter 2 'Practising Groupwork Values', pp. 27–44
- http://www.aaswg.org/files/AASWG_Standards_for_Social_Work_Practice_with_Groups.pdf

virtual groups

SEE ALSO **confidentiality; process; researching groups; self-help; silence**

In the early days of personal computing, technologically minded people with shared interests formed special interests groups and communicated through bulletin boards or used Internet Relay Chat (IRC). These activities were primarily the domain of the early adopters of interactive computer technology (ICT). Since then the world has been transformed and there is a wide range of technology to facilitate online groups and possible to find virtual groups related to any hobby, leisure activity, social cause, personal problem, health condition or interest. This burgeoning of online groups has been increasingly *researched* (Kelly et al., 2006).

Face-to-face and online groups have many things in common: a group identity, mutual aid, group norms, culture and intimacy can all develop in virtual groups, similar to face-to-face groups. There are many differences as well due to the nature of the medium. In face-to-face groups people must be in the same room at the same time, whilst online groups allow members to participate from all around the globe. In addition, because communication can be in the form of text and posted to a shared virtual space, the meetings can be asynchronous, which means that members do not have to be 'together' at the same time (Levine, 2005; Meier, 2000; Regan, 1997; Smokowski, Galinski and Harlow, 2001).

Some of the advantages of online groups include:

- Continuous, 24 hours a day access;
- Ease of attendance – from home, work or any internet connection;
- Privacy – in particular, stigmaized groups can protect their identities;
- Accessibility – homebound people can participate without having to leave the home and people living in remote areas are not isolated;
- Finding others in similarly unusual circumstances – the 'all in the same boat' phenomenon for people with, for instance, rare conditions;
- Lurking – *silent* or unseen members can benefit from the conversations between other group members without inhibiting group *processes*.

Some of the disadvantages of online groups include:

- Social exclusion – some socially disadvantaged people do not have access to computers or are not able to operate them.
- Literacy – illiterate people are excluded from online groups that use text; some literate people have difficulty writing their thoughts and feelings.

- Equipment failures can interfere with virtual group participation.
- Privacy concerns – *confidentiality* of communication can easily be breached.
- Miscommunication is more likely in the absence of verbal and visual cues and without the restraint that face-to-face contact is more likely to produce.
- Fantasy – members can more easily present an inaccurate, untruthful picture of themselves.

Whatever the balance of advantage and disadvantage, virtual groups are increasing. Further technological change is leading to face-to-face groups that are virtual (such as Skype). These need people to be present at the same time, but not in the same room. Currently, most virtual groups are self-directed, *self-help* groups, but it is likely that professional groupworkers will discover the potential of virtual groups, too.

Implications for practice

- Online groups can be useful in working with stigmaized populations or those isolated due to distance or mobility, and professionals should keep abreast of online group resources and consider referring people to them;
- Potential leaders and users of online groups need to be aware of the limitations and take steps to minimize these limitations.

FURTHER READING

- Colón, Y. and Stern, S. (2010) 'Counseling Groups Online: Theory and Framework' in R. Kraus, G. Stricker and C. Speyer (eds), *Online Counseling: A Handbook for Mental Health Professionals* (London: Elsevier)
- McKenna, K.Y.A. and Green, A.S. (2002) 'Virtual Group Dynamics', *Group Dynamics: Theory Research, and Practice,* 6 (1): pp. 116–127

work groups

SEE ALSO **activities; cohesion; collective; context; outcome; purpose; resources; roles; task; teamwork; time**

Not all groups are naturally occurring. Some are formed for a specified purpose – to complete a range of tasks or to accomplish a particular piece of work. These work groups or working groups are often formed within a single organization, though they can also reach across to other interest groups, such as clubs, residential associations and the like. A key feature of these work groups is that they are focused on an agreed outcome and they are time-limited, so there is a deadline for the work. What draws group members together is the interest in the work or necessity of the tasks that they must accomplish – and the fact that this can best be achieved by a group rather than a set of individuals. In short, a team is formed. We suggest the equation: teamwork = groupwork.

Work groups can work really well or they can flounder – just like any group, success depends on harnessing group process. Even with a highly focused, task-oriented group, process is what drives the success – or thwarts it.

When work groups are conceived as *groups* (the clue is in the name), it is possible for explicit groupwork principles to be applied. These include:

- Establishing a clear purpose (which might be different from the initial one);
- Ensuring participation of all members in *activities* that are meaningful to them;
- Fostering *cohesion* by having people work together on some tasks;
- Developing a common way of working together – a group culture or norms (Kozlowski and Bell, 2003).

Work groups need to be composed of members based on the range of skills needed, not because of job descriptions or organizational politics. *Roles* should not be allocated unthinkingly to agency hierarchy (e.g., it may be appropriate for a person to take a leadership role who is not necessarily a manager in the agency). Successful multi-professional teams have members who are clear about their role, yet team members can comfortably blur the lines when needed (Bronstein, 2003).

The *context* of the work group is significant and there should be sufficient *resources* and organizational or community support. In addition, there needs to be an appropriate mix of shared and individual tasks.

The leadership style can vary among authoritarian, democratic or laissez-faire, just like group leadership, with exactly the same impact on the team members' levels of compliance, resistance, efficiency and participation. Common difficulties in groups are mirrored in difficulties in teams and work groups, in particular conflict and similar roles are taken on by individuals in the team (such as 'internal leadership'), with a similar propensity for subgroups to develop. In short, team dynamics have all the characteristics of group process. The functions of work groups are not dissimilar to some kinds of problem-solving groups.

Implications for practice

- Understanding a work group *as a group* can help make work groups more productive;
- Clarity about the central purpose of a work group and the roles of its members is central to successful outcomes;
- A mindshift to team as group can significantly improve relationships in a team, and a possible catalyst for this shift is the joining of a new team member.

FURTHER READING

- Campion, M.A., Medsker, G.J. and Higgs, A.C. (2001) 'Relations between Work Group Characteristics and Effectiveness: Implications for Designing Effective Work Groups', *Personnel Psychology*, 46: pp. 823–850
- Ephross, P.H. and Vassil, T.V. (2004) 'Group Work and Working Groups' in C. D. Garvin, L.M. Gutiérrez and M.J. Galinsky (eds),

Handbook of Social Work with Groups (New York: The Guilford Press), pp. 400–414

- Wagner, J.A. *et al.* (2012) 'Individualism–Collectivism and Team Member Performance: Another Look', *Journal of Organizational Behaviour,* 33 (7): pp. 946–963

appendix 1

methods and models

The following sources provide examples of particular groupwork methods:

Argyle, E. and Bolton, G. (2004) 'The Use of Art within a Groupwork Setting' *Groupwork,* 14(1): pp. 46–62

Atkinson, D. (1993) 'Life History Work with a Group of People with Learning Disabilities', *Groupwork,* 6(3): pp. 199–210

DeVere, M. and Rhonne, O. (1991) 'The Use of Photographs as a Projective and Facilitative Technique in Groups', *Groupwork,* 4(2): pp. 129–140

Drower, S. (1991) 'Groupwork and Oral History: Raising the Consciousness of Young People during Social Transition', *Groupwork,* 4(2): pp. 119–128

Edgar, I. (1992) 'The Dream in Groupwork Practice', *Groupwork,* 5(2): pp. 54–64

Evans, K. (2009) 'Rhythm "N" Blues: Bringing Poetry into Groupwork', *Groupwork,* 19(3): pp. 27–38

Fitzsimmons, J. and Levy, R. (1996) 'An Art Therapy Group for Young People with Eating Difficulties', *Groupwork,* 9(3): pp. 283–291

Gibson, F. (1992) 'Reminiscence Groupwork with Older People', *Groupwork,* 5(3), 28–40.

Henchman, D. and Walton, S. (1993) 'Critical Incident Analysis and Its Application in Groupwork', *Groupwork,* 6(3), 189–198

Huntington, A. (1999) 'Action Methods and Interpersonal Processes in Groups: An Exploration of Pyschodramatic Concepts', *Groupwork,* 11(2): pp. 49–67

Lange, R. (2004) 'Using Narrative Therapy in an Educational Parenting Group', *Groupwork,* 14(1): pp. 63–79

Lordan, N. (1996) 'The Use of Sculpts in Social Groupwork Education', *Groupwork,* 9(1): pp. 62–79

Marshall, M. and Holmes, G. (2009) 'An Evaluation of a Mindfulness Group', *Groupwork,* 19(1): pp. 40–58

Parkinson, F. (1993) 'Coping with Trauma', *Groupwork,* 6(2): pp. 140–151

Ruch, G. (2006) 'Nothing New Under the Sun: Using Sculpts in Post-Qualification Child Care Social Work Groups', *Groupwork,* 16(2): pp. 8–24

Sharry, J. (2008) *Solution-Focused Groupwork* (London: Sage)

Shik, A.W.Y., Yue, J.S.C. and Tang, K.L. (2009) 'Life Is Beautiful: Using Reminiscence Groups to Promote Well-Being Among Chinese Older People with Mild Dementia', *Groupwork*, 19(2): pp. 8–27

Smokowski, P.R., Galinsky, M. and Harlow, K. (2001) 'Using Technologies in Groupwork Part I: Face to Face Groups', *Groupwork*, 13(1): pp. 73–97

Sunderland, C.C. (1997) 'Brief Group Therapy and the Use of Metaphor', *Groupwork*, 10(2): pp. 126–141

Thomas, N.D. and Coleman, S. (1997), 'Using the Sensory Orientation Group with a Frail Elderly Population', *Groupwork*, 10(2): pp. 95–106

Towl, G.J. and Dexter, P. (1994) 'Anger Management Groupwork with Prisoners: An Empirical Evaluation', *Groupwork*, 7(3): pp. 256–269

populations

Children and young people

Chowns, G. (2008) '"No You Don't Know How We Feel": Groupwork with Children Facing Parental Loss', *Groupwork*, 18(1): pp. 14–37

Clerkin, E. and Knaggs, B. (1991) 'Working Creatively with Children', *Groupwork*, 4(1): pp. 48–56

Dixon, G. and Phillips, M. (1994) 'A Psychotherapeutic Group for Boys Who Have Been Sexually Abused', *Groupwork*, 7(1): 79–95

Dwivedi, K.N. (ed) (1993) *Groupwork with Children and Adolescents* (London: Jessica Kingsley)

Ferraro, G. and Tucker, J. (1993) 'Groupwork with Siblings of Children with Special Needs: A Pilot Study', *Groupwork*, 6(1): pp. 43–50

Gilroy, C. and Johnson, P. (2004) 'Listening to the Language of Children's Grief', *Groupwork*, 14(3): pp. 91–111

Harmey, N. and Price, B. (1992) 'Groupwork with Bereaved Children', *Groupwork*, 5(3): pp. 19–27

Malekoff, A. (1997) *Group Work with Adolescents: Principles and Practice* (New York/London: The Guilford Press)

Mullender, A. (1995) 'Groups for Children Who Have Lived with Domestic Violence: Learning from North America', *Groupwork*, 8(1): pp. 79–98

Pollard, N. (2007) 'Voices Talk, Hands Write: Sustaining Community Publishing with People with Learning Difficulties', *Groupwork*, 17(2): pp. 51–73

Pennells, Sister M. (1995) 'Time and Space to Grieve: A Bereavement Group for Children', *Groupwork*, 8(3): pp. 243–254

Robertson, R. (1990) 'Groupwork with Parents of Sleepless Children', *Groupwork*, 3(3): pp. 249–259

Springer, D.W., Pomeroy, E.C. and Johnson, T. (1999) 'A Group Intervention for Children of Incarcerated Parents: Initial Blunders and Subsequent Solutions', *Groupwork,* 11(1): pp. 54–70

St Thomas, B. and Johnson, P. (2008) *Empowering Children Through Art and Expression: Culturally Sensitive Ways of Healing Trauma and Grief* (London: Jessica Kingsley)

Westergaard, J. (2009) *Effective Groupwork with Young People* (Maidenhead: Open University Press)

People with learning difficulties

Cormack, E. (1993) 'Group Therapy with Adults with Learning Difficulties Who Have Committed Sexual Offences', *Groupwork,* 6(2): pp. 162–175

Gobat, H. (1993) 'Groupwork with Parents of Learning Disabled Adolescents', *Groupwork,* 6(3): pp. 221–231

Gobat, H. (1994) 'Ourselves and Others', *Groupwork,* 7(3): pp. 210–222

Olsen, A. (2009) 'The Changing of the Guard: Groupwork with People Who Have Intellectual Disabilities', *Groupwork,* 19(3): pp. 39–56

Read, S., Papakosta-Harvey, V. and Bower, S. (2000) 'Using Workshops on Loss for Adults with Learning Disabilities', *Groupwork,* 12(2): pp. 6–26

Schonfeld, H. and Morrissey, M.C. (1992) 'Social Workers and Psychologists as Facilitators of Groupwork with Adults with a Learning Difficulty: A Survey of Current Practice', *Groupwork,* 5(3): pp.41–61

Wilson, M., *et al.* (2004) '"Funzone": Using Groupwork for Teaching and Learning', *Groupwork,* 14(1): pp. 9–29

Marginalized populations

Breton, M. (1991) 'Toward a Model of Social Groupwork Practice with Marginalised Populations', *Groupwork,* 4(1): pp. 31–47

Medical and health

Belchamber, C. (2009) 'Particpants' Perceptions of Groupwork in the Management of Cancer Symptoms in Older People', *Groupwork,* 19(2): pp. 79–100

Firth, P. (2000) 'Picking Up the Pieces: Groupwork in Palliative Care', *Groupwork,* 12(1): pp. 26–41

Martin, N. and O'Neill, E. (1992) 'Groupwork with Teenage Cancer Patients', *Groupwork,* 5(3): pp. 62–73

Neal, D. (2009) 'Groupwork to Support Self-Care after Stroke', *Groupwork,* 19(2): pp. 101–120

Reverand, E.E. and Levy, L.B. (2000) 'Developing the Professionals: Groupwork for Health Promotion', *Groupwork,* 12(1): pp. 42–57

Men's groups

Bensted, J., *et al.* (1994) 'Men Working with Men in Groups: Masculinity and Crime', *Groupwork*, 7(1): pp. 37–49

Fleming, J. and Luczynski, Z. (1999) 'Men United: Father's Voices', *Groupwork*, 11(2): pp. 21–37

Lindsay, J., *et ai.* (2006) 'Therapeutic Factors in the First Stage of Men's Domestic Violence Groups: Men Talk about Universality and How It Becomes Operational in the Group', *Groupwork*, 16(1): pp. 29–47

Mullender, A. (1995A) 'Groupwork with Male "Domestic" Abusers: Models and Dilemmas', *Groupwork*, 9(1): pp. 27–47

Oborne, M. and Maidment, J. (2007) 'C'mon Guys! a Program to Facilitate Father Involvement in the Primary School Environment', *Groupwork*, 17(3): pp. 8–24

Prinsloo, C.R. (2007) 'Strengthening the Father–Child Bond: Using Groups to Improve the Fatherhood Skills of Incarcerated Fathers', *Groupwork*, 17(3): pp. 25–42

Mental health

Ball, J. and Norman, A. (1996) '"without the Group I'd Still Be Eating Half the Co-Op": An Example of Groupwork with Women Who Use Food', *Groupwork*, 9(1): pp. 48–61

Manor, O. (1999) 'Help as Mutual Aid: Groupwork in Mental Health', *Groupwork*, 11(3): pp. 30–49

Manor, O. and Carson, J. (2003) 'Groupwork in Mental Health', *Groupwork*, 13(3): pp. 128, (special issue)

Mason, S. (2000) 'Groupwork with Schizophrenia: Clinical Aspects', *Groupwork*, 12(2): pp. 27–44

Morgan, S. and Carson, J. (2009) 'The Recovery Group: A Service User and Professional Perspective', *Groupwork*, 19(1): pp. 26–39

Phillips, J.H. and Corcoran, J. (2000) 'Multi-Family Group Interventions with Schizophrenia', *Groupwork*, 12(2): pp. 45–63

Radcliffe, J. *et al.* (eds) (2010) *Psychological Groupwork with Acute Psychiatric Inpatients* (London: Whiting and Birch)

Valinejad, C. and Smith, J. (2008) 'It Is Possible for People Diagnosed with Schizophrenia to Recover', *Groupwork*, 18(1): pp. 38–58

Offenders and gangs

Brown, A. and Caddick, B. (1993) *Groupwork with Offenders* (London: Whiting and Birch)

Cowburn, M. (1990) 'Work with Male Sex Offenders in Groups', *Groupwork*, 3(2): pp. 157–171

Drakeford, M. (1994) 'Groupwork for Parents of Young People in Trouble: A Proposal', *Groupwork*, 7(3): pp. 236–247

Lee, F.W.L., Lo, T.W. and Wong, D.S.W. (1996) 'Intervention in the Decision-Making of Youth Gangs', *Groupwork*, 9(3): pp. 292–302

Yates, J. (2004) 'Evidence, Effectiveness and Groupwork Developments in Youth Justice', *Groupwork*, 14(3): pp. 112–132

Older people and people with dementia

Bender, M. (2004) *Therapeutic Groupwork for People with Cognitive Losses: Working with People with Dementia* (Oxford: Speechmark)

Crimmens, P. (1998) *Storymaking and Creative Groupwork with Older People* (London: Jessica Kingsley)

Geyer, S. (2010) 'Strengths-Based Groupwork with Alcohol Dependent Older Persons: Solution to an Age-Old Problem?', *Groupwork*, 20(1): pp. 63–86

Heathcote, J. and Hong, C.S. (2009) 'Groupwork as a Tool to Combat Loneliness Among People: Initial Observations', *Groupwork*, 19(2): pp. 121–130

Kelly, T. B. (2004) 'Mutual Aid Groups for Older Persons with a Mental Illness', *Journal of Gerontological Social Work*, 44(1/2): pp. 111–126

Parker, J. (2006) '"I Remember That ... " Reminiscence Groups with People with Dementia: A Valuable Site for Practice Learning', *Groupwork*, 16(1): pp. 7–28

Parker, J. (ed) (2009) 'Groupwork with Older People', *Groupwork*, 19(2): p. 136, (special issue)

Rishty, A.C. (2000) 'The Strengths Perspective in Reminiscence Groupwork with Depressed Older Adults', *Groupwork*, 12(3): pp. 37–55

Parents and families

Beatty, D. and King, A. (2008) 'Supporting Fathers Who Have a Child with a Disability: The Development of a New Parenting Program', *Groupwork*, 18(3): pp. 69–87

Bunston, W. and Heynatz, A. (eds) (2006) *Addressing Family Violence Programs: Groupwork Interventions for Infants, Children and Their Parents* (Melbourne: Royal Children's Hospital)

Dennison, C. and Ingledew, H. (1999) 'Groupwork with the Mothers of Teenage Mothers', *Groupwork*, 11(2): pp. 5–20

Dobbin, D. and Evans, S. (1994) 'Staying Alive in Difficult Times: The Experience of Groupwork with Mothers of Children Who Have Been Sexually Abused', *Groupwork*, 7(2): pp. 256–269

Finlayson, S. (1993) 'Working with a Family Group of Bereaved Children', *Groupwork*, 6(2): pp. 93–106

Hadlow, J. (1995) 'Groupwork to Facilitate Family Reconstitution: A Social Work Response', *Groupwork*, 8(3): pp. 313–323

Hopmeyer, E. and Werk, A. (1993) 'A Comparative Study of Four Family Bereavement Groups', *Groupwork*, 6(2): pp. 107–121

Norman, C. (1994) 'Groupwork with Young Mothers', *Groupwork*, 7(3): pp. 223–235

Prinsloo, C. R. (2007) 'Strengthening the Father–Child Bond: Using Groups to Improve the Fatherhood Skills of Incarcerated Fathers', *Groupwork*, 17(3): pp. 25–42

Sharry, J. (1999) 'Building Solutions in Groupwork with Parents', *Groupwork*, 11(2): pp. 68–89

Refugees

Ajdukovic, M., Cevizovic, M. and Kontak, K. (1995) 'Groupwork in Croatia: Experiences with Older Refugees', *Groupwork*, 8(1): pp. 152–165

Pecnik, N. and Miskulin, M. (1996) 'Psychosocial Assistance to Refugee and Displaced Women in Croatia', *Groupwork*, 9(3): pp. 328–351

Reynolds, J. and Shackman, J. (1994) 'Partnership and Training and Practice with Refugees', *Groupwork*, 7(1): pp. 23–36

Sex abuse

Donaldson, M.A. and Codes-Green, S. (1993) *Group Treatment of Adult Incest Survivors* (London: Sage)

Women's groups

Barnett, S., Corder, F. and Jehu, D. (1990) 'Group Treatment for Women Sex Offenders against Children', *Groupwork*, 3(2): pp. 191–203

Batsleer, J. (2005) 'Peace within Her Borders? Faith Discourses in the Context of Inter-Cultural Groupwork with Women Survivors', *Groupwork*, 15(3): pp. 6–22

Blazina, C. (2001) 'Analytic Psychology and Gender Role Conflict: The Development of the Fragile Masculine Self', *Psychotherapy: Theory, Research, Practice, Training* 38(1): pp. 50–59

Butler, S. (1994) 'All I've Got in My Purse Is Mothballs! the Social Action Women's Group', *Groupwork*, 7(2): pp. 163–179

Chew, J. (1998) *Women Survivors of Childhood Sexual Abuse* (New York: Haworth Press)

Groves, P.A. and Schondel, C. (1997) 'Feminist Groupwork with Lesbian Survivors of Incest', *Groupwork*, 10(3): pp. 215–230

Prendergast, M.L., *et al.* (2011) 'The Relative Effectiveness of Women-Only and Mixed-Gender Treatment for Substance-Abusing Women', *Journal of Substance Abuse Treatment*, 40(4): pp. 336–348

Roy, V., Gourde, M-A. and Couto, E. (2011) 'Engagement of Men in Group Treatment Programs: A Review of the Literature', *Groupwork*, 21(1): pp. 28–45

Schiller, L.Y. (1995) 'Stages of Development in Women's Groups: A Relational Model', in R. Kurland and R. Salmon (eds), *Group Work Practice in a Troubled Society: Problems and Opportunities* (New York: The Haworth Press, Inc.), pp. 117–138

Schiller, L.Y. (1997) 'Rethinking Stages of Group Development in Women's Groups: Implications for Practice', *Social Work with Groups,* 20(3): pp. 3–19

Suk-Ching, E.A.L. (1995) 'An Integrated, Feminist Socio-Economic Model: Groupwork with Nurses in Hong Kong', *Groupwork,* 8(3): pp. 285–301

Trevithick, P. (1995) '"Cycling Over Everest": Groupwork with Depressed Women', *Groupwork,* 8(1): pp. 15–33

Wintram, C., *et al.* (1994) 'A Time for Women: An Account of a Group for Women on an Out of City Housing Development in Leicester', *Groupwork,* 7(2): pp. 125–135

Zilberleyt, L.M. and Fung, L.W. (2011) 'Community Social Service Projects: Working in Task Groups to Create Change', in C.F. Kuechler (ed), *Group Work: Building Bridges of Hope* (London: Whiting and Birch), pp. 116–130

Other populations

Grindley, G. (1994) 'Working with Religious Communities', *Groupwork,* 7(1): pp. 50–62

Kohli, K. (1993) 'Groupwork with Deaf People', *Groupwork,* 6(3): pp. 232–247

Larkin, M. (2007) 'Group Support during Caring and Post-Caring: The Role of Carers' Groups', *Groupwork,* 17(2): pp. 28–51

Nkouth, B.N., St-Onge, M. and Lepage, S. (2010) 'the Group as a Place of Training and Universality of the Experience of Voice Hearers', *Groupwork,* 20(2): pp. 45–64

O'Connor, I. (1992) 'Bereaved by Suicide: Setting Up an "Ideal" Therapy Group in a Real World', *Groupwork,* 5(3): pp. 74–86

Williamson, C. and Baker, L.M. (2008) 'Helping Victims of Prostitution and Trafficking: It Takes a Community', *Groupwork,* 18(3): pp. 10–29

setting

The following source provide examples of groupwork in particular settings:

Brown, A. (1990) 'Groupwork with a Difference: The Group "Mosaic" in Residential and Day Care Settings', *Groupwork,* 3(3): pp. 269–285

Brown, A. and Clough, R. (1989) *Groups and Grouping: Life and Work in Day and Residential Centres* (London: Tavistock/Routledge)

Cary, C., Reid, C. and Berdan, K. (2004) 'Involving School Students in Social Action in America: The Youth Dreamers Group', *Groupwork,* 14(2): pp. 64–79

Clarke, P. and Aimable, A. (1990) 'Groupwork Techniques in a Residential Primary School for Emotionally Disturbed Boys', *Groupwork,* 3(1): pp. 36–48

Earnshaw, J. (1991) 'Evolution and Accountability: Ten Years of Groups in a Day Centre for Young Offenders,' *Groupwork* 2(4): pp. 231–239

Garrett, P.J.T. (1995) 'Group Dialogue within Prisons', *Groupwork,* 8(1): pp. 49–66

Lo, T.W. (1992) 'Groupwork with Youth Gangs in Hong Kong', *Groupwork,* 5(1), 68–71

Payne, M., Hartley, N. and Heal, R. (2008) 'Social Objectives of Palliative Day Care Groups', *Groupwork,* 18(1): pp. 59–75

Radcliffe, J., Hajek, K. and Carson, J. (eds) (2007) 'Inpatient groupwork', *Groupwork,* 17(1): p. 68, (special issue)

Rees, P. (2009) 'Student Perspectives on Groupwork: Findings of a School Improvement Initiative', *Groupwork,* 19(1): pp. 59–81

St Thomas, B. and Johnson, P. (2006) '"Changing Perceptions" Creating New Identities in the Work Place', *Groupwork,* 16(2): pp. 25–42

Towl, G. (1990), 'Culture Groups in Prison', *Groupwork,* 3(3): pp. 260–268

Towl, G. (ed) (1995) *Groupwork in Prisons* (London: The Chameleon Press)

Ward, P. (2008) '"It's Not Just What You Do, It's the Way That You Do It": Groupwork and the Dental Career Journey', *Groupwork,* 18(2): pp. 81–100

appendix 2

GROUPWORK LOG

Name of the group:

My name:

Group session number:

Date/time of session:

Who was present and who sat where?

Draw a diagram in the box
If somebody was absent, do you know why?
Is there a need to follow up?
Consider who contributed
most – – – – least?
Is there a pattern?
Where does power lie in the group?

What was the general atmosphere and **feeling** of this session of the group?

What were the main **aims** of this session?

1

2

3

What **themes** are emerging for the group?

What was **my** main contribution to the session?

What did my **co-leader** particularly contribute?

What I **learned** most from this session as a group leader was....

Future plans include....

Adapted from Doel and Sawdon (1999: 236)

bibliography

AASWG (2010) *Standards for Social Work Practice with Groups.* 2nd edn (Alexandria, VA: AASWG) (available at www.aaswg.org)

Abu-Samah, A. (1996) 'Empowering Research Process: Using Groups in Research to Empower the People', *Groupwork,* 9(2): pp. 221–252

Adams, J. (2004) 'Participant-Focussed Questionnaires', *Groupwork,* 14(3): pp. 11–17

Adams, R. (2008) *Empowerment, Participation and Social Work,* 4th edn (Basingstoke: Palgrave Macmillan)

Ajdukovic, M., Cevizovic, M. and Kontak, K. (1995) 'Groupwork in Croatia: Experiences with Older Refugees', *Groupwork,* 8(1): pp. 152–165.

Alissi, A.S. (2009) 'Group Work History: Past, Present, and Future – United States', in A. Gitterman and R. Salmon (eds), *Encyclopaedia of Group Work,* Kindle edn (New York: Taylor and Francis)

Argyle, E. and Bolton, G. (2004) 'The use of art within a groupwork setting', *Groupwork,* 14(1): pp. 46–62

Ashmore, R., *et al.* (2012) 'Lecturers' Accounts of Facilitating Clinical Supervision Groups within a Pre-Registration Mental Health Nursing Curriculum', *Nurse Education Today,* 32: pp. 2224–2228

Association for Specialists in Group Work (ASGW) (2000) ASGW professional standards for the training of group workers, *The Journal for Specialist in Group Work,* 25: pp. 237–244

Association for Specialists in Group Work (ASGW) (1990) 'Ethical Guidelines for Group Counsellors: ASGW 1989 Revision', *The Journal for Specialist in Group Work,* 15(2): pp. 119–126

Atherton, S. (2006) *Putting Group Learning into Practice* (Birmingham: West Midlands Learning Resource Network/Skills for Care)

Atkinson, D. (1993) 'Life History Work with a Group of People with Learning Disabilities', *Groupwork,* 6(3): pp. 199–210

Bach, G.R. (1967) 'Marathon Group Dynamics: I. Some Functions of the Professional Group Facilitator', *Psychological Reports,* 20: pp. 995–999

Ball, J. and Norman, A. (1996) '"Without the Group I'd Still Be Eating Half the Co-Op": An Example of Groupwork with Women Who Use Food', *Groupwork,* 9(1): pp. 48–61

Bamber, J. (2004) 'Framing Educational Groupwork', *Groupwork,* 14(2): pp. 80–94

Barlow, S.H. (2010) 'Evidence Bases for Group Practice', in R.K. Conyne (ed), *The Oxford Handbook of Group Counseling* (New York: Oxford University Press): pp. 207–230

Barnett, S., Corder, F. and Jehu, D. (1990) 'Group Treatment for Women Sex Offenders against Children', *Groupwork,* 3(2): pp. 191–203

Batsleer, J. (1994) 'Silence in Working across Difference', *Groupwork,* 7(3): pp. 197–209

Beal, D.J., *et al.* (2003) 'Cohesion and Performance in Groups: A Meta-Analytic Clarification of Construct Relations', *Journal of Applied Psychology,* 88(6): pp. 989–1004

Beatty, D. and King, A. (2008) 'Supporting Fathers Who Have a Child with a Disability: The Development of a New Parenting Program', *Groupwork,* 18(3): pp. 69–87

Behroozi, C.S. (1992) 'Groupwork with Involuntary Clients: Remotivating Strategies', *Groupwork,* 5(2): pp. 31–41

Belchamber, C. (2009) 'Particpants' Perceptions of Groupwork in the Management of Cancer Symptoms in Older People', *Groupwork,* 19(2): pp. 79–100.

Bender, M. (2004) *Therapeutic Groupwork for People with Cognitive Losses: Working with People with Dementia* (Oxford: Speechmark)

Bennis, W. and Shepard, H. (1956) 'A Theory of Group Development', *Human Relations,* 9(4): pp. 415–437

Benson, J. (2001) *Working More Creatively with Group.* 2nd edn (Abingdon: Routledge)

Benson, J. (1992) 'The Group Turned Inwards: A Consideration of Some Group Phenomena as Reflective of the Northern Irish Situation', *Groupwork,* 5(3): pp. 5–18

Bensted, J., *et al.* (1994) 'Men Working with Men in Groups: Masculinity and Crime', *Groupwork,* 7(1): pp. 37–49

Berg, R.C., Landreth, G.L. and Fall, K.A. (2013) *Group Counseling: Concepts and Procedures.* 5th edn (New York: Routledge)

Berger, R. (2009) 'Encounter of a Racially Mixed Group with Stressful Situations', *Groupwork,* 19(3): pp. 57–76

Berger, R. (1997) 'Suddenly the Light Went on: Using Groupwork to Empower Returning Students', *Groupwork,* 10(1): pp. 21–29

Berman-Rossi, T. (2001) 'Older Persons in Need of Long-Term Care', in A. Gitterman (ed), *Handbook of Social Work Practice with Vulnerable and Resilient Populations.* 2nd edn (New York: Columbia University Press), pp. 715–758

Berman-Rossi, L. (1995) Mutual-Aid in Toddler Groups (check title). Paper presented at AASWG 17th Annual Symposium on Social Work with Groups. San Diego, CA.

Berman-Rossi, T. (1993) 'The Tasks and Skills of the Social Worker across Stages of Group Development', in S. Wenocur, P.H. Ephross, T.V. Vassil, R.K. Varghese (eds), *Social Work with Group: Expanding Horizons* (New York: Haworth Press), pp. 69–95

Berman–Rossi, T. and Cohen, M. (1988) 'Group Development and Shared Decision Making with Homeless Mentally Ill Women', *Social Work with Groups,* 11(4): pp. 63–78

Berman-Rossi, T. and Kelly, T.B. (2004) 'Using Groups to Teach the Connection between Private Troubles and Public Issues', in J. Ramey *et al.* (eds), *Growth and Development Through Group Work* (New York: Haworth Press), pp. 105–124

Berman-Rossi, T. and Kelly, T.B. (2003) Teaching Students the Link Between Group Composition, Diversity, and Group Development. Paper presented at Council of Social Work Education, Annual Program Meeting, February 2003 (Atlanta, GA, USA)

Berry, M. and Letendre, J. (2004) 'Lambs and Lions: The Role of Psychoeducational Groups in Enhancing Relationship Skills and Social Networks', *Groupwork,* 14(1): pp. 30–45

Bertcher, H.J. (1994) *Group Participation: Techniques for Leaders and Members* (Thousand Oaks, CA: Sage)

Berteau, G. and Villeneuve, L. (2006) 'Integration of the Learning Process and the Group Development Process in Group Supervision', *Groupwork,* 16(2): pp. 43–60

Bieling, P.J., McCabe, R.E. and Antony, M.M. (2009) *Cognitive–Behavioral Therapy in Groups* (New York: Guilford Press)

Bilides, D.G. (1991) 'Race, Color, Ethnicity, and Class: Issues of Biculturalism Is School-Based Adolescent Counseling Groups', in K.L. Chau (ed), *Ethnicity and Biculturalism: Emerging Perspectives of Social Group Work* (New York: Haworth Press), pp. 105–124

Bion, W.R. (1959) *Experiences in Groups* (New York: Ballantine Books)

Birnbaum, M.L. and Auerbach, C. (1994) 'Group Work in Graduate Social Work Education: The Price of Neglect', *Journal of Social Work Education,* 36(2): pp. 347–356

Birnbaum, M.L. and Cicchetti, A. (2008) 'The Power of Purposeful Sessional Endings in Each Group Encounter', *Social Work with Groups,* 23(3): pp. 37–52

Birnbaum, M.L. and Cicchetti, A. (2005) 'A Model for Working with the Group Life Cycle in Each Group Session across the Life Span of the Group', *Groupwork,* 15(3): pp. 23–43

Birnbaum, M., Cicchetti, A. and Mason, S. (2007) *Working with the Group: Beginning, Middle and Ending Phases in Each Group Encounter* (New York: Wurzeiler School of Social Work)

Bodinham, H. and Weinstein, J. (1991) 'Making Authority Accountable: The Experience of a Statutory Based Women's Group', *Groupwork,* 4(1): pp. 22–30

Bollmann, L. (1989) 'Supportive Groups for Dialysis Patients', *Groupwork* 2(3): pp. 212–219

Bourassa, D.B. and Clements, J. (2010) 'Supporting Ourselves: Groupwork Interventions for Compassion Fatigue', *Groupwork,* 20(2): pp. 7–23

Boyd, R.D. (1991) *Personal Transformation in Small Groups* (London: Routledge)

Breton, M. (1991) 'Toward a Model of Social Groupwork Practice with Marginalised Populations', *Groupwork,* 4(1): pp. 31–47

Bronstein, L.R. (2003, July) 'A Model for Interdisciplinary Collaboration', *Social Work,* 48(3): pp. 297–306

Brower, A.M., Arndt, R.G. and Ketterhagen, A. (2004) 'Very Good Solutions Really Do Exist for Group Work Research Design Problems', in C.D. Garvin, L.M. Gutiérrez and M.J. Galinsky (eds), *Handbook of Social Work with Groups* (New York: The Guilford Press), pp. 435–446

Brown, A. (1994) *Groupwork.* 3rd edn (Aldershot: Arena)

Brown, A. (1990) 'Groupwork with a Difference: The Group "Mosaic" in Residential and Day Care Settings', *Groupwork,* 3(3): pp. 269–285

Brown, A. and Caddick, B. (1993) *Groupwork with Offenders* (London: Whiting and Birch)

Brown, A. and Caddick, B. (1986) 'Models of Social Groupwork in Britain: A Further Note', *British Journal of Social Work,* 16: pp. 99–103

Brown, A., *et al.* (1982) 'Towards a British Model of Groupwork', *British Journal of Social Work,* 12: pp. 587–603

Brown, A. and Clough, R. (1989) *Groups and Grouping: Life and Work in Day and Residential Centres* (London: Tavistock/Routledge)

Brown, A. and Mistry, T. (2005) 'Group Work with "Mixed Membership Groups": Issues of Race and Gender', in A. Malekoff and R. Kurland (eds), *A Quarter Century of Classics (1978–2004): Capturing the Theory, Practice and Spirit of Social Work with Groups* (Binghamton: The Haworth Press), pp. 133–148

Brown, N. (1998) *Psychoeducational Groups: Accelerated Development* (Philadelphia: Taylor and Francis)

Brown, S., Garvey, T. and Harden, T. (2011) 'A Sporting Chance: Exploring the Connection between Social Work with Groups and Sports for at-Risk Urban Youth', *Groupwork,* 21(3): pp. 62–77

Buckingham, J. and Parsons, J. (2005) 'Groupwork with Female Adult Survivors of Childhood Abuse: A Small Study with Statistical Evaluation of Outcome', *Groupwork,* 15(1): pp. 7–23

Bullock, A. and Bannigan, K. (2011) 'Effectiveness of Activity-Based Group Work in Community Health: A Systematic Review', *American Journal of Occupational Therapy,* 65(3): pp. 257–266

Bunston, W. and Heynatz, A. (eds) (2006) *Addressing Family Violence Programs: Groupwork Interventions for Infants, Children and Their Parents* (Melbourne: Royal Children's Hospital)

Burgess, H. and Taylor, I. (1995) 'Facilitating Enquiry and Action Learning Groups for Social Work Education', *Groupwork,* 8(2): pp. 117–133

Burlingame, G.M., Kapetanovic, S. and Ross, S. (2005) 'Group Psychotherapy' in S. Wheelan (ed), *The Handbook of Group Research and Practice* (London: Sage Publications), pp. 387–406

Butler, S. (1994) 'All I've Got in My Purse Is Mothballs! the Social Action Women's Group', *Groupwork,* 7(2): pp. 163–179

Butler, S. and Wintram, C. (1991) *Feminist Groupwork* (London: Sage)

Campion, M.A., Medsker, G.J. and Higgs, A.C. (2001) 'Relations between Work Group Characteristics and Effectiveness: Implications for Designing Effective Work Groups', *Personell Psychology,* 46: pp. 823–850

Canning, J.J. (2012) 'Teaching Social Work from a Group-as-a-Whole Perspective: A Classroom Case Study', in G.J. Tully, K. Sweeney and S. Palombo (eds), *Gateways to Growth* (London: Whiting and Birch), pp. 39–54

Canton, R., Mack, C. and Smith, J. (1992) 'Handling Conflict: Groupwork with Violent Offenders', *Groupwork,* 5(2): pp. 42–53

Caplan, T. (2005a) 'Active or Passive Intervention in Groups: The Group Leader's Dilemma', *Groupwork* 15(1): pp. 24–41

Caplan, T. (2005b) 'First Impressions: Treatment Considerations from First Contact with a Groupworker to First Group Experience', *Groupwork,* 15(3): pp. 44–57

Caplan, T. and Thomas, H. (1997) 'Don't Worry, It's Just a Stage He's Going through: A Reappraisal of the Stage Theory of Group Work as Applied to an Open Model Treatment Group for Men Who Abuse Women,' *Groupwork,* 10(3): pp. 231–250

Carson, J. and Dennison, P. (2008) 'The Role of Groupwork in Tackling Organisational Burnout: Two Contrasting Perspectives', *Groupwork,* 18(2): pp. 8–25

Carson, J. and Hopkinson, P. (2005) 'Self-Esteem Workshops for Mental Health Professionals: Here Are the Outcomes, but Where Is the Process? an Open Letter', *Groupwork,* 15(3): pp. 58–72

Cary, C., Reid, C. and Berdan, K. (2004) 'Involving School Students in Social Action in America: The Youth Dreamers Group', *Groupwork*, 14(2): pp. 64–79

Casstevens, W.J. and Cohen, M.B. (2011) 'A Groupwork Approach to Focus Group Research in the Context of a Psychiatric Clubhouse Program', *Groupwork*, 21(1): pp. 46–58

Chau, K.L. (1990) 'Social Work with Groups in Multicultural Contexts', *Groupwork*, 3(1), 8–21

Chew, J. (1998) *Women Survivors of Childhood Sexual Abuse* (New York: Haworth Press)

Chorcora, M.N, Jennings, E. and Lordan, N. (1994) 'Issues of Empowerment: Anti-Oppressive Groupwork by Disabled People in Ireland', *Groupwork*, 7(1): pp. 63–78 (cartoons by S. O'Shaughnessy)

Chowns, G. (2008) '"No You Don't Know How We Feel": Groupwork with Children Facing Parental Loss', *Groupwork*, 18(1): pp. 14–37

Clapton, G. and Daly, M. (2007) 'Bridging the Theory–Practice Gap: Student Placement Groups Co-Facilitated by Lecturers and Practice Teachers', *Groupwork*, 17(3): pp. 60–75

Clarke, P. and Aimable, A. (1990) 'Groupwork Techniques in a Residential Primary School for Emotionally Disturbed Boys', *Groupwork*, 3(1): pp. 36–48

Clerkin, E. and Knaggs, B. (1991) 'Working Creatively with Children', *Groupwork*, 4(1): pp. 48–56

Cohen, C., *et al.* (2012) 'Global Group Work: Honouring Processes and Outcomes', in A.M. Bergart, S.R. Simon and M. Doel (eds), *Group Work: Honoring Our Roots, Nurturing Our Growth* (London: Whiting and Birch), pp. 107–127

Cohen, M.B. and Mullender, A. (eds) (2003) *Gender and Groupwork* (London/New York: Routledge)

Cole, M.B. (2012) *Group Dynamics in Occupational Therapy: The Theoretical Basis and Practice Application of Group Intervention* (Thorofare, NJ: Slack Books)

Colón, Y. and Stern, S. (2010) 'Counseling Groups Online: Theory and Framework', in R. Kraus, G. Stricker and C. Speyer (eds), *Online Counseling: A Handbook for Mental Health Professionals* (London: Elsevier)

Comer, E., Meier, A. and Galinsky, M.J. (2004) 'Development of Innovative Group Work Practice Using the Intervention Research Paradigm', *Social Work*, 49(2): pp. 250–260

Conyne, R.K. (1999) *Failures in Groupwork: How Can We Learn from Our Mistakes?* (Thousand Oaks, CA: Sage)

Corey, G. (2011) *Theory and Practice of Group Counseling*. 8th edn (Belmont, CA: Brooks/Cole, Cengage Learning)

Corey, M., Corey, G. and Corey, C. (2010) *Groups: Process and Practice*. 8th edn (Belmont, CA: Brooks/Cole, Cengage Learning)

Cormack, E. (1993) 'Group Therapy with Adults with Learning Difficulties Who Have Committed Sexual Offences', *Groupwork*, 6(2): pp. 162–175

Cowburn, M. (1990) 'Work with Male Sex Offenders in Groups', *Groupwork*, 3(2): pp. 157–171

Cox, C.B. and Ephross, P.H. (1998) *Ethnicity and Social Work Practice* (New York: Oxford University Press)

Coyle, G.L. (1930) *Social Process in Organized Groups* (New York: Richard R. Smith)

Craig, C. (2009) *Exploring the Self Through Photography: Activities for Use in Group Work* (London: Jessica Kingsley)

Craig, E. (1990) 'Starting the Journey: Enhancing the Therapeutic Elements of Groupwork for Adolescent Female Child Sexual Abuse Victims', *Groupwork*, 3(1): pp. 103–117

Craig, R. (1988) 'Structured Activities with Adolescent Boys', *Groupwork*, 1(1): pp. 48–59

Creswell, J. (1997) *Creating Worlds, Constructing Meaning: The Scottish Storyline Method* (Portsmouth, NH: Heinemann)

Crimmens, P. (1998) *Storymaking and Creative Groupwork with Older People* (London: Jessica Kingsley)

Crouch, E.C., Bloch, S. and Wanlass, J. (1994) 'Therapeutic Factors: Interpersonal and Intrapersonal Mechanisms', in A. Fuhriman and G.M. Burlingame (eds), *Handbook of Group Psychotherapy: An Empirical and Clinical Synthesis* (New York: John Wiley Publishers), pp. 269–315

Cwikel, J. and Oron, A. (1991) 'A Long-Term Support Group for Chronic Schizophrenic Outpatients: A Quantitative and Qualitative Evaluation', *Groupwork*, 4(2): pp. 163–177

Daste, B. (1995) 'Creative Short-Term Group Therapy in a Managed Care Environment', *Groupwork*, 8(3): pp. 302–312

Davies, P. (1999) *70 Activities for Tutor Groups* (London: Gower)

Day, P. (2005) 'Coping with Our Kids: A Pilot Evaluation of a Parening Programme Delivered by School Nurses', *Groupwork*, 15(1): pp. 42–60

de Bono, E. (2000) *Six Thinking Hats* (London: Penguin Books)

Delbecq, A.L. and Van de Ven, A.H. (1971) 'A Group Process Model for Problem Identification and Program Planning', *Journal of Applied Behavioural Science*, 7(4): pp. 466–492

Dennison, C. and Ingledew, H. (1999) 'Groupwork with the Mothers of Teenage Mothers', *Groupwork*, 11(2):pp. 5–20

DeVere, M. and Rhonne, O. (1991) 'The Use of Photographs as a Projective and Facilitative Technique in Groups', *Groupwork*, 4(2): pp. 129–140

Dixon, L. (2000) 'Punishment and the Question of Ownership: Groupwork in the Criminal Justice System', *Groupwork*, 12(1): pp. 6–25

Dixon, G. and Phillips, M. (1994) 'A Psychotherapeutic Group for Boys Who Have Been Sexually Abused', *Groupwork*, 7(1): pp. 79–95

Dobbin, D. and Evans, S. (1994) 'Staying Alive in Difficult Times: The Experience of Groupwork with Mothers of Children Who Have Been Sexually Abused', *Groupwork*, 7(2): pp. 256–269

Doel, M. (2012) 'when Is a Group Not a Group', in G.J. Tully, K. Sweeney and S. Palombo (eds), *Gateways to Growth* (London: Whiting and Birch), pp. 129–138

Doel, M. (2009a) 'Assessing Skills in Groupwork: A Program of Continuing Professional Development', in C.S. Cohen, M.H. Phillips and M. Hanson (eds), *Strength and Diversity in Social Work with Groups* (New York and London: Routledge), pp. 69–80

Doel, M. (2009b) 'Co-working', in A. Gitterman and R. Salmon (eds), *Encyclopaedia of Group Work*, Kindle edn (New York: Taylor and Francis)

Doel, M. (2007) 'Flash Groups', *Groupwork*, 17(3): pp. 3–7

Doel, M. (2006) *Using Groupwork* (London: Routledge/Community Care)

Doel, M. (2005) *Using Groupwork* (London: Routledge/Community Care), Chapter 5 'Do', pp. 75–98

Doel, M. (2004) 'Difficult Behaviour in Groups', *Groupwork*, 14(1): pp. 80–100

Doel, M. and Orchard, K. (2007) 'Participant Observation and Groupwork: Researchers as Temporary Insiders', *Groupwork*, 16(3): pp. 46–70

Doel, M. and Sawdon C. (1999) 'Action Techniques' in *The Essential Groupworker* (London: Jessica Kingsley), Chapter 7: pp. 130–159

Doel, M. and Sawdon C. (1999a) *The Essential Groupworker* (London: Jessica Kingsley)

Doel, M. and Sawdon, C. (1999b) 'No Group Is an Island: Groupwork in a Social Work Agency', *Groupwork*, 11(3): pp. 50–69

Doel, M. and Sawdon, C. (1995) 'A Strategy for Groupwork Education and Training in a Social Work Agency', *Groupwork*, 8(2): pp. 189–204

Donaldson, M.A. and Codes-Green, S. (1993) *Group Treatment of Adult Incest Survivors* (London: Sage)

Douglas, T. (1994) *Survival in Groups: The Basics of Group Membership* (Buckingham: Open University Press)

Douglas, T. (1993) *A Theory of Groupwork Practice* (Houndmills: Macmillan)

Douglas, T. (1991) *A Handbook of Common Groupwork Problems* (London: Routledge)

Douglas, T. (1983) *Groups: Understanding People Gathered Together* (London: Tavistock)

Drakeford, M. (1994) 'Groupwork for Parents of Young People in Trouble: A Proposal', *Groupwork,* 7(3): pp. 236–247

Drower, S. (1991) 'Groupwork and Oral History: Raising the Consciousness of Young People during Social Transition', *Groupwork,* 4(2): pp. 119–128

Drum, D., Swanbrow-Becker, M. and Hess, E. (2011) 'Expanding the Application of Group Interventions: Emergence of Groups in Health Care Settings', *Journal for Specialist in Groupwork,* 36(4): pp. 247–263

Drysdale, J. and Purcell, R. (1999) 'Breaking the Culture of Silence: Groupwork and Community Development', *Groupwork,* 11(3): pp. 70–87

Dubus, N. (2009) 'Professional/Paraprofessional Team Approach in Groupwork with Cambodian Refugee Women', *Groupwork,* 19(2): pp. 46–62

Duffy, B. and McCarthy, B. (1993) 'From Group Meeting to Therapeutic Group', *Groupwork,* 6(2): pp. 152–161

Dyson, S. and Harrison, M. (1996) 'Black Community Members-as-Researchers: Working with Community Groups in the Research Process', *Groupwork,* 9(2): pp. 203–220

Earnshaw, J. (1991) 'Evolution and Accountability: Ten Years of Groups in a Day Centre for Young Offenders', *Groupwork* 2(4): pp. 231–239

Edgar, I. (1992) 'The Dream in Groupwork Practice', *Groupwork,* 5(2): pp. 54–64

Ellis, A. and Dryden, W. (2007) *The Practice of Rational Emotive Behavior Therapy,* Kindle edn (New York: Springer Publishing)

Ephross, P.H. and Vassil, T.V. (2004) 'Group Work and Working Groups', in C.D. Garvin, L.M. Gutiérrez and M.J. Galinsky (eds), *Handbook of Social Work with Groups* (New York: The Guilford Press), pp. 400–414

Erford, B.T. (2011) 'Outcome Research in Group Work', in B.T. Erford (ed), *Group Work: Process and Applications* (New York: Pearson), pp. 312–321

Erford, B.T. (ed) (2001) *Group Work: Process and Applications* (New York: Pearson)

Evans, K. (2009) 'Rhythm "N" Blues: Bringing Poetry into Groupwork', *Groupwork,* 19(3): pp. 27–38

Fatout, M.F. (1998) 'Exploring Worker Responses to Critical Incidents', *Groupwork,* 10(3): pp. 183–195

Fatout, M.F. (1989) 'Decision-Making in Therapeutic Groups', *Groupwork,* 2(1): pp. 70–79

Fawcett, J. (1994) 'Promoting Positive Images: The Role of Groupwork in Promoting Women Managers within Organisations', *Groupwork,* 7(2): pp. 145–152

Ferraro, G. and Tucker, J. (1993) 'Groupwork with Siblings of Children with Special Needs: A Pilot Study', *Groupwork*, 6(1): pp. 43–50

Finlay, L. (1999) 'When Actions Speak Louder: Groupwork in Occupational Therapy', *Groupwork*, 11(3): pp. 19–29

Finlayson, S. (1993) 'Working with a Family Group Of Bereaved Children', *Groupwork*, 6(2), 93–106.

Finley, R. and Payne, M. (2010) 'A Retrospective Records Audit Of Bereaved Carers' Groups', *Groupwork*, 20(2): pp. 65–84

Firth, P. (2000) 'Picking Up the Pieces: Groupwork in Palliative Care', *Groupwork*, 12(1): pp. 26–41

Fischer, J. and Corcoran, K. (2007) *Measures for Clinical Practice*. 4th edn (New York: Free Press)

Fitzsimmons, J. and Levy, R. (1996) 'An Art Therapy Group for Young People with Eating Difficulties', *Groupwork*, 9(3): pp. 283–291

Fleming, J. (2004) 'The Beginning Stages of a Social Action Training Event', *Groupwork*, 14(2): pp. 24–41

Fleming, J. and Luczynski, Z. (1999) 'Men United: Father's Voices', *Groupwork*, 11(2): pp. 21–37

Forsyth, D. (1999) *Group Dynamics*. 3rd edn (Belmont, CA: Brooks/Cole-Wadsworth)

Foulkes, S.H. and Anthony, E.J. (2003) *Group Psychotherapy: The Psychoanalytic Approach*. 2nd edn (London: Karnac)

France, A. (1996) 'Exploitation or Empowerment? Gaining Access to Young People's Reflections on Crime Prevention Strategies', *Groupwork*, 9(2): pp. 169–185

Francis-Spence, M. (1994) 'Groupwork and Black Women Viewing Networks as Groups: Black Women Meeting Together for Affirmation and Empowerment', *Groupwork*, 7(2): pp. 109–116

Francis-Spence, M. and Goldstein, B.P. (1995) 'Managing the Tension between Being Task-Centred and Being Anti-Oppressive', *Groupwork*, 8(2): pp. 205–216

Frank, M.D. (2011) 'Community Social Service Projects: Working in Task Groups to Create Change', in C.F. Kuechler (ed), *Group Work: Building Bridges of Hope* (London: Whiting and Birch), pp. 67–80

Freire, P. (1972) *Pedagogy of the Oppressed* (Harmonsworth: Penguin)

Fulcher, L.C. and Ainsworth, F. (eds) (2006) *Group Care Practice with Children and Young People* (New York: Haworth Press)

Fyfe, I. (2004) 'Social Action and Education for Citizenship in Scotland', *Groupwork*, 14(2): pp. 42–63

Galinsky, M. and Schopler, J. (1989) 'Developmental Patterns in Open-Ended Groups', *Social Work with Groups*, 12(2): pp. 99–114

Galinsky, M. and Schopler, J. (1985) 'Patterns of Entry and Exit in Open-Ended Groups', *Social Work with Groups,* 8(2): pp. 67–80

Galinsky, M., Terzian, M. and Fraser, M. (2006) 'The Art of Group Work Practice with Manualized Curricula', *Social Work with Groups,* 29(1): pp. 11–26

Gant, L.M. (2004) 'Evaluation of Group Work', in C.D. Garvin, L.M. Gutiérrez and M.J. Galinsky (eds), *Handbook of Social Work with Groups* (New York/London: Guilford Press), pp. 461–476

Garland, J., Jones, H. and Kolodny, R. (1965) 'A Model for Stages of Development in Social Work Groups', in S. Bernstein (ed), *Explorations in Group Work: Essays in Theory and Practice* (Boston: Boston University School of Social Work), pp. 12–53

Garrett, P.J.T. (1995) 'Group Dialogue within Prisons', *Groupwork,* 8(1): pp. 49–66

Garvin, C. (1996) *Contemporary Group Work.* 3rd edn (Boston: Allyn and Bacon)

Garvin, C., Gutiérrez, L.M. and Galinsky, M.J. (eds) (2004) *Handbook of Social Work with Groups* (New York: The Guilford Press)

Garvin, C. and Reed, B.G. (1994) 'Small Group Theory and Social Work Practice: Promoting Diversity and Social Justice or Recreating Inequities?' In R.R. Greene (ed), *Human Behavior Theory: A Diversity Framework* (New York: Aldine de Gruyter), pp. 173–191

Garvin, C. and Reed, B.G. (1983) 'Gender Issues in Social Group Work: An Overview', *Social Work with Groups,* 6(3–4): pp. 5–18

Gazda, G.M., Ginter, E.J. and Horne, A.M. (2001) *Group Counseling and Group Psychotherapy* (Boston, MA: Allyn and Bacon)

Geirdal, A.O. (1989) 'Supportive Groupwork with Young Arthritic Mothers', *Groupwork* 2(3): pp. 220–236

Germain, C.B. and Bloom, M. (1999) *Human Behavior in the Social Environment.* 2nd edn (New York: Columbia University Press)

Geyer, S. (2010) 'Strengths-Based Groupwork with Alcohol Dependent Older Persons: Solution to an Age-Old Problem?', *Groupwork,* 20(1): pp. 63–86

Gibson, F. (1992) 'Reminiscence Groupwork with Older People', *Groupwork,* 5(3): pp. 28–40

Gilroy, C. and Johnson, P. (2004) 'Listening to the Language of Children's Grief', *Groupwork,* 14(3): pp. 91–111

Gitterman, A. (2005a) 'The Life Model, Oppression, Vulnerabililty and Resiliency, Mutual Aid, and the Mediating Function', in A. Gitterman and L. Shulman (eds), *Mutual Aid Groups, Vulnerable and Resilient Populations, and the Life Cycle.* 3rd edn (New York: Columbia University Press), pp. 3–37

Gitterman, A. (2005b) 'Group Formation: Tasks, Methods, and Skills', in A. Gitterman and L. Shulman (eds), *Mutual Aid Groups, Vulnerable and Resilient Populations, and the Life Cycle*. 3rd edn (New York: Columbia Univesity Press), pp. 73–110

Gitterman, A. (ed) (2001) *Handbook of Social Work Practice with Vulnerable and Resilient Populations*. 2nd edn (New York: Columbia University Press)

Gitterman, A. and Germain, C. (2008) *The Life Model of Social Work Practice: Advances in Theory and Practice*. 3rd edn (New York: Columbia University Press)

Gitterman, A. and Salmon, R. (eds) (2009) *Encyclopaedia of Social Work with Groups* (New York: Routledge)

Gitterman, A. and Shulman, L. (eds) (2005) *Mutual Aid Groups, Vulnerable and Resilient Populations and the Life Cycle*. 3rd edn (New York: Columbia University Press)

Glassman, U. (2010) 'Relevance of Group Work's Humanistic Values and Democratic Norms to Contemporary Global Crises', in D. M. Steinberg, *Orchestrating the Power of Groups: Beginnings, Middles and Endings (Overture, Movements and Finales)* (London: Whiting and Birch), pp. 136–147

Glassman, U. (2008) *Group Work: A Humanistic and Skills Building Approach*. 2nd edn (Thousand Oaks, CA: SAGE Publications)

Gobat, H. (1994) 'Ourselves and Others', *Groupwork*, 7(3): pp. 210–222

Gobat, H. (1993) 'Groupwork with Parents of Learning Disabled Adolescents', *Groupwork*, 6(3): pp. 221–231

Goodman, H. (2006) 'Organizational Insight and the Education of Advanced Group Work Practitioners' in A. Malekoff, R. Salmon and D.M. Steinberg (eds), *Making Joyful Noise: The Art, Science and Soul of Group Work* (Binghamton: The Haworth Press), pp. 91–104

Gordon, K.H. (1992) 'Evaluation for the Improvement of Groupwork Practice', *Groupwork*, 5(1): pp. 34–49

Gray, I., Parker, J. and Immins, T. (2008) 'Leading Communities of Practice in Social Work: Groupwork or Management?', *Groupwork*, 18(2): pp. 26–40

Grey, S.J. (2007) 'A Structured Problem-Solving Group for Psychiatric Inpatients', *Groupwork*, 17(1): pp. 20–33

Grindley, G. (1994) 'Working with Religious Communities', *Groupwork*, 7(1): pp. 50–62

Groupwork journal (1999) 'Learning from Mistakes' theme, 11 (1): pp. 54–93

Groves, P.A. and Schondel, C. (1997) 'Feminist Groupwork with Lesbian Survivors of Incest', *Groupwork*, 10(3): pp. 215–230

Gutiérrez, L.M., Parsons, R.J. and Cox, E.O. (1989) *Empowerment in Social Work Practice* (Belmont, CA: Brooks/Cole)

Habermann, U. (1990) 'Self Help Groups: A Minefield for Professionals', *Groupwork,* 3(3): pp. 221–235

Hackman, J.R. (1990) *Groups that Work (and Those that Don't): Creating Conditions for Effective Teamwork* (San Francisco: Jossey-Bass)

Hadlow, J. (1995) 'Groupwork to Facilitate Family Reconstitution: A Social Work Response', *Groupwork,* 8(3): pp. 313–323

Hajek, K. (2007) 'Interpersonal Group Therapy on Acute Inpatient Wards', *Groupwork,* 17(1): pp. 7–19

Hare, P., Borgatta, E.F. and Bales, R.F. (eds) (1955) *Small Groups: Studies in Social Interaction* (New York: Alfred Knopf)

Harmey, N. and Price, B. (1992) 'Groupwork with Bereaved Children,' *Groupwork,* 5(3): pp. 19–27

Harris, B. (2007) 'Inpatient Groups: Working with Staff, Patients and the Whole Community: Personal Reflections of a Group Analyst', *Groupwork,* 17(1): pp. 45–56

Harrison, M. and Ward, D. (1999) 'Values as Context: Groupwork and Social Action', *Groupwork,* 11(3): pp. 88–103

Hartley, P. and Dawson, M. (2010) *Success in Groupwork* (Basingstoke: Palgrave Macmillan)

Hawkins, P. and Shohet, R. (2000) *Supervision in the Helping Professions* (Maidenhead: Open University Press)

Heap, K. (1988a) 'The Worker and the Group Process', *Groupwork,* 1(1): pp. 17–29

Heap, K. (1988b) 'Short-Term Groupwork in the Treatment of Chronic Sorrow: A Norwegian Experience', *Groupwork,* 1(3): pp. 197–214

Heap, K. (1985) *The Practice of Social Work with Groups: A Systematic Approach* (London: Unwin Hyman)

Heathcote, J. and Hong, C.S. (2009) 'Groupwork as a Tool to Combat Loneliness Among People: Initial Observations', *Groupwork,* 19(2): pp. 121–130

Henchman, D. and Walton, S. (2008) 'Problematic Behaviour at Work: A Reflective Approach for Team-Group Leaders', *Groupwork,* 18(2): pp. 58–80

Henchman, D. and Walton, S. (1997) 'Effective Groupwork Packages and the Importance of Process', *Groupwork,* 10(1): pp. 70–80

Henchman, D. and Walton, S. (1993) 'Critical Incident Analysis and Its Application in Groupwork', *Groupwork,* 6(3): pp. 189–198

Henderson, P. and Foster, G. (1992) 'Training Techniques in Groupwork', The Effective Trainer Series, National Extension College

Henry, M. (1988) 'Revisiting Open Groups', *Groupwork,* 1(3): pp. 215–228

Hickson, A. (1995) *Creative Action Methods in Groupwork* (Oxon: Winslow Press)

Hodge, J. (1985) *Planning for Co-leadership: A Practice Guide for Groupworkers* (Newcastle: Groupvine)

Hogan, B. (2012) 'Reflective Practise and Mutual Aid in Educational Groups: A Gateway to Constructed Knowledge', in G.J. Tully, K. Sweeney and S. Palombo (eds), *Gateways to Growth* (London: Whiting and Birch), pp. 25–38

Holmes, G. and Gahan, L. (2006) 'Psychology in the Real World: Understanding Yourself and Others: An Attempt to Have an Impact on Stigma and Social Inclusion', *Groupwork,* 16(3): pp. 9–25

Home, A.M. (1996) 'Enhancing Research Usefulness with Adapted Focus Groups', *Groupwork,* 9(2): pp. 128–138

Home, A. and Biggs, T. (2005) 'Evidence-Based Practice in the Real World: A Group for Mothers of Children with Invisible Disabilities', *Groupwork,* 15(2): pp. 39–60

Hopmeyer, E. and Werk, A. (1993) 'a Comparative Study of Four Family Bereavement Groups', *Groupwork,* 6(2): pp. 107–121

Housen, S. (2009) 'The Use of Reminiscence in the Prevention and Treatment of Depression in Older People Living in Care Homes: A Literature Review', *Groupwork,* 19(2): pp. 28–45

Huntington, A. (1999) 'Action Methods and Interpersonal Processes in Groups: An Exploration of Pyschodramatic Concepts', *Groupwork,* 11(2): pp. 49–67

IRISS (2012) Leading for Outcomes. Guidance on Leading Teams towards an Outcomes-Focused Approach. http://www.iriss.org.uk/project/leading-outcomes

Ixer, G. (1999) 'There's No Such Thing as Reflection', *British Journal of Social Work,* 29 (4), 523–537

Jagendorf, J. and Malekoff, A. (2005) 'Groups-on-the-Go: Spontaneously Formed Mutual Aid Groups for Adolescents in Distress', in A. Malekoff, and R. Kurland (eds), *A Quarter Century of Classics (1978–2004): Capturing the Theory, Practice and Spirit of Social Work with Groups* (Binghamton: The Haworth Press), pp. 229–246

Janis, I. (1972) *Victims of Groupthink* (Boston: Houghton Mifflin)

Jefford, A., Pharwaha, B.K. and Grandison, A. (2007) 'Inpatient Groupwork: The Groupworker as a Consultant to the Group', *Groupwork,* 17(1): pp. 57–67

Johnson, D.W. and Johnson, F.P. (1994) *Joining Together: Group Theory and Group Skills* (Boston: Allyn and Bacon)

Johnson, D.W. and Johnson, R.T. (2005) 'Learning Groups', in S.A. Wheelan (ed), *The Handbook of Group Research and Practice* (Thousand Oaks and London: Sage), pp. 441–461

Johnson, P. (2008) 'Debate: Flash Groups', *Groupwork*, 18(1): pp. 10–13

Johnson, P. and Wilson, M. (eds) (2011) *Groupwork Student Writing, Groupwork*, 21(2) (special issue)

Johnson, P., Beckerman, A. and Auerbach, C. (2001) 'Researching Our Own Practice: Single System Design for Groupwork', *Groupwork*, 13(1): pp. 57–72

Jones, J.E. (1972) 'Types of Growth Groups', in J.W. Pfeiffer and J.E. Jones (eds), *The 1972 Annual Handbook for Group Facilitators* (San Diego, CA: Pfeiffer and Company)

Jones, M., *et al.* (1971) *Small Group Psychotherapy* (Harmondswoth: Penguin)

Kalcher, J. (2004) 'Social Group Work in Germany: An American Import and Its Historical Development', in C. Carson, *et al.* (eds), *Growth and Development Through Group Work* (New York: Haworth Press), pp. 51–72

Kamau, C. (2010) 'Ingroup Attraction, Coordination and Individualism as Predictors of Student Task Group Performance', *Groupwork*, 20(1): pp. 34–62

Keenan, E. and Pinkerton, J. (1988) 'Social Action Groupwork as Negotiation: Contradictions in the Process of Empowerment', *Groupwork*, 1(3): pp. 229–238

Kellman, G. (2012) 'The Power of Group Work and Community Organizing in the 2008 US Presidential Race', in A. Bergart, S. Simon and M. Doel (eds), *AASWG Symposium Proceedings, Chicago 2009* pp. XX–YY (London: Whiting and Birch)

Kelly, T.B. (2005) 'Accumulated Risk: Mutual Aid Groups for Elderly Persons with a Mental Illness', in A. Gitterman and L. Shulman (eds), *Mutual Aid Groups, Vulnerable Populations, and the Life Cycle*. 3rd edn (New York: Columbia University Press), pp. 536–572

Kelly, T.B. (2004) 'Mutual Aid Groups for Older Persons with a Mental Illness', *Journal of Gerontological Social Work*, 44(1/2): pp. 111–126

Kelly, T.B. and Berman-Rossi, T. (1999) 'Advancing Stages of Group Development Theory: The Case of Institutionalized Older Persons', *Social Work with Groups*, 22(2/3): pp. 119–138

Kelly, T.B., Lowndes, A. and Tolson, D. (2005) 'Advancing Stages of Group Development: The Case of Virtual Nursing Community of Practice Groups', *Groupwork*, 15(2): pp. 17–38

Kelly, T.B., *et al.* (2011) 'Using the Research Process to Develop Group Services for Older Persons with a Hearing Disability', in D. Steinberg (ed), *Orchestrating the Power of Groups* (London: Whiting and Birch)

Kelly, T.B., *et al.* (2006) 'The Use of Online Groups to Involve Older People in Influencing Nursing Care Guidance', *Groupwork*, 16(1): pp. 69–94

Kerslake, A. (1990) 'Groupwork Training: A Case Study', *Groupwork*, 3(1): pp. 65–76

Kindred, M. (2011) *A Practical Guide to Working with Involuntary Clients in Health and Social Care* (London: Jessica Kingsley), Chapter 13

Klein, A.F. (1972) *Effective Group Work* (New York: Association Press)

Klein, A.F. (1953) *Society, Democracy, and the Group* (New York: Morrow)

Kohli, K. (1993) 'Groupwork with Deaf People', *Groupwork*, 6(3): pp.232–247

Kolb, D.A. (1984) *Experiential Learning: Experience as the Source of Learning and Development* (Englewood Cliffs, NJ: Prentice Hall)

Kozlowski, S.W.J. and Bell, B.S. (2003) 'Work Groups and Teams in Organizations', in W.C. Borman, D.R. Ilgen and R.J. Klimoski (eds), *Handbook of Psychology (Vol. 12): Industrial and Organizational Psychology* (New York: Wiley), pp. 333–375

Kreeger, L. (ed) (1994) *The Large Group: Dynamics and Therapy* (London: Karnac Books)

Krueger, R.A. and Casey, M.A. (2009) *Focus Groups*. 4th edn (Thousand Oaks, CA: Sage)

Kurland, R. (2005) 'Planning: The Neglected Component of Group Development', in A. Malekoff, and R. Kurland (eds), *A Quarter Century of Classics (1978–2004): Capturing the Theory, Practice and Spirit of Social Work with Groups* (Binghamton: The Haworth Press), pp. 9–16

Kurland, R. (2003) 'Racial Difference and Human Commonality: The Worker–Client Relationship', *Social Work with Groups*, 21(1/2): pp. 113–118

Kurland, R. (1978) 'Planning: The Neglected Component of Group Development', *Social Work with Groups*, 1(2): pp. 173–178

Kurland, R. and Malekoff, A. (eds) (2002) *Stories Celebrating Group Work: It's not always Easy to Sit on Your Mouth* (Binghamton, NY: The Haworth Press)

Kurland, R. and Salmon, R. (2006) 'Purpose: A Misunderstood and Misused Keystone of Group Work Practice', in A. Malekoff, R. Salmon and D.M. Steinberg (eds), *Making Joyful Noise: The Art, Science and Soul of Group Work* (Binghamton: The Haworth Press), pp. 105–120

Kurland, R. and Salmon, R. (2005) 'Group Work Vs Casework in a Group: Principles and Implications for Teaching and Practice', in A. Malekoff, and R. Kurland (eds), *A Quarter Century of Classics (1978–2004): Capturing the Theory, Practice and Spirit of Social Work with Groups* (Binghamton: The Haworth Press), pp. 121–132

Kurland, R and Salmon, R. (1998) *Teaching a Methods Course in Social Work with Groups* (Alexandria VA: Council on Social Work Education)

Kurtz, L.F. (1997) *Self-Help and Support Groups: A Handbook for Practitioners* (Thousand Oaks, CA: Sage)

Lam, D.O.B. (1995) 'Social Groupwork Practice in Hong Kong: Application of Western Ideas in an Asian Population', *Groupwork,* 8(3): pp.273–284

Lange, R. (2004) 'Using Narrative Therapy in an Educational Parenting Group', *Groupwork,* 14(1): pp. 63–79

Larkin, M. (2007) 'Group Support during Caring and Post-Caring: The Role of Carers' Groups', *Groupwork,* 17(2): pp. 28–51

Lavoie, F., Borkman, T. and Gidron, B. (1994) *Self-Help and Mutual Aid Groups* (New York: The Haworth Press)

Lebacq, M. and Shah, Z. (1989) 'A Group for Black and White Sexually Abused Children', *Groupwork,* 2(2): pp. 123–133

Lee, C., *et al.* (2009) 'An Innovative Approach to Support Social Groupwork: A University Groupwork Club', *Groupwork,* 19(3): pp. 11–26

Lee, F.W.L. (2000) 'Working with Natural Groups of Youth-at-Risk: An RGC Approach', *Groupwork,* 12(3): pp. 21–36

Lee, F.W.L. and Li, R.C. (2008) 'The Use of "Play" with a Group of Young New Arrival Students in Hong Kong', *Groupwork,* 18(3): pp. 30–51

Lee, F.W.L., Lo, T.W. and Wong, D.S.W. (1996) 'Intervention in the Decision-Making of Youth Gangs', *Groupwork,* 9(3): pp. 292–302

Lee, F.W.L. and Yim, E.L. (2004) 'Experiential Learning Group for Leadership Development of Young People', *Groupwork,* 14(3): pp. 63–90

Lee, J.A.B. (2001) *The Empowerment Apporach to Social Work Practice: Builiding the Beloved community.* 2nd edn (New York: Columbia University Press)

Lee, J.A.B. (1991) 'Empowerment through Mutual Aid Groups: A Practice Grounded Conceptual Framework', *Groupwork,* 4(1): pp. 5–21

Lee, J.A.B. and Berman-Rossi, T. (1999) 'Empowering Adolescent Girls in Foster Care: A Short-Term Group Record', in C.W. LeCroy (ed), *Case Studies in Social Work Practice.* 2nd edn (Pacific Grove, CA: Brooks/Cole)

Leszcz, M. and Kobos, J.C. (2008) 'Evidence-Based Group Psychotherapy: Using AGPA's Practice Guidelines to Enhance Clinical Effectiveness', *Journal of Clinical Psychology,* 64(11): pp. 1238–1260

Letendre, J. (2009) 'Curricular-Based Approach', in A. Gitterman and R. Salmon (eds), *Encyclopeadia of Social Work with Groups* (New York: Routledge)

Letendre, J., Gaillard, B.V. and Spath, R. (2008) 'Getting the Job Done: Use of a Work Group for Agency Change', *Groupwork,* 18(3): pp. 52–68

Levin, K.G. (2006), 'Involuntary Clients Are Different: Strategies for Group Engagement Using Individual Relational Theories in Synergy with Group Development Theories', *Groupwork,* 16(2): pp. 61–84

Levine, J. (2005) 'an Exploration of Female Social Work Students' Participation in Online and Face-to-Face Self-Help Groups', *Groupwork,* 15(2): pp. 61–79

Lewin, K. (1947a) 'Frontiers in Group Dynamics: Concept, Method and Reality in Social Science; Social Equilibria and Social Change', *Human Relations*, 1(1): pp. 5–41

Lewin, K. (1947b) 'Group Decision and Social Change', in T.M. Newcomb and E.L. Hartley (eds), *Readings in Social Psychology* (New York: Holt, Rinehart and Winston)

Lewin, K., Lippit, R. and White, R.K. (1939) 'Patterns of Aggressive Behavior in Experimentally Created Social Climates', *Journal of Social Psychology*, 10: pp. 271–301

Lewis, C. (2006) 'What Works in Groupwork? towards an Ethical Framework for Measuring Effectiveness', *Groupwork*, 16(3): pp. 71–89

Lewis, G. (1992) 'Groupwork in a Residential Home for Older People: Building on the Positive Aspects of Group Living', *Groupwork*, 5(1): pp. 50–57

Liles, R.E. and Wahlquist, L. (2006) 'Twenty-Five Years in Parents Anonymous', *Groupwork*, 16(3): pp. 26–45

Lindsay, J., Roy, V., Turcotte, D. and Montminy, L. (2006) 'Therapeutic Factors in the First Stage of Men's Domestic Violence Groups: Men Talk about Universality and How It Becomes Operational in the Group', *Groupwork*, 16(1): pp. 29–47

Lindsay, T. (2005) 'Group Learning on Social Work Placements', *Groupwork*, 15(1): pp. 61–89

Lindsay, T. and Orton, S. (2011) *Groupwork Practice in Social Work*. 2nd edn (Exeter: Learning Matters)

Lindsay, T. and Orton, S. (2008) *Groupwork Practice in Social Work* (Exeter: Learning Matters), Chapter 8 'Coping with Unexpected or Unhelpful Responses', pp. 109–119

Liu, F.L.W.C. (2002) 'Closing a Cultural Divide: Enhancing Mutual Aid while Working with Groups in Hong Kong', *Groupwork*, 13(2): pp. 72–92

Lizzio, A. and Wilson, K. (2001) 'Facilitating Group Beginnings', *Groupwork*, 13(1): pp. 6–31

Lo, T.W. (1993) 'Neutralisation of Group Control in Youth Gangs', *Groupwork*, 6(1): pp. 51–63

Lo, T.W. (1992) 'Groupwork with Youth Gangs in Hong Kong', *Groupwork*, 5(1): pp. 68–71

Longres, J.F. (2000) *Human Behavior in the Social Environment*. 3rd edn (New York: Wadsworth Publishing)

Lordan, N. (1996) 'The Use of Sculpts in Social Groupwork Education', *Groupwork*, 9(1): pp. 62–79

Lordan, N., Quirke, D. and Wilson, M. (2009) 'Mask Making and Social Groupwork', in C.S. Cohen, M.H. Phillips and M. Hanson (eds),

Strength and Diversity in Social Work with Groups (New York and London: Routledge), pp. 103–119

Lumley, J. and Marchant, H. (1989) 'Learning about Groupwork', *Groupwork*, 2(2): pp. 134–144

MacGowan, M.J. (2008) *A Guide to Evidence Based Group Work* (New York: Oxford University Press)

MacGowan, M.J. (2000) 'Evaluation of a Measure of Engagement for Group Work', *Research on Social Work Practice*, 10(3): pp. 348–361

McCarthy, C.Y. and Hart, S. (2011) 'Designing Groups to Meet Evolving Challenges in Health Care Settings', *Journal for Specialist in Group Work*, 36(4): pp. 352–367

McCaughan, N. (1988) 'Swimming Upstream: A Survey of Articles on Groupwork in Social Work Journals 1986–87', *Groupwork*, 1(1): pp. 77–89

McCaughan, N. (ed) (1978) *Group Work: Learning and Practice* (London: George Allen and Unwin), National Institute Social Servce Library #33

McDermott, F. (2005) 'Researching Groupwork: Outsider and Insider Perspectives', *Groupwork*, 15(1): pp. 91–109

McDermott, F. (2002) *Inside Group Work: A Guide to Reflective Practice* (St Leonard's NSW: Allen and Unwin)

McKenna, K.Y.A. and Green, A.S. (2002) 'Virtual Group Dynamics', *Group Dynamics: Theory Research, and Practice*, 6(1): pp. 116–127

McMahon, A. (2003) 'Redefining the Beginnings of Social Work in Australia', *Advances in Social Work and Welfare Education*, 5(1): pp. 86–94

McMorris, L.E., Gottlieb, N.H. and Sneden, G.G. (2005) 'Developmental Stages in Public Health Partnerships: A Practical Perspective', *Health Promotion Practice*, 6(2): pp. 219–226

Machery, E. and Faucher, L. (2005) 'Social Construction and the Concept of Race', *Philosophy of Science*, 72: pp. 1208–1219

Magen, R.H. and Mangiardi, E. (2005) 'Groups and Individual Change', in S.A. Wheelan (ed), *The Handbook of Group Research and Practice* (Thousand Oaks and London: Sage), pp. 351–361

Maidment, J. and Crisp, B.R. (2007) 'Not Just for Romance: Applications of "Speed Dating" in Social Work Education', *Groupwork*, 17(2): pp. 13–27

Maidment, J. and Macfarlane, S. (2009) 'Craft Groups: Sites of Friendship, Belonging and Learning for Older Women', *Groupwork*, 19(1): pp. 10–25

Malekoff, A. (2006) 'Putting Ideas to Paper: A Guideline for Practitioners (and Others) Who Wish to Write for Publication', in A. Malekoff, R. Salmon and D.M. Steinberg (eds), *Making Joyful Noise: The Art, Science and Soul of Group Work* (Binghamton: The Haworth Press), pp. 57–72

Malekoff, A. (2004) *Group Work with Adolescents: Principles and Practice*, 'The Use of "Program" in Group Work' (New York: Guilford Press), Chapter 9

Malekoff, A. (1999) 'Expressing Our Anger: Hindrance or Help in Groupwork with Adolescents?', *Groupwork*, 11(1): pp. 71–82

Malekoff, A. (1997) *Group Work with Adolescents: Principles and Practice* (New York/London: The Guilford Press)

Malekoff, A. and Kurland, R. (eds) (2005) *A Quarter Century of Classics (1978–2004): Capturing the Theory, Practice and Spirit of Social Work with Groups* (Binghampton, NY: The Haworth Press)

Manor, O. (2010) 'The Single Session Format: Common Features of Groupwork in Acute Psychiatric Wards', in J. Radcliffe, *et al. Psychological Groupwork with Acute Psychiatric Inpatients* (London: Whiting and Birch), pp. 132–155

Manor, O. (2007) 'Flash Groups: A Quick Response', *Groupwork*, 17(3): pp. 79–80

Manor, O. (2001) *Ripples: Groupwork in Different Settings* (London: Whiting and Birch)

Manor, O. (2000) *Choosing a Groupwork Approach* (London: Jessica Kingsley)

Manor, O. (1999) 'Help as Mutual Aid: Groupwork in Mental Health', *Groupwork*, 11(3): pp. 30–49

Manor, O. (1996) 'Storming as Transformation: A Case Study of Group Relationships', *Groupwork*, 9(3): pp. 128–138

Manor, O. (1989) 'Organising Acountability for Social Groupwork: More Choices', *Groupwork*, 2(2): pp. 108–122

Manor, O. (1988) 'Preparing the Client for Social Groupwork: An Illustrated Framework', *Groupwork*, 1(2): pp. 100–114

Manor, O. and Carson, J. (2003) 'Groupwork in Mental Health', *Groupwork*, 13(3): pp. 128 (special issue)

Manor, O. and Dumbleton, M. (1993) 'Combining Activities and Growth Games: A Systems Approach', *Groupwork*, 6(3): pp. 248–265

Maram, M. and Rice, S. (2002) 'To Share or Not to Share: Dilemmas of Facilitators Who Share the Problem of Group Members', *Groupwork*, 13(2): pp. 6–33

Marsh, P. and Doel, M. (2005) *The Task-Centred Book* (London: Routledge)

Marshall, M. and Holmes, G. (2009) 'An Evaluation of a Mindfulness Group', *Groupwork*, 19(1): pp. 40–58

Marsiglia, F.F. and Kulis, S. (2009) *Diversity, Oppression, and Change: Culturally Grounded Social Work* (Chicago: Lyceum Books)

Martin, N. and O'Neill, E. (1992) 'Groupwork with Teenage Cancer Patients', *Groupwork*, 5(3): pp. 62–73

Martin, R. and Harrington, M. (2001) 'Group Work in a Residential Setting: The Twenty-Four Hour Group', in T.B. Kelly, T. Berman-Rossi and S. Palombo (eds), *Strengthening Resiliency Through Groupwork* (New York: Haworth Press)

Mason, K. and Adler, J.R. (2012) 'Groupwork Therapeutic Engagement in a High Secure Hospital: Male Service User Perspectives', *British Journal of Forensic Practice,* 14(2): pp. 92–102

Mason, S. (2000) 'Groupwork with Schizophrenia: Clinical Aspects', *Groupwork,* 12(2): pp. 27–44

Massa, H. (1995) 'Social Work with Groups in France: A Critical Historical Perspective', *Groupwork,* 8(3): pp. 255–272

Matzat, J. (1993) 'Away with the Experts? Self-Help Groupwork in Germany', *Groupwork,* 6(1): pp. 30–42

Matzat, J. (1989) 'Self-Help Groups as Basic Care in Psychotherapy and Social Work', *Groupwork,* 2(3): pp. 248–256

Meier, A. (2000) 'Offering Social Support Via the Internet: A Case Study of an Online Support Group for Social Workers', *Journal of Technology in Human Services,* 17(2/3): pp. 237–266

Middleman, R. (2005) 'The Use of Program: Review and Update', in A. Malekoff and R. Kurland (eds), *A Quarter Century of Classics (1978–2004): Capturing the Theory, Practice and Spirit of Social Work with Groups* (Binghamton: The Haworth Press), pp. 29–48

Middleman, R. and Wood, G.G. (1990) *Skills for Direct Practice in Social Work,* Part III, 'Skills for Working with Groups' (New York: Columbia University Press)

Miller, R. and Mason, S.E. (2012) 'Open-Ended and Open-Door Treatment Groups for Young People with Mental Illness', *Social Work with Groups,* 35(1): pp. 50–67

Mistry, T. (1989) 'Establishing a Feminist Model of Groupwork in the Probation Service', *Groupwork* 2(2): pp. 145–158

Mistry, T. and Brown, A. (1997a) 'Groupwork with "Mixed Membership" Groups: Issues of Race and Gender', in T. Mistry and A. Brown (eds), *Race and Groupwork* (London: Whiting and Birch), pp. 12–25

Mistry, T. and Brown, A. (eds) (1997b) *Race and Groupwork* (London: Whiting and Birch)

Mistry, T. and Brown, A. (1991) 'Black/White Co-Working in Groups', *Groupwork,* 4(2): pp. 101–118

Moe, R.G. (1989) 'Groupwork as Early Intervention in High Risk Families', *Groupwork,* 2(3): pp. 263–275

Mondros, J.B. and Wilson, S. (1994) *Organizing for Power and Empowerment* (New York: Columbia University Press)

Morgan, S. and Carson, J. (2009) 'The Recovery Group: A Service User and Professional Perspective', *Groupwork,* 19(1): pp. 26–39
Moxley, D.P., *et al.* (2011) 'Quilting in Self-Efficacy Group Work with Older African American Women Leaving Homelessness', *Art Therapy: Journal of the American Art Therapy Association,* 28(3): pp. 113–122
Muir, L. (2000) 'Evolving the Curriculum: Groupwork and Community Based Learning', *Groupwork,* 12(1): pp. 72–82
Muir, L. and Notta, H. (1993) 'An Asian Mothers' Group', *Groupwork,* 6(2): pp. 122–132
Mullender, A. (1995a) 'Groupwork with Male "Domestic" Abusers: Models and Dilemmas', *Groupwork,* 9(1): pp. 27–47
Mullender, A. (1995b) 'Groups for Children Who Have Lived with Domestic Violence: Learning from North America', *Groupwork,* 8(1): pp. 79–98
Mullender, A. (1990) 'Groupwork in Residential Settings for Elderly People', *Groupwork,* 3(3): pp. 286–301
Mullender, A. (1988) 'Groupwork as the Method of Choice with Black Children in White Foster Homes', *Groupwork,* 1(2): pp. 158–172
Mullender, A., Ward, D. and Fleming, J. (2013) *Self-Directed Groupwork Revisited: A Model for Service User Empowerment* (Basingstoke: Palgrave Macmillan)
Muskat, B. and Mesbur, E.S. (2011) 'Adaptations for Teaching Social Work with Groups in the Age of Technology', *Groupwork,* 21(1): pp. 6–27
Neal, D. (2009) 'Groupwork to Support Self-Care after Stroke', *Groupwork,* 19(2): pp. 101–120
Neary, M. and Brandon, G. (1997) 'A Group's Journey through Separation and Loss: Therapeutic Groupwork with Children as a Social Work Intervention', *Groupwork,* 10(1): pp. 20–30
Nitsum, N. (1997) *The Anti-Group* (London/New York: Routledge)
Nkouth, B.N., St-Onge, M. and Lepage, S. (2010) 'The Group as a Place of Training and Universality of the Experience of Voice Hearers', *Groupwork,* 20(2): pp. 45–64
Norman, C. (1994) 'Groupwork with Young Mothers', *Groupwork,* 7(3): pp. 223–235
Northen, H. (2004) 'Ethics and values in group work', in C.D. Garvin, L.M. Gutiérez and M.J. Galinsky, *Handbook of Social Work with Groups* (New York: The Guilford Press), pp. 76–89
Northen, H. and Kurland, R. (2001) *Social Work with Groups.,*3rd edn (New York: Columbia University Press)
Norton, C.L. and Tucker, A.R. (2010) 'New Heights: Adventure-Based Groupwork in Social Work Education and Practice', *Groupwork,* 20(2): pp. 24–44

Norton, K. (2003) 'Henderson Hospital: Greater Than the Sum of Its Sub-Groups', *Groupwork*, 13(3): pp. 65–100

Nosco, A. and Breton, M. (1997) 'Applying a Strengths, Competence and Empowerment Model', *Groupwork*, 10(1): pp. 55–69

Nylund, M. (2000) 'The Mixed-Based Nature of Self-Help Groups in Finland', *Groupwork*, 12(2): pp. 64–85

Oborne, M. and Maidment, J. (2007) 'C'mon Guys! a Program to Facilitate Father Involvement in the Primary School Environment', *Groupwork*, 17(3): pp. 8–24

O'Connor, I. (1992) 'Bereaved by Suicide: Setting Up an "Ideal" Therapy Group in a Real World', *Groupwork*, 5(3): pp. 74–86

O'Dee, M. (1995) 'Using Groupwork Methods in Social Work Education', *Groupwork*, 8(2): pp. 166–176

Olsen, A. (2009) 'The Changing of the Guard: Groupwork with People Who Have Intellectual Disabilities', *Groupwork*, 19(3): pp. 39–56

Omsted, M.S. and Hare, A.P. (1978) *The Small Group*. 2nd edn (New York: Random House)

O'Neal, G.S. (2006) 'Using Multicultural Resources in Groups', *Groupwork*, 16(1): pp. 48–68

O'Neal, G.S. (1999) 'Parent Education Groups: Using Cultural Literature during the Engagement Phase', *Groupwork*, 11(2): pp. 38–48

Otway, O. (1993) 'Art Therapy: Creative Groupwork for Women', *Groupwork*, 6(3): pp. 221–220

Otway, O. and Peake, A. (1994) 'Using a Facilitated Self-Help Group for Women Whose Children Have Been Sexually Abused', *Groupwork*, 7(2): pp. 153–162

Palmer, S.E. (1983) 'Authority: An Essential Part of Practice', *Social Work*, March/April, 120–125.

Papell, C. (2011) 'More Than Sixty Years with Social Group Work: Personal and Professional History', in C.F. Kuechler (ed), *Group Work: Building Bridges of Hope* (London: Whiting and Birch), pp. 3–25

Papell C. and Rothman, B. (1980) 'Relating the Mainstream Model of Social Work with Groups to Group Psychotherapy and Structured Groups', *Social Work with Groups*, 3(2): pp. 5–23

Papell, C. and Rothman, B. (1966) 'Social Group Work Models: Possession and Heritage', *Journal for Education for Social Work*, 2(2): pp. 66–77

Parker, J. (ed) (2009) 'Groupwork with Older People', *Groupwork*, 19(2): pp. 136 (special issue)

Parker, J. (2006) 'I Remember That... Reminiscence Groups with People with Dementia: A Valuable Site for Practice Learning', *Groupwork*, 16(1): pp. 7–28

Parkinson, F. (1993) 'Coping with Trauma', *Groupwork*, 6(2): pp. 140–151

Paul, R. (2012) 'Reflective Insights on Group Clinical Supervision; Understanding Transference in the Nursing Context', *Reflective Practice,* 13(5): pp. 679–691

Payne, M., Hartley, N. and Heal, R. (2008) 'Social Objectives of Palliative Day Care Groups', *Groupwork,* 18(1): pp. 59–75

Peake, A. and Otway, O. (1990) 'Evaluating Success in Groupwork: Why Not Measure the Obvious?', *Groupwork,* 3(2): pp. 118–133

Peavy, R.V. (1971) 'Encounter Groups', *Conseiller Canadien,* 5(4): pp. 245–299

Pecnik, N. and Miskulin, M. (1996) 'Psychosocial Assistance to Refugee and Displaced Women in Croatia', *Groupwork,* 9(3): pp. 328–351

Penn State University (2005) *Building Blocks for Teams: Student Tips.* http://tlt.its.psu.edu/suggestions/teams/student/index.html.

Pennells, Sister M. (1995) 'Time and Space to Grieve: A Bereavement Group for Children', *Groupwork,* 8(3): pp. 243–254

Phillips, J. (2001) *Groupwork in Social Care* (London: Jessica Kingsley Publishers)

Phillips, J. (1989) 'Targeted Activities in Group Contexts: The Analysis of Activities to Meet Consumer Need', *Groupwork,* 2(1): pp. 48–57

Phillips, J.H. and Corcoran, J. (2000) 'Multi-Family Group Interventions with Schizophrenia', *Groupwork,* 12(2): pp. 45–63

Pines, M. (2000) *The Evolution of Group Analysis* (London: Jessica Kingsley Publishers)

Pollard, N. (2010) 'Occupational Narratives, Community Publishing and Worker Writing Groups: Sustaining Stories from the Margins', *Groupwork,* 20(1): pp. 9–33

Pollard, N. (2007) 'Voices Talk, Hands Write: Sustaining Community Publishing with People with Learning Difficulties', *Groupwork,* 17 (2): pp. 51–73

Popplestone-Helm, S.V. and Helm, D.P. (2009) 'Setting Up a Support Group for Children and Their Well Carers Who Have a Significant Adult with a Life-Threatening Illness', *International Journal of Palliative Nursing,* 15(5): pp. 214–221

Prendergast, M.L., Messina, N.P., Hall, E.A. and Warda, U.S. (2011) 'The Relative Effectiveness of Women-Only and Mixed-Gender Treatment for Substance-Abusing Women', *Journal of Substance Abuse Treatment,* 40 (4): pp. 336–348

Preston-Shoot, M. (2007) *Effective Groupwork.* 2nd edn (Basingstoke: Palgrave Macmillan)

Preston-Shoot, M. (2004) 'Evidence: The final Frontier? Star Trek, Groupwork and the Mission of Change', *Groupwork,* 14 (3): pp. 18–40

Preston-Shoot, M. (1992) 'On Empowerment, Partnership and Authority in Groupwork Practice: A Training Contribution', *Groupwork,* 5 (2): pp. 5–30

Preston-Shoot, M. (1989) 'Using Contracts in Groupwork', *Groupwork,* 2 (1): pp. 36–47

Preston-Shoot, M. (1988) 'A Model for Evaluating Groupwork', *Groupwork,* 1(2): pp. 147–157

Prinsloo, C.R. (2007) 'Strengthening the Father–Child Bond: Using Groups to Improve the Fatherhood Skills of Incarcerated Fathers', *Groupwork,* 17(3): pp. 25–42

Pritchard, D. (2004) 'Critical Incident Analysis and Secondary Trauma: An Analysis of Group Process', *Groupwork,* 14(3): pp. 44–62

Pullen-Sansfaçon, A. and Ward, D. (2012) 'Making Interprofessional Working Work: Introducing a Groupwork Perspective', *British Journal of Social Work,* doi: 10.1093/bjsw/bcs194.

Radcliffe, J. (ed) (2010) *Psychological Groupwork with Acute Psychiatric Inpatients* (London: Whiting and Birch)

Radcliffe, J. and Diamond, D. (2007) 'Psychodynamically-Informed Discussion Groups on Acute Inpatient Wards', *Groupwork,* 17(1): pp. 34–44

Radcliffe, J., Hajek, K. and Carson, J. (eds) (2007) 'Inpatient Groupwork', *Groupwork,* 17(1): pp. 68 (special issue)

Radcliffe, J., Hajek, K., Carson, J. and Manor, O. (eds) (2010) *Psychological Groupwork with Acute Psychiatric Patients* (London: Whiting and Birch)

Read, S., Papakosta-Harvey, V. and Bower, S. (2000) 'Using Workshops on Loss for Adults with Learning Disabilities', *Groupwork,* 12(2): pp. 6–26

Reamer, F.G. (2006) *Social Work Values and Ethics.* 3rd edn (New York: Columbia University Press)

Rees, P. (2009) 'Student Perspectives on Groupwork: Findings of a School Improvement Initiative', *Groupwork,* 19(1): pp. 59–81

Regan, S. (1997) 'Teleconferencing Group Counselling: Pre-Group Public Phase', *Groupwork,* 10(1): pp. 5–20

Regan, S. and Young, J. (1990) 'Siblings in Groups: Children of Separated/ Divorced Parents', *Groupwork,* 3(1): pp. 22–35

Reid, K. (1988) 'But I Don't Want to Lead a Group! Some Common Problems of Social Workers Leading Group', *Groupwork,* 1(2): pp. 124–134

Reverand, E.E. and Levy, L.B. (2000) 'Developing the Professionals: Groupwork for Health Promotion', *Groupwork,* 12(1): pp. 42–57

Reynolds, J. and Shackman, J. (1994) 'Partnership and Training and Practice with Refugees', *Groupwork,* 7(1): pp. 23–36

Reynolds, M. (1993) *Groupwork in Education and Training* (London: Kogan Page)

Rhule, C. (1988) 'A Group for White Women with Black Children', *Groupwork,* 1(1): pp. 41–47

Rice, S. and Goodman, C. (1992) 'Support Groups for Older People: Is Homogeneity or Heterogeneity the Answer?', *Groupwork,* 5(2): pp. 65–77

Rimmer, J. (1993) 'A Cruse Family Circle', *Groupwork,* 6(2): pp. 133–139

Ringer, T.M. (2002) *Group Action: The Dynamics of Groups in Therapeutic, Educational and Corporate Settings* (London: Jessica Kingsley)

Rishty, A.C. (2000) 'The Strengths Perspective in Reminiscence Groupwork with Depressed Older Adults', *Groupwork,* 12(3): pp. 37–55

Roberts, J. and Pines, M. (eds) (1991) *The Practice of Group Analysis* (London: Routledge)

Roberts, R.W. and Northen, H. (eds) (1976) *Theories of Social Work with Groups* (New York: Columbia University Press)

Robertson, R. (1990) 'Groupwork with Parents of Sleepless Children', *Groupwork,* 3(3): pp. 249–259

Robotham, D. (2008) 'from Groups to Teams to Virtual Teams', *Groupwork,* 18(2): pp. 41–57

Robson, M. (2002) *Problem-Solving in Groups.* 3rd edn (Aldershot: Gower)

Robson, M. and Beary, C. (1995) *Facilitating* (Aldershot: Gower)

Rogers, C.R. (1970) *Carl Rogers on Encounter Groups* (New York: Harper and Row)

Rogers, C.R. (1970) *Encounter Groups* (London: Penguin)

Roman, C.P. (2006) 'A Worker's Personal Grief and Its Impact on Processing a Group's Termination', in A. Malekoff, R. Salmon and D.M. Steinberg (eds), *Making Joyful Noise: The Art, Science and Soul of Group Work* (Binghamton: The Haworth Press), pp. 235–242

Rooney, R.H. (2009) *Strategies for Work with Involuntary Clients.* 2nd edn (New York: Columbia University Press)

Rose, C. (2008) *The Personal Development Group: The Students' Guide* (London: Karnac Books)

Rose, C. (2003) 'The Personal Development Group', *Counselling and Psychotherapy Journal,* 14(5): pp. 13–15

Rose, S. (1977) *Group Therapy: A Behavioral Approach* (Englewood, NJ: Prentice Hall)

Ross, S. (1991), 'The Termination Phase in Groupwork: Tasks for the Groupworker', *Groupwork,* 4(1): pp. 57–70

Ross, S. and Thorpe, A. (1988) 'Programming Skills in Social Groupwork', *Groupwork,* 1(2): pp. 135–146

Rowan, J. (1999) 'Crossing the Great Gap: Groupwork for Personal Growth', *Groupwork,* 11(3): pp. 6–18

Rowland, D. (1995) 'An Outdoor Teamwork Programme for a Group of First Year Sixth Formers', *Groupwork,* 8(2): pp. 177–188

Roy, V., Gourde, M-A. and Couto, E. (2011) 'Engagement of Men in Group Treatment Programs: A Review of the Literature', *Groupwork,* 21(1): pp. 28–45

Ruch, G. (2006) 'Nothing New Under the Sun: Using Sculpts in Post-Qualification Child Care Social Work Groups', *Groupwork,* 16(2): pp. 8–24

Rutan, J.S., Stone, W.N. and Shay, J.J. (2007) *Psychodynamic Group Psychotherapy.* 4th edn (New York: Guilford Press)

Schiller, L.Y. (1997) 'Rethinking Stages of Group Development in Women's Groups: Implications for Practice', *Social Work with Groups,* 20(3): pp. 3–19

Schiller, L.Y. (1995) 'Stages of Development in Women's Groups: A Relational Model', in R. Kurland and R. Salmon (eds), *Group Work Practice in a Troubled Society: Problems and Opportunities* (New York: The Haworth Press, Inc.), pp. 117–138

Schimmel, C.J. and Jacobs, E.E. (2011) 'When Leaders Are Challenged: Dealing with Involuntary Members in Groups', *Journal for Specialists in Group Work,* 36(2): pp. 144–158

Schön, D. (1983) *The Reflective Practitioner: How Professionals Think in Action* (London: Temple Smith)

Schonfeld, H. and Morrissey, M.C. (1992) 'Social Workers and Psychologists as Facilitators of Groupwork with Adults with a Learning Difficulty: A Survey of Current Practice', *Groupwork,* 5(3): pp. 41–61

Schopler, J. and Galinsky, M. (2005) 'Meeting Practice Needs: Conceptualising the Open-Ended Group', in A. Malekoff and R. Kurland (eds), *A Quarter Century of Classics (1978–2004): Capturing the Theory, Practice and Spirit of Social Work with Groups* (Binghamton: The Haworth Press), pp. 49–60

Schopler, J. and Galinsky, M. (1984) 'Meeting Practice Needs: Conceptualizing the Open-Ended Group', *Social Work with Groups,* 7(2): pp. 3–19

Schutz, W.C. (1986) 'Encounter Groups', in I.L. Kutash and A. Wolf (eds), *Psychotherapist's Casebook* (San Francisco, CA: Jossey-Bass)

Schwartz, W. (1976) 'Between Client and System: The Mediating Function', in R. Roberts and H. Northen (eds), *Theories of Social Work with Groups* (New York: Columbia University Press) pp. 171–197

Seabury, B. (1981) 'Arrangement of Physical Space in Social Work Settings', *Social Casework,* 62(4): pp. 227–234

Shaffer, J. and Galinsky, M.D. (1989) *Models of Group Therapy.* 2nd edn (Englewood Cliffs, NJ: Prentice-Hall)

Sharry, J. (2008) *Solution-Focused Groupwork.* 2nd edn (London: Sage)

Sharry, J. (1999) 'Building Solutions in Groupwork with Parents', *Groupwork,* 11(2): pp. 68–89

Shik, A.W.Y., Yue, J.S.C. and Tang, K.L. (2009) 'Life Is Beautiful: Using Reminiscence Groups to Promote Well-Being Among Chinese Older People with Mild Dementia', *Groupwork,* 19(2): pp. 8–27

Shirley, S. (2012) 'Groupwork in Graduate Social Work Education: Where Are We Now?' in A.M. Bergart, S.R. Simon and M. Doel (eds), *Group Work: Honoring Our Roots, Nurturing Our Growth* (London: Whiting and Birch), pp. 95–106

Shulman, L. (2009) *The Skills of Helping Individuals, Families, Groups, and Communities.* 6th edn (Belmont, CA: Brookes/Cole)

Shulman, L. (2002) 'Learning to Talk about Taboo Subjects: A Lifelong Professional Challenge', *Social Work with Groups,* 25 (1–2): pp. 139–150

Shulman, L. (1967) 'Scapegoats, Group Workers, and Pre-Emptaive Intervention', *Social Work,* 12: pp. 37–43

Simon, S. and Stauber, K.W. (2011) 'Technology and Groupwork: A Mandatae and an Opportunity', *Groupwork,* 21 (3): pp. 7–21

Simpson, I. (2010) 'Containing the Uncontainable: A Role for Staff Support Goups', in J. Radcliffe, K. Hajek, J. Carson and O. Manor (eds), *Psychological Groupwork with Acute Psychiatric Inpatients* (London: Whiting and Birch), pp. 87–105

Singh, P. (2007) 'Groupwork in Multicultural Classrooms: A South African Case Study', *Groupwork,* 17(3): pp. 43–59

Smith, C.K. and Davis-Gage, D. (2008) 'Experiential Group Training: Perceptions of Graduate Students in Counselor Education Programs', *Groupwork,* 18 (3): pp. 88–106

Smith, L.C. and Shin, R.Q. (2008) 'Social Privilege, Social Justice, and Group Counselling: An Inquiry', *Journal for Specialists in Group Work,* 33 (4): pp. 351–366

Smith, M.K. (2004) 'The Early Development of Group Work', *The Encyclopedia of Informal Education,* www.infed.org/groupwork/early_group_work.htm. Values.

Smokowski, P.R., Galinsky, M. and Harlow, K. (2001) 'Using Technologies in Groupwork Part I: Face to Face Groups', *Groupwork,* 13(1): pp. 73–97

Springer, D.W., Pomeroy, E.C. and Johnson, T. (1999) 'A Group Intervention for Children of Incarcerated Parents: Initial Blunders and Subsequent Solutions', *Groupwork,* 11(1): pp. 54–70

St Thomas, B. and Johnson, P. (2008) *Empowering Children Through Art and Expression: Culturally Sensitive Ways of Healing Trauma and Grief* (London: Jessica Kingsley)

St Thomas, B. and Johnson, P. (2006) '"Changing Perceptions" Creating New Identities in the Work Place', *Groupwork,* 16(2): pp. 25–42

St Thomas, B. and Johnson, P. (2002) 'In Their Own Voices: Play Activities and Art with Traumatised Children', *Groupwork,* 13 (2): pp. 34–34

Stacey, R. (2005) 'Social Selves and the Notion of the Group-as-a-Whole', *Group,* 29(1): pp. 187–209

Stark-Rose, R.M., Livingston-Sacin, T.M., Merchant, N. and Finley, A.C. (2012) 'Group Counselling with United States Racial Minority Groups: A 25-Year Content Analysis', *Journal for Specialists in Group Work,* 27 (4): pp. 277–296

Steinberg, D.M. (2005) 'She's Doing All the Talking, So What's in It for Me? (the Use of Time in Groups)', in A. Malekoff and R. Kurland (eds), *A Quarter Century of Classics (1978–2004): Capturing the Theory, Practice and Spirit of Social Work with Groups* (Binghamton: The Haworth Press), pp. 173–186

Steinberg, D.M. (2004) *The Mutual-Aid Approach to Working with Groups: Helping People Help One Another.* 2nd edn (New York: Haworth Press)

Steinberg, D.M., Tully, G. and Salmon, R. (eds) (2011) 'Voices from the Classroom: Students Speak', *Social Work with Groups,* 34 (3–4) (special issue)

Stewart, C. (2009) 'Some Critical Perspectives on Social Work and Collectives', *British Journal of Social Work,* 39 (2): pp. 334–352

Stoller, F.J. (1972) 'Marathon Groups: Toward a Conceptual Model' in L.N. Solomon and B. Berzon (eds), *New Perspectives on Encounter Groups* (San Francisco: Jossey-Bass)

Streng, I. (2008) 'Using Therapeutic Board Games to Promote Child Mental Health', *Journal of Public Mental Health,* 7 (4): pp. 4–16

Suk-Ching, E.A.L. (1995) 'An Integrated, Feminist Socio-Economic Model: Groupwork with Nurses in Hong Kong', *Groupwork,* 8 (3): pp. 285–301

Sullivan, N. (2004) 'Conflict as an Expression of Difference: A Desirable Group Dynamic in Anti-Oppression Social Work', in C.J. Carson, *et al.* (eds), *Growth and Development Through Group Work* (New York: The Haworth Press), pp. 75–90

Sullivan, N.E., Mesbur E.S. and Lang, N.C. (2009) 'Group Work History: Past, Present, and Future – Canada', in A. Gitterman and R. Salmon (eds), *Encyclopaedia of Group Work,* Kindle edn (New York: Taylor and Francis)

Sunderland, C.C. (1997) 'Brief Group Therapy and the Use of Metaphor', *Groupwork,* 10 (2): pp. 126–141

Swift, P. (1996) 'Focusing on Groups in Social Policy Research', *Groupwork,* 9 (2): pp. 154–168

Szymkiewicz-Kowalska, B. (1999) 'Working with Polarities, Roles and Timespirits: A Process Oriented Approach to Emotions in the Group', *Groupwork,* 11(1): pp. 24–40

Taylor, G. (1996) 'Ethical Issues in Practice: Participatory Social Research and Groups', *Groupwork,* 9 (2): pp. 110–127

Taylor, J., Miles, D. and Eastgate, J. (1988) 'A Team Development Exercise', *Groupwork,* 1(3): pp. 251–261

Taylor, P. (1994) 'The Linguistic and Cultural Barriers to Cross-National Groupwork', *Groupwork,* 7(1): pp. 7–22

Theodoratou-Bekou, M. (2008) 'Psychological Maturing and Coping Strategies: Study Based on Group Process', *Groupwork,* 18(1): pp. 76–98

Thomas, C. (2010) *Groups and Team Coaching: The Essential Guide* (London: Routledge)

Thomas, N.D. and Coleman, S. (1997) 'Using the Sensory Orientation Group with a Frail Elderly Population', *Groupwork,* 10(2): pp. 95–106

Thompson, N. (2007) *Power and Empowerment* (Lyme Regis: Russell House Publishing)

Thompson, N. (2006) *Anti-Discriminatory Practice.* 4th edn (Houndmills: Palgrave Macmillan)

Thompson, S. (1995) 'Living with Loss: A Bereavement Support Group', *Groupwork,* 9(1): pp. 5–14

Tindale, R.S., Dkyema-Engblade, A. and Wittkowski, E. (2005) 'Conflict within and between Groups', in S Wheelan (ed), *The Handbook of Group Research and Practice* (London: Sage Publications), pp. 313–328

Tolson, D., *et al.* (2006) 'Constructing a New Approach to Developing Evidence Based Practice with Nurses and Older People', *Worldviews on Evidence-Based Nursing,* 3(2): pp. 62–72

Toseland, R.W., Jones, L.V. and Gellis, Z.D. (2006) 'Group Dynamics', in C.D. Garvin, L.M. Gutiérrez and M.J. Galinsky (eds), *Handbook of Social Work with Groups* (New York: The Guilford Press), pp. 13–31

Toseland, R.W. and Rivas, R.F. (2001) *An Introduction to Group Work Practice.* 4th edn (Boston: Allyn and Bacon)

Towl, G. (ed) (1995) *Groupwork in Prisons* (London: The Chameleon Press)

Towl, G. (1990) 'Culture Groups in Prison', *Groupwork,* 3(3): pp. 260–268

Towl, G.J. and Dexter, P. (1994) 'Anger Management Groupwork with Prisoners: An Empirical Evaluation', *Groupwork,* 7(3): pp. 256–269

Trevithick, P. (2012) *Social Work Skills and Knowledge: A Practice Handbook.* 3rd edn (Maidenhead: Open University Press)

Trevithick, P. (2005) 'The Knowledge Base of Groupwork and Its Importance within Social Work', in *Groupwork,* 15(2): pp. 80–107

Trevithick, P. (1995) '"Cycling Over Everest": Groupwork with Depressed Women', *Groupwork,* 8(1): pp. 15–33

Tribe, R. (1997) 'A Critical Analysis of a Support and Clinical Supervision Group for Interpreters Working with Refugees Located in Britain', *Groupwork,* 10(3): pp. 196–214

Tropp, E. (1976) 'A Developmental Theory', in R. Roberts and H. Northen (eds), *Theories of Social Work with Groups* (New York: Columbia University Press), pp. 198–237

Tucker, S. (ed) (2000) *A Therapeutic Community Approach to Care in the Community* (London: Jessica Kingsley)

Tuckman, B. (1965) 'Developmental Sequence in Small Groups', *Psychological Bulletin*, 63: pp. 384–399

Tuckman, B.W. and Jensen, M.C. (1977) 'Stages of Small Group Development Revisited', *Group and Organizational Studies*, 2: pp. 419–427

Tudor, K. (1999) *Group Counselling: Professional Skills for Counsellors* (London: Sage)

Turkie, A. (1995) 'Dialogue and Reparation in the Large, Whole Group', *Groupwork*, 8(2): pp. 152–165

Turkie, A. (1992) 'Supporting Those Who Support Others: The Groupwork Consultant's Role in Facilitating Work Groups', *Groupwork*, 5(1): pp. 24–33

Turner, M. and Pratkanis, A. (1998) Twenty five years of groupthink research, *Organizational Behavior and Human Decision Processes*, 73(2): pp. 105–115

Valinejad, C. and Smith, J. (2008) 'It Is Possible for People Diagnosed with Schizophrenia to Recover', *Groupwork*, 18(1): pp. 38–58

Van de Ven, A.H. and Delbecq, A.L. (1974) 'The Effectiveness of Nominal, Delphi and Interacting Group Decision-Making Processes', *Anatomy of Management Journal*, 17: pp. 605–621

Vinter, R.D. (1959) 'Group Work: Perspectives and Prospects', in *Social Work with Small Groups* (New York: National Association of Social Workers), pp. 128–149

Wadesango, N. (2011) 'Groupwork: Myth or Reality in School Based Decision-Making', *Groupwork*, 21(1): pp. 59–82

Wagner, J.A., *et al.* (2012) 'Individualism–Collectivism and Team Member Performance: Another Look', *Journal of Organizational Behaviour*, 33(7): pp. 946–963

Walmsley, J. (1990) 'the Role of Groupwork in Research with People with Learning Difficulties', *Groupwork*, 3(1): pp. 49–64

Walton, P. (1996) 'Focus Groups and Familiar Social Work Skills: Their Contribution to Practitioner Research', *Groupwork*, 9(2): pp. 139–153

Ward, A. (1995) 'Establishing Community Meetings in a Children's Home', *Groupwork*, 8(1): pp. 67–78

Ward, A. (1993), 'The Large Group: The Heart of the System in Group Care', *Groupwork*, 6(1): pp. 64–77

Ward, D. (ed) (2008) 'Groupwork in Management and Organisational Change', *Groupwork,* 18(2): pp. 124 (special issue)

Ward, D. (ed) (2004) 'Groupwork and Social Action', *Groupwork,* 14(2): p. 96 (special issue)

Ward, D. and Mullender, A. (1991) 'Facilitation in Self-Directed Groupwork', *Groupwork,* 4(2): pp. 141–151

Ward, P. (2008) 'It's Not Just What You Do, It's the Way That You Do It: Groupwork and the Dental Career Journey', *Groupwork,* 18(2): pp. 81–100

Wayne, J. and Cohen, C. (2001) *Groupwork Education in the Field* (Alexandria, VA: Council on Social Work Education)

Weigel, R.G. (2002) 'The Marathon Encounter Group – Vision and Reality: Exhuming the Body for a Last Look', *Consulting Psychology Journal: Practice and Research,* 54(3): pp. 186–198

Weinstein, J. (1994) 'a Dramatic View of Groupwork', *Groupwork,* 7(3): pp. 248–255

Wenger, E. (1998) *Communities of Practice: Learning, Meaning, and Identity* (Cambridge: Cambridge University Press)

Westergaard, J. (2010) 'Providing Support to Young People through Groupwork: Delivering Personalised Learning and Development in the Group Context', *Groupwork,* 20(1): pp. 87–102

Westergaard, J. (2009) *Effective Groupwork with Young People* (Maidenhead: Open University Press)

Wetherell, M. (1996) *Identities, Groups and Social Identity* (London: Sage/OUP)

Wheelan, S.A. (ed) (2005a) *The Handbook of Group Research and Practice* (Thousand Oaks/London: Sage)

Wheelan, S.A. (2005b) 'The Developmental Perspective', in S.A. Wheelan (ed), *The Handbook of Group Research and Practice* (Thousand Oaks/ London: Sage), pp. 119–132

Whitaker, D.S. (1985) *Using Groups to Help People* (London: Routledge and Kegan Paul)

Williams, A. (1991) Forbidden *Agendas: Strategic Action in Groups* (London: Routledge)

Williamson, C. and Baker, L.M. (2008) 'Helping Victims of Prostitution and Trafficking: It Takes a Community', *Groupwork,* 18(3): pp. 10–29

Williamson, T. (2008) 'Strengthening Group Decision-Making within Shared Governance: A Case Study', *Groupwork,* 18(2): pp. 101–120

Wilson, M. (2009) 'Flash Groups: Copenhagen Skole Bus', *Groupwork,* 19(1): pp. 8–9

Wilson, M., *et al.* (2004) '"Funzone": using groupwork for teaching and learning', *Groupwork,* 14(1): pp. 9–29

Wintram, C., *et al.* (1994) 'a Time for Women: An Account of a Group for Women on an Out of City Housing Development in Leicester', *Groupwork,* 7(2): pp. 125–135

Worden, B. (2000) 'Using Fieldwork Experience as a Tool for Teaching: A Multi-Layered Approach', *Groupwork,* 12(3): pp. 56–76

Yalom, I.D. and Leszcz, M. (2005) *The Theory and Practice of Group Therapy* (New York: Basic Books)

Yalom I.D. and Lieberman M.A. (1971) 'A Study of Encounter Group Casualties', *Archives of General Psychiatry,* 25: pp. 16–30

Yanca S.J. and Johnson, L.C. (2012) 'Generalist Social Work Practice with Groups', in A. Bergart, S. Simon and M. Doel (eds), *Group Work: Honoring Our Roots, Nurturing Our Growth* (London: Whiting and Birch), pp. 209–230

Yates, J. (2004) 'Evidence, Effectiveness and Groupwork Developments in Youth Justice', *Groupwork,* 14(3): pp. 112–132

Yip, K. (2002) 'Strengths and Weaknesses of Self-Help Groups in Mental Health: The Case of Grow', *Groupwork,* 13(2): pp. 93–113

Young, T.L., *et al.* (2013) 'Personal Growth Groups: Measuring Outcome and Evaluating Impact', *The Journal for Specialists in Group Work,* 38(1): pp. 52–67

Zastrow, C. (2001) *Social Work with Groups: A Comprehensive Workbook* (Pacific Grove, CA: Brooks Cole Publishers)

Zilberleyt, L.M. and Fung, L.W. (2011) 'Community Social Service Projects: Working in Task Groups to Create Change', in C.F. Kuechler (ed), *Group Work: Building Bridges of Hope* (London: Whiting and Birch), pp. 116–130

index

Made in the USA
Middletown, DE
29 August 2017